Agile Development & Business Goals

About the Authors

Bill Holtsnider is an experienced writer, educator, and software professional with more than 26 years of experience working in the computer industry. His IT expertise includes working in such diverse areas as stock portfolio management, identity management, and software development. He is the author of six books and a wide range of technical and marketing documentation.

Tom Wheeler has a long track record of building organizations to develop commercial software, including products for financial services and contact centers. He has built, sold, and been a senior manager in a variety of different types of companies, including international conglomerates and garage-sized start-ups. He first created the Six Week Solution back in the 1980s and has been fine-tuning it ever since.

George Stragand is a manager and software developer with over 20 years of producing and managing the delivery of commercial software on time. He has worked for companies ranging in size from start-ups to multinationals, creating software for both external and in-house use. He still hasn't found a problem that couldn't be solved by one more level of indirection or a suitable amount of explosives in the correct location.

Joseph Gee has spent the last 10 years of his career leading and coaching teams through a variety of successful projects and Agile transitions. His advocacy for software craftsmanship has equipped teams for success in small custom shops, large telecom enterprise systems, commercial shrink-wrap modeling software, and, most recently, cutting-edge behavioral analytics.

Agile Development & Business Goals
The Six Week Solution

Bill Holtsnider

Tom Wheeler

George Stragand

Joseph Gee

AMSTERDAM • BOSTON • HEIDELBERG • LONDON
NEW YORK • OXFORD • PARIS • SAN DIEGO
SAN FRANCISCO • SINGAPORE • SYDNEY • TOKYO
Morgan Kaufmann Publishers is an imprint of Elsevier

Morgan Kaufmann Publishers is an imprint of Elsevier.
30 Corporate Drive, Suite 400, Burlington, MA 01803, USA

This book is printed on acid-free paper.

Library of Congress Cataloging-in-Publication Data
Agile development and business goals : the six week solution / by Bill Holtsnider ... [et al.].
    p. cm.
  ISBN 978-0-12-381520-0
  1. Management information systems. 2. Business–Computer programs. 3. Agile software development.
I. Holtsnider, Bill, 1956-HD30.213.A37 2010
    005.068′4–dc22
                                                                                                2010008497

British Library Cataloguing-in-Publication Data
A catalogue record for this book is available from the British Library.

ISBN: 978-0-12-381520-0

For information on all Morgan Kaufmann publications,
visit our Web site at www.mkp.com or www.elsevierdirect.com

Printed in the United States of America
10   11   12   13   5   4   3   2   1

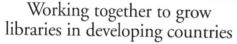

Brief Table of Contents

Complete Contents

Preface

This is a book about a powerful type of software development—an approach we call the "Six Week Solution."

WHO IS THIS BOOK WRITTEN FOR?

Types of Individuals

- This book is for CEOs—to give to their COOs and CTOs.
- This book is for CTOs—to give to their *software development managers*.

This book is for software development managers to *use*. They are the ones who have to make the software work: they have to build the teams, define the roles, buy the tools, and get the software written and up and running. They gotta make it all fly. *They* are the ones we really wrote this book for.

Types of Development Teams

We have two key audiences in mind:

- Start-ups putting a software development team in place for the first time. (You are "greenfielding" it.)
- Internal software development teams with established development methodologies delivering updates to an internal or external product.

Start-Ups

If you are "greenfielding" it, there are many important things you must do. This book is not written to cover all of the issues you will face, but it *is* written to help you design, implement, and manage a state-of-the-art method of creating world-class software.

If you have not yet started building your team, we suggest you read the chapters mostly in the order in which they are written. Specifically, read Chapters 1–10. Then, when you are ready to adopt the Six Week Solution, read Chapter 11, "Transitioning to the Six Week Solution."

Internal Software Development Groups

If you are running a classic internal development team and you are reading this book, you are looking for a better way of doing what you are currently doing. This process is just what you are looking for.

If you already have a team(s) working, you can read the chapters in any order you want and only the ones you feel are most appropriate for your organization.

As a side note, if you are an internal software development team, software industry wisdom says act like a start-up. *Do the same things start-ups do.* While there are important differences between a start-up development team and an internal one, in some keys ways they are very much the same. When building teams and attracting talent, for example, the developers who thrive in a start-up environment are often (although not always) the types of programmers you will need to make a dynamic process like this work.

CHAPTER SUMMARY

Chapter	Description
Chapter One: Introduction	The Six Week Solution is a unique and powerful process of creating software. To determine if this process is right for you, ask yourself the following questions about *your current method of creating software*. Does it: 1. Align software development with business needs? 2. Compensate your development team based on delivering on their commitments? 3. Have both Business and Technical components? 4. Lend itself to a description so simple that everyone in the company can understand it? 5. Produce revenue-generating results that address real-world needs? 6. Tie your investment in your software development to the delivery of the software you need? 7. Account directly for Quality? 8. Hit Your Short-Term Goals While - 9. Addressing Your Long-Term Goals at the Same Time? 10. Reward success and make the effects of failure tangible?
Chapter Two: The Problem	This chapter discusses why developing software is difficult, much more difficult than it appears and more difficult than many other complex undertakings. Through this chapter (and the entire book, for that matter), we compare getting workable, useful software out the door to other demanding challenges; we do so in order to learn (and have you learn along with us), to get some perspective on the challenge we are facing, and thereby to better execute on the task ahead of us.
Chapter Three: Expectations	It is no secret that software is often released late, in less-than-ideal conditions, and way over budget. This chapter discusses briefly how software used to be done. Specifically, we talk about how software development often fails, it sometimes (accidentally) succeeds, and is seldom aligned with business needs. We talk about why waterfall processes often fail, why other Agile methodologies often fail, that they don't manage the cost of change, and they don't factor quality into the core of the process.
Chapter Four: Overview of the Six-Week Solution	We discuss how to ship software in a timely manner, align your company with business and ship at least quarterly, and automate the build process. We discuss why six weeks was chosen as the length of the cycle, as well as what the key deadlines are in the process.

Continued

Chapter	Description
Chapter Five: The Solution's Critical Pieces	The Six Week Solution has the following critical pieces that are discussed in this chapter: the entire company must buy into the idea, work space, personnel roles, hiring smart, compensation, development tools, and cycle commitments.
Chapter Six: Managing the Cost of Change	This chapter outlines strategies on how to tame the exponentially growing cost of the change curve and maximize the return on your investment of your software project.
Chapter Seven: Assuring Software Quality	Software that functions as it should, every time, in every situation, is boring (and, of course, unheard of). At the same time, some people might use the term "reliable" for software that functions every time. But that turns out to be exactly what everyone wants: software so boring and reliable you don't think about it. This chapter describes tools, techniques, and methods for making sure you focus on the quality of your software.
Chapter Eight: Integrating Automation into Your Development Process	Much software in the 21st century is still built, reviewed, and tested manually. Tools and techniques exist now to automate almost every step of the software development process. Automating these steps can radically enhance not only the quality of your end result, but have a measurable effect on your bottom line. Read this chapter for details.
Chapter Nine: Other Software Development Approaches	In this chapter, the Six Week Solution is compared not only to the classic approach to software development ("waterfall"), but also to various "flavors" of Agile.
Chapter Ten: Risks with Using This Approach	No method for developing software is fool-proof, and no process exists without some risks. The Six Week Solution is no exception. This chapter discusses the following: small risks; large risks; things that appear to be risks but actually are not; and things that do not appear to be risks, but are actually potential landmines. We also provide methods of mitigating these risks.
Chapter Eleven: Transitioning to the Six Week Solution	As you may know by now, the Six Week Solution is a unique approach. Transitioning from your current approach to this one will involve some specific actions, but we promise that the initial pain of the transition will be well worth it. This chapter discusses some of the common challenges we have seen companies face when making this changeover.
Chapter Twelve: Conclusions	This chapter discusses the benefits the Six Week Solution offers: • Aligns Software Development with Business Needs • Developers Are Compensated Based on Their Performance • Addresses Both Core Business and Core Technical Components • Simple to Describe to Everyone in the Company • Designed from the Ground Up to Produce Revenue-Generating Software • Ties Directly into Your Investment in Your Software Development • Accounts Directly for Quality • Allows You to Hit Your Short-Term Goals While Addressing Your-Long-Term Goals at the Same Time • Rewards Success and Penalizes Failure • What to Do Next

ACKNOWLEDGMENTS

As we note in the book, the four us have nearly a century of combined years of corporate experience. Along the way, we have been fortunate enough to meet some exceptional individuals who have helped us significantly both professionally and personally. They have mentored us, supported us, and generally kept us on the Path. Without those very special people, we would not be where we are now and we certainly could not have written this book. To them we owe our undying gratitude.

Reviewers

We would like to thank the following individuals who helped review our book at its various stages: Peter Gallanis (Chief Architect and Co-Founder, Aha! Software), Robin George (Vice President of Engineering and Chief Architect, AIMCO), Bruce Bacon (Vice President of Product Strategy and Management, Aha! Software), Steve Ropa (Agile Consultant, VersionOne), Prashant Natarajan, Cameron Skinner (Product Unit Manager, Microsoft), and Bill Wood (Vice President, Product Development, Ping Identity).

Graphics

We want to thank Erick Stragand (estragand.com) for his excellent drafts of the cover art.

But we especially want to express our gratitude to Tish Gance for taking time away from painting original automotive artwork at ferrarti.com to create our compelling chapter graphics—this technical book is much friendlier and warmer because of her efforts.

People at MKP

We would also like to thank the people at the publishing team: Acquisitions Editor Greg Chalson, Assistant Editor Heather Scherer, Production Editor André A. Cuello, and copy editor Melissa Revell.

Families

Most importantly, we are tremendously indebted to our family and friends for their support and understanding during the difficult period that this book was being written.

Introduction: Ask Yourself These 10 Key Questions

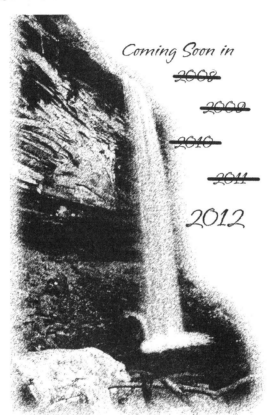

Coming Soon in
~~2008~~
~~2009~~
~~2010~~
~~2011~~
2012

CHAPTER CONTENTS

Agile Development and Business Goals. DOI: 10.1016/B978-0-12-381520-0.00001-1

INTRODUCTION

Creating software is a difficult, expensive, and time-consuming process fraught with perils for your budgets and your deadlines. It is also challenging, potentially very rewarding financially, and filled with pockets of excitement and unpredictability that will keep you on your corporate toes. It is not for the faint of heart.

The Six Week Solution is a unique and powerful process of creating software. To determine if this process is right for you, ask yourself the following questions:

TEN QUESTIONS TO ASK ABOUT YOUR SOFTWARE DEVELOPMENT PROCESS

Does *your* process:

1. Align software development with business needs?
2. Compensate your development team based on delivering on their commitments?
3. Lend itself to a description so simple that everyone in the company can understand it?
4. Have both core Business *and* core Technical components?
5. Produce revenue-generating results that address real-world needs?
6. Tie your investment in your software development to the delivery of the software you need?
7. Account directly for Quality?
8. Hit your short-term goals while...
9. Addressing your long-term goals at the same time?
10. Reward success and make tangible the effects of failure?

The Six Week Solution does all of the above—and more.

1. Align software development with business needs

Is your development entirely focused on the needs for your business or do these needs fall second to cool technical solutions, "architectural" roadblocks, and technology wars? Steering a development team can often be challenging; simple requests seem to always get refused with obscure technical roadblocks. Despite it being the reason for a project's existence, actually delivering what the business needs seems to somehow slip behind other esoteric concerns.

The Six Week Solution formally ties the needs of your business with the goals of your software development team. The section called "Deliver Something of Value" on page 34 discusses this connection in detail.

With software delivery happening every six weeks, the business gets new software, including bug fixes, enhancements, and entirely new features and functionality, on a predictable schedule. The concept that something will be delivered and the schedule is known from the start allows planning for deployment, through upgrading and finally through product launch. No department is held hostage to the software development organization and can proceed independently with their own responsibilities.

For further details on this topic, see the following sections: "Why the Six Week Solution Is Different" on page 28, "Software Development Sometimes (Accidentally) Succeeds" on page 32, and "True Negotiation" on page 83.

2. Compensate aggressively

How tangible to the development team is the business impact of the development effort? Is the delivery of the business needs that define success for every member of your development team or is that an incidental aspect of their efforts? Are you sure? Developer motivations can frequently surprise business-minded people. One of the unique features of the Six Week Solution is its implementation of a risk/reward compensation system for the development team. While it is a radical approach—some companies reward technical people for performance, but not very many—the compensation piece of the Six Week Solution is not a random technique. It is a core component of the process.

Note that currently all of the *critical* people in your company are probably paid like this: they are incented monetarily. This is true of your upper management and your salespeople, just to list a few. Why are you not doing this with your software developers?

Further, software developers who lived through the dot bomb crash have probably collected a lot of useless paper in the form of stock options that never paid off like they were promised. While those who had success with options would relish another opportunity, those who have all this worthless paper are not as interested in working for yet another piece of paper promising a payoff in the faraway future. Compensating aggressively, quickly, and with every cycle proves your money is where your mouth is and dispels any notion that your developers are working toward some nebulous goal.

Another reason to compensate aggressively is that good developers have realized that they are in an environment where they are "free agents." They are free to get traded, go to another team, or hold out and not work at all, much like a professional athlete. The top talent has achieved this freedom without unionizing and understands that they make their own deals and can create their own future. The base pay and bonus structure allow them to have a say in how they are compensated, how much risk they are willing to assume, and how much confidence they have in their own abilities. This approach to compensation is a tool you can use to attract and retain the top talent.

For further details on this topic, see the section called "Compensation" on page 79.

3. Addresses both core business and core technical components

Is your development process entirely focused on the technical needs of the development effort? Is it instead focused on serving the needs of the business and compromising the technical concerns to get there? Both aspects must be intertwined to make the most successful, effective project that you can. This duality is a critical component of the Six Week Solution and one of its key differentiators from other Agile processes. Scrum, for example, addresses some of the business components the Six Week Solution does, but does not fully address the critical aspect of bringing technical disciplines to the process.

For a detailed discussion of differences between the Six Week Solution and other types of software development, see Chapter 9, "Other Software Development Approaches" on page 161.

- The *business components* of this process are critical to the sustainability of your product. They are examined throughout the book, but are discussed in detail in Chapter 4, "Overview of the Six Week Solution" on page 37 and Chapter 8, "Integrating Automation" on page 135.

- The *technical components* of this process are critical to the sustainability of your product. They are examined throughout the book, but are discussed in detail in Chapter 7, "Assuring Software Quality" on page 117 and Chapter 8, "Integrating Automation" on page 135.

4. Make it simple to describe

Does everyone in your business, from the CEO down, understand how your software development interacts with and affects their work? Do they know how to leverage the development team effectively or are they working around the development process? Are they surprised by having new things air dropped on them that may or may not be what they needed?

If you need a one-sentence description of the Six Week Solution to sell it to your boss on the elevator, here it is:

The Six Week Solution is a unique methodology that aligns the goals of the software development division with the goals of the business.

The process is intended to be simple enough that everyone in your organization will grasp it quickly. They will be able to articulate it both internally and externally without requiring everyone involved to have a master's degree in Computer Science or Software Project Management.

The key point here is that the Six Week Solution is giving the business side of the company predictability; business needs *some* predictability in order to function. They need to understand when to submit sales estimates by, when to close out quarters, how many people will be needed for a particular task, etc. In the past, the software development department has not provided enough information in a reliable manner for other parts of the company to give them the respect they deserve.

For further details on this topic, see Chapter 4, "Overview of the Six Week Solution" on page 37.

5. Produce revenue-generating software

Is your software process delivering the features that you know would make the biggest impact on your user experience or market segment? Is it even delivering working software? There is a lot of software being written these days and some of it actually addresses real-world needs and, as a consequence, generates revenue. But a lot of software is not like that. Like any other part of the business, a software project needs to manage the basic components of profitability. A process for developing software needs to be able to:

- Raise revenue
- Reduce expenses
- Increase profit

The key formula:

$$R - E = P$$

Revenue minus Expenses equals Profit

While this formula is always present in the mind of a businessperson, it isn't even the top 10 concerns of your average software developer. Programmers generally don't see the need to apply this formula while performing their daily tasks. But anyone—developer, businessperson, sales rep, janitor—who has started their own company and who is responsible for meeting payroll understands it all too well.

In order to keep your company/organization/department going, you have to be profitable. You have to make money. How much money you need to make, in what format, how fast, and so on—those factors all vary from organization to organization. But the basic requirement to generate a profit does not change.

Founders at Work, a book of interviews with start-up founders in the tech world, refers often to the idea that as a founder, you can have *too much* money initially. Not having a lot of money enforces a discipline that does not exist if all of the cash you need is readily available. The book is filled with stories of founders working in their parent's basements, taking out second and third mortgages, borrowing money from family—all trying to make their particular software dream work. It is also common for businesses, as they grow, to hit a size where they lose the focus on efficient, streamlined work as political maneuvering trumps an increasingly less tangible impact on the bottom line.

For further details on this topic, see the section called "Successful Software Development: Manages the Cost of Change" on page 33.

A note for nonprofits

The meaning of the word "profit" can change, too. Do you work for a "nonprofit"? Do not kid yourself or your teammates—you still need to generate a "profit." You might not have to generate cash, but you have to add to the greater good—you need to help people, the environment, society, etc. If you do not, you are only taking up space. Unfortunately, there is a large amount of space-taking up going on in today's software industry workplace. The dot bomb cut down on some, but it is still extremely common.

6. Tie your investment to software delivery

What are the primary artifacts being created by your software process? Are they extensive requirements documents, design documents, or endless review meetings? Are they piles of "sign-off" agreements? You do not need extensive documents in return for your investment in your software development. You cannot extract any cash value from those things and they do not increase the value of your company. Your investment needs to deliver you *working software* that you can quickly put to work for you.

For further details on this topic, see the section called "Avoid Speculative Investments" on page 100.

7. Account directly for quality

You get functional software that works instead of half-baked functionality with dead ends. The quality is measurable within the code base when all the tenets of the Six Week Solution are followed.

Does your current process make this critical yet often invisible element of your project visible?

Quality keeps your project from costing more in support than it generates. It not only affects how people see your software, but also shapes the perceptions of the reliability and professionalism of your business. Most importantly, the quality of the code in your project decides whether that project will still be viable in a few short months time. Allowing poor work from your developers is like deciding your surgeon does not need to worry about sterile hands or tools. The job might get done, but the damage done will kill you later.

For further details on this topic, see Chapter 7, "Assuring Software Quality" on page 117.

8. Hit your short-term goals while...

This process allows you to quickly release software. It should be obvious that if a unit of work fits within six weeks, it can directly appear in the release at the end of the cycle. Appropriately sized features, bug fixes, tweaks, and so on would all fit within the six week time frame and would be released in less than a quarter. When users are used to waiting more than a year for an upgrade, the ability to deliver quality functional software in a quarter (or less, depending on when the request came into the company) is truly revolutionary!

For further details on this topic, see "Why Six Weeks?" on page 41.

9. Addressing your long-term goals at the same time

With only six weeks allocated for developing a bit of functionality, it may seem like a stretch to imagine that long-term work would ever get done. But we have done it consistently, cycle after cycle, year after year. Using the development disciplines outlined in this book (such as keeping a build viable at all times), the Six Week Solution allows you to execute long-term work.

Two strategies help:

- You can release bits and pieces
- You can go for the big bang all-at-once approach (especially attractive for breakthrough features) and "hide" the work behind licensing or configuration.

Both of these approaches keep the current software functional while new abilities are added.

This allows for creating releasable software today, while still working toward larger features that may appear three, six, or even nine months in the future. Furthermore, with each cycle producing a functional software artifact, it is possible to keep the stakeholders aware of and involved in the progress as you work toward a long-term goal.

For further details on this topic, see Chapter 6, "Managing the Cost of Change" on page 89.

10. Reward success and make tangible the effects of failure

Does the structure of your project allow people to shine or hide? Do you know who your star performers really are? Are you sure those are not just the loudest ones? How about your dead weight? Do you know who is just coasting?

If you use traditional software development models, two things typically happen:

- You are not rewarded for success. (No bonuses are paid.)
- You are not penalized for failure. ("Oh, well, we missed our deadline. Never mind. Let's just do the same thing again and see if it works this time.")

When a measurement point exists twice a quarter, it keeps the performance of your employees in your consciousness. Areas with a large number of bug reports every cycle will be clearly exposed. Areas of code that are of poor quality will likewise be exposed. Who is shouldering the responsibility for the group may not be equal, but you'll know who is working to the best of their ability and who is loafing.

For further details on this topic, see the section called "Compensation" on page 79.

Our answer to these problems? The Six Week Solution.

By the way, what does the Six Week Solution add to the Agile Paradigm?

We discuss how the Six Week Solution compares to other software methodologies, including Agile, throughout the book. We also compare the Six Week Solution and Agile Development in detail in Chapter 9, "Other Software Development Approaches" on page 161. So read those sections to get a more in-depth presentation of this topic.

In the meantime, here is an overview of the differences:

- **Compensation Piece:** Performance is rewarded and, on the flip side, failure is penalized. Bonuses are paid (or not) every six weeks, not at some vague future annual date.
- **No Reward for Success:** Other processes do not reward success; what is the difference in classic development for the next sprint if everything was or was not delivered?
- **No Risk in Failure:** Other processes do not have to share the business' cost with the team when it fails; they just do another sprint and hope for the best again.
- **If Cycle Fails Developers, Lose Money:** Developers have a vested interest in delivering, not some vague promise of some future payoff.
- **Other Agile Processes Iterate a Lot but Let the Boxes Fall Where They May:** If a sprint fails to meet the objective, what happens? A boss stomps and shouts, everybody feels bad, and then they do the same thing all over again.
- **Other Agile Processes Do Not Align with Business:** Sure there may be an on-site customer, but there is nothing to enforce exposure of what is being developed outside of the development group. With the Six Week Solution, the work done is what you really need done.

Of course, without many of these high-level engineering concepts, *any* software development environment—Agile or not—is going to fail.

WHY LISTEN TO US?
Our experience

We have seen a software release or two: between us, we have over 95 years of software development experience.

We have done waterfall, Agile, scrums, stand-ups, sit-downs, two-a-days—you name it, we have been involved in it. If there is a technique to get quality software written, tested, and released, we have tried it.

We are extensively experienced professionals

We have started, restarted, and restored many software shops to successful, sustainable, money-making enterprises in contracting models, product development models, and internal development models.

We have rescued dying products, as well as created new ones, and we have done it in close business relationships to ensure satisfied stakeholders. We are currently managing teams of between nine and 30 people and, by using it every day in a real-world environment, further refining this methodology.

This process is different

The Six Week Solution is different from anything else we have tried. It works, for one thing, which is more than you can say for some of the other things we have tried. It works very well.

And it has been tested, tested, and tested again. So it is not just a theory, either.

But what truly sets this technique apart are two things:

- The goals of the software development division are closely aligned to the goals of the business.
- Developers get paid—they get "incented" to use today's terms—for their performance. If they meet the goals they said they would meet, they get a bonus. If they miss the goals, they get nothing.

Note that we did *not* say the "*performance* of the company," we said the "*goals* of the company"; those are two different things.

We discuss these two differences in more detail later as well as throughout the book, but take a moment to think about just how different those two items are. If you tell someone who is not in the software industry that you are aligning the goals of your development team to your company's goals, their reactions might be: "So? Of course you are! Doesn't everyone do that?"

No, they don't and if you spend 30 seconds in a software company, you will discover that getting software written, tested, and released is a *lot* harder than it seems. And getting useful software, software people actually want, is even harder. Much more rewarding, challenging, painful, fun, frustrating, artistic, exciting—in general, very different from what it looks like from the outside.

The process has been vetted

Our book is designed to provide you with a time-tested method of releasing timely, quality software.

It has been used in many settings to navigate the minefields that cause project failure, including cutthroat competition, complex technical challenges, thorny personnel issues, shifting code standards, and conflicting customer demands.

This book is about one way to do software development right. But it is *not* a theoretical book. This is a book about a process that has been developed in the field—in real-world software development shops—for over 20 years. It discusses the plusses and minuses of various software development issues and details how one particular approach—the "Six Week Solution"—offers some time-tested solutions to those issues.

Always know whose problem you're solving.

Lisa Waits, Nokia's director of corporate business development

You will need to run your development shop very differently, but it works and works very well.

Grosch's law, paraphrased

Computing power increases as the square of the cost increases. If you want to do it twice as cheaply, you have to do it four times as fast.
http://en.wikipedia.org/wiki/Herb_Grosch

This was as true in 1965 as it is today. Many times, going quicker isn't an effort of putting a bigger engine into a drag racer; sometimes you have to rethink your entire approach to go faster.

The other half

There are plenty of great books detailing how to design software and they are crucially important. This isn't one of them. Fundamentally, software development is a people problem. People have to manage the complexity of the task. People have to work in teams to coordinate their efforts and keep their pieces in sync. People have to coordinate on their methods of work. People have to evaluate priorities and gauge business value. People have to all be pulling in the same direction. This is a book on how to create teams and an environment where people work very hard to deliver the high-quality software in a timely manner that your business actually needs.

The Problem: Why Software Projects Fail

CHAPTER CONTENTS

Agile Development and Business Goals. DOI: 10.1016/B978-0-12-381520-0.00002-3

INTRODUCTION

This chapter discusses why developing software is difficult, why it is much more difficult than it appears and is more difficult than many other complex undertakings. Throughout this chapter (and the entire book, for that matter), we compare getting workable, useful software out the door to other demanding challenges; we do so in order to learn (and have you learn along with us), to get some perspective on the challenge we are facing, and thereby to better execute on the task ahead of us.

It is no secret that software is often released late, in less-than-ideal condition, and way over budget. Google addressed this problem by releasing several of its initial products with the "beta" label on them. Microsoft's problems getting a workable upgrade to Windows XP are well documented. (XP was released in 2001, Windows 7 came out *nine years* later.)

HISTORICAL PERSPECTIVE

To first understand why developing software is hard, we must look back in history. The Great Pyramids of Egypt were not built in a day or even a year; by most accounts, it was a 20-year project. The Great Wall of China was built, maintained, and rebuilt from sixth century BC to the 16th century in various locations; in other words, it was a "10-century project."

Inevitability, both were constructed in sections, and not in a single big bang of caffeine and inspiration. And yet today it is routinely expected that software is constructed quickly, cheaply, and with a minimum of resources. The effort spent on planning large construction projects dwarfs most software and just coordinating all of the people involved must have been a monumental task by itself.

In other words, both the Great Pyramids and the Great Wall took an enormous amount of planning and careful execution; today's software projects, however, often get started after only an hour of "planning." Clearly many software projects do not do enough forecasting, let along successful execution of the plan.

THE SCOPE OF SOFTWARE

Put another way, the scope of most software is difficult to comprehend. Most adults grasp what $1000 looks like, but move that number to the $12 trillion deficit of the U.S. National Debt in January of 2010 (www.usdebtclock.org) and most people have a hard time understanding it.

Taking the number down to the typical office, it may be possible to find people who can write a macro of 30–40 lines in their own spreadsheet, although even this skill is fairly rare. But the approaches used in a spreadsheet macro do not scale to even a small product: the small macro doesn't address the issues, for example, of email, password resets, user permissions, different browsers, security, and a host of other topics that a commercially viable product has to address. Simply put, the large majority of workers in a software development team cannot grasp the size and complexity of the software they make. The conceptual disconnect between the expectations and the delivery of software should therefore be clear.

Software is expected to be useful, to produce something of value, or to provide some insight that would be difficult to do manually. (For more details on this topic, see Chapter 3, "The Expectations: What It Means for Software to Succeed" on page 31.) More importantly, creating a complete software product is a much more complex task than writing a spreadsheet macro or simple SQL query.

Everyone involved in the defining of the requirements may fully understand the concept of the matrix or graph that needs to be produced. From that point on the complexities grow because only certain users should be able to see the output, certain others may only be able to load data, while at the same time there is a requirement to log everyone who ever had the chance to see any data. And "Oh, by the way, everybody should not be required to log in again." None of this comes close to appearing on the spreadsheet macro "programmer's" radar.

Complexity

Software is mind-numbingly complex. A U.S. space shuttle has two million moving parts and is considered one of the most complex machines ever built. Mac OS X, however, now has over 86 million lines of code—each one being a virtual moving part. The number of moving parts running currently on your desktop that allows you to see movies of cats dancing to 1980s music is staggering. The expectation is that we can casually add almost anything to that operating system software. We can, but not only with extreme discipline can everything be kept working together.

Delivery

While we manage all that complexity, we also have to get something of value shipped, and shipped soon. It needs to actually address the end user's needs, it needs to work well, and it needs to get out the door.

The perfect is the enemy of the deadline.
Bill Wallace, engineering group manager for GM's Volt battery
(source: http://blogs.techrepublic.com.com/tech-manager/?p=2321&tag=nl.e053)

Even developers seldom understand the scope of the software they work with

The truth about what the typical worker (and even management) thinks about software becomes crystal clear when a new requirement is uncovered. It is amazing to hear management—while well versed in overcoming objections in sales, finances, and all the trappings of running a business that software developers typically do not spend time thinking about—become annoyed when developers push back on a schedule.

Management may have actually invested some time to look over a database developer's shoulder and see him or her type in a simple statement such as "`select * from foo_table`" and be amazed that almost instantly data begin appearing on the monitor. As a result, they often can't understand that it's really not just a "couple lines of SQL code" to summarize an enormous data set, trending it month by month, shipping that data to a browser, and having it display a graph. Clearly, a mechanism to increase communication is necessary.

SOFTWARE DEVELOPMENT OFTEN FAILS

Software fails, and not just by producing an incorrect number or crashing outright, but *entire software* projects fail. It has been estimated that in 2009, information technology (IT) failures cost $6.2 trillion a year worldwide and over $1 trillion in the United States alone (IT Complexity Crisis: Danger and Opportunity, Roger Sessions, November 2009). Many other studies do not agree on the percentage of software projects that fail, but they also put the cost in the $50 to $80 billion range annually. In 2008, it was suggested that 68% of IT projects fail (http://blogs.zdnet.com/project-failures/?p=1175) and that the cause of the failure is poor requirements. Given these numbers, it would be easy to expect that software developers are the most downtrodden members of a company, marching off to the next project with eyes downcast and mumbling like Eeyore from *Winnie the Pooh*. Instead, developers are wildly optimistic, eager to jump onto something new. The cost of failure is high, but the rewards of success are higher still.

In short, software projects are too expensive to let fail, and yet an enormous proportion do exactly that: a 2009 survey of IT projects by the Standish Group (CHAOS Summary 2009) showed an industry failure rate of 68%. Las Vegas casinos give significantly better odds than that! IT project failures can frequently take their companies down with them. It is an old cliché, but it still holds true:

A successful software project has to build the right software and build the software right.

THE NEED FOR PROCESS

Without process, software development spirals down into a quagmire of work orders to add this or that unrelated feature as quickly as possible. Some development teams even think they are successful until they have to take the next major leap in their project: that is when they are shocked at the cost to get to the next level. Clearly, a process is necessary to help all involved understand what is going on throughout the company.

Software development requires many things to be successful. There is the hard knowledge of how to write a for loop or how to parse a string, along with a plethora of other minutiae. With the advent of modeling techniques such as UML (Unified Modeling Language), there even is an approach of how to break out a piece of software and decompose it into manageable bits.

However, there is also a soft side to creating software that is hard to quantify. How do you measure the spark of inspiration that takes an enormous data problem and breaks it down into smaller problems to achieve a much quicker response time? Other sparks of creativity make leaps to entirely new forms of presentation that provide previously unimagined insights to users.

The time frame for most development also constrains the work. Too little time and the temptation is to bang something out quickly that will probably not be maintainable in the long term. Too much time and the old adage of "work expands to fill the available time" becomes true. Here again, a balance must be struck to avoid falling to either side.

To solve the problem of developing useful quality software, a holistic approach is necessary to use the contributions of everyone across all departments of an organization.

A COMMON QUESTION

A frequent frustration for business and programmers alike arises early on when discussing any software process. The question goes like this:

> "I have good programmers and a business need, why do I have to do anything except put them in a room and tell them to go?"

It is an important question. Nobody wants to drag around a lot of extra administrative headache for no reason.

Delivery

Developing software is an enormous investment. Programmers are not inexpensive, and systems of any size take a significant amount of time to develop and cost in infrastructure and manpower. This is true whether you are an internal IT department with a big training and rollout program to manage or a single-product shop with marketing schedules and sales deadlines to meet.

Build the right software—that is, the software you need

This point seems so obvious and yet it is a large problem. If we don't build software we actually need, we have failed. However, building software that we need is difficult. For one thing, the needs of the system are rarely as clear as we think. For another, software is frequently automating or replacing human effort. Humans excel at making vague decisions based on partial information, patterns of previous experience, and unrelated contextual information. Breaking down the decisions that a human makes to the degree that a computer can make them exposes many surprising things.

A tangential point: software has been developed that allows computers to defeat humans at chess. But poker, because it is a game of "incomplete information"—such as pulling off a bluff successfully—has proven much more difficult to design a winning program for.

Writing business software is often like this: you are operating with "incomplete information," such as what the user's real needs are (as opposed to what the user *thinks* they are).

Designing state-of-the-art software faces this quandary all the time; before you were shown it to be possible, for example, did you even understand you wanted email on your phone? Now you cannot imagine a phone without it.

Poorly understood requirements

Requirements are tricky things. Far too much gets implied and not enough gets detailed. Attempting to document everything before anything can start is also a losing proposition; by the time some requirements get fully fleshed out, the underlying technology has evolved to a different form and the requirements are out of date. Worse yet, a competitor has delivered (or at least announced delivery— see "FUD" in the glossary) a version of the same feature. Somehow, a balance must be struck.

Some development methods attempt to address this apparent conflict by time-boxing development. The Six Week Solution process wholeheartedly embraces this approach by enforcing deliverables of what may be a functioning piece of software without every bell and whistle tacked on the software. This approach helps drive the construction of what is really important and provides value for the company and its customers.

The Six Week Solution approach believes it is far better to release software that provides value and learn what is really important as time goes on than to spend time arguing over the final form and not producing working software on time.

When a requirement is being driven by only one person (or a single department), it is limited in scope and thought and will only specify the horizon of that originator. (If nobody understands what is being requested, chances are that it will miss the mark.) The alternative of attempting to discover every use case and define everything up front before any work begins leads to another problem: "analysis paralysis."

Unless the requirement is so clear that everyone presented with the request would instantly understand the need and value of the requirement, the originator has a responsibility to flesh out details. Presenting a couple of bullet points for a complex problem and speaking briefly only show a lack of investment from the presenter and will not resonate with development. There should be no surprise that if a requirement lacks sufficient detail it will not be addressed; "sufficient detail" is difficult to quantify, for much may go unsaid and implied in a team that has been working together for a long time. Until enough details are worked out, the request will never get traction.

Striking a balance between the desire to know everything about a request and the need to move quickly into a new opportunity is a key skill and is core to the Six Week Solution.

Adapting software development to business processes

Businesses think and plan for quarters, but typically software development departments do not. (For further discussion of this topic, see the section called "Why Six Weeks?" on page 41.)

- Software developers may think that the functionality will take two or three sprints, but they rarely worry about what can be delivered for marketing by the start of Q3 to meet a tradeshow deadline.
- However, the *business side of the company* commonly plans for events, press releases, salesperson's compensation, etc.

Putting a time horizon to development, including penalties and rewards, allows alignment of your business needs and software development. Further, it allows you to gauge where you are frequently and make game-changing decisions.

Another issue: needs change over time

Once a product is in the field, the needs of the product change. It has long been an adage in software development that "Any running program is obsolete and should be documented, and that if the program is useful, it must be modified." As humorous as that statement is, the awful truth is that it is true.

When a piece of software is first envisioned, it is pure, true to the original concept creator's ideas and goals. This is a glorious time to be involved in the creation of a product because each new feature is a milestone and nothing is a problem. Then it gets into the hands of a (paying) customer and the needs are changed instantly.

When customers get the software, it might not work like they thought:

> Imagine that the product is so close in many ways to a spreadsheet program that the user is familiar with, but it is delivered in a browser; inevitably, the customer will complain because Ctrl-*whatever* key doesn't work the same in your product as the spreadsheet program. In past approaches, the only response from the company would be "Sorry, you have to wait until the next release." And that release may be six months or more than a year away.

One theory is that pushing it into the next release is the only sure way to get the quality where it needs to be. However, that method comes at a risk: the temperature of a client continues to escalate and small problems become big problems.

Another approach is to recognize that this is a reasonable request and could be defined to be built and delivered within one or more cycles, while simultaneously delivering functional and improved software to the customer. Sometimes, you don't have to fix *all* the bugs, but you do need to fix *enough of them* so that the customer knows you are working hard and will wait until the next release. And if that release is only six weeks away, they don't have to wait long.

Newly exposed opportunities

Frequently, the product can solve an unexpected problem with just a few tweaks from the existing design and be far more robust as a consequence.

When envisioned originally, using the input for the industries that you were targeting, the product needed to have a well-known set of features. Then industries outside of that original target audience saw your product; it was so close to what they needed that they bought it. But it wasn't exactly what they wanted and they need this or that changed slightly.

The worst thing to do in this situation is to think that that's not the business you're in and that the people need to go pound sand. Instead, take a real look at what they are saying and abstract the question. More often than not, it will benefit your original customers as well as give the new customers what they really need. Use these opportunities to improve the product and sell it to new customers.

SOFTWARE DEVELOPMENT IS HARD—VERY HARD

Excellent software development is even harder. Throwing something together quickly is done all the time, and there are many objectives that a quick-and-dirty script can solve. Crafting a quality, valuable, sustainable software product is something else altogether.

Developers and product managers are notorious for overdesigning and underbuilding. Perhaps the hardest single thing to have done is to create new things that fit right into the existing program instead of starting over from scratch every time. Greenfield development or "cut, paste, and tweak" work is easy, but projects rarely stay in these phases for very long. True mastery of developing software is adding dramatic, useful new features in a reliable, incremental fashion.

It requires an unusual mix of art and science

To produce exceptional software you need two things:

- artistic inspiration
- hard science

Artistic inspiration does not necessarily mean a background in art (and therefore enabling the creation of beautiful-looking GUIs), and hard science does not require a mastery of particle physics (although if your product deals with radiation, you had better have people who understand it). You need to strike a balance.

The artistic

The artistic, inspired element provides the creative spark to come up with new ideas and solve complex problems. Many times, software development gets to stand on the shoulders of giants who came before in order to enable the current generation to reach further. Putting together all prior advances in software, from the low-level guts of memory management, linked lists, sorting, and so on, and applying it to delivering data through a Web page, for example, require many artistic leaps.

Much like the creation of a painting, the moment of inspiration cannot be forced. It is frequently true that after a good night's sleep the solution to a problem is evident the next morning. The ability to realize that you are not making progress and need to walk away for a while is critical, yet many developers continue to sit in front of a keyboard vainly attempting to produce a solution to meet an artificial deadline imposed by managers eager to show progress to *their* boss.

The scientific

Equally, you need the hard science component to develop software, for at its most basic level the computer is a binary machine. Mathematics—and not just arithmetic for adding, subtracting, multiplying, and dividing—can frequently solve a problem that would be nearly impossible (or take too long) to solve in a brute force manner. The ability to find patterns in something that looks completely unstructured at first glance is often crucial to taking the necessary leaps to move a product forward.

Another scientific skill necessary to craft software is the ability to observe and change assumptions. Technology advances quickly, and in six months there may be a better solution that can be applied to your problem. What was true a few years ago may no longer be true today, and nowhere is this more evident than in the area of parallel programming. (This is true regardless of whether it is inside a single computer or distributed across many machines.) This particular advance is not yet universally understood in software development, and the old approaches that led to good performance may not be relevant in a massively parallel environment. The ability to realize that an approach is no longer working and needs to change is required.

WHY OTHER AGILE METHODOLOGIES OFTEN FAIL

It is very popular today to approach development in sprints or iterations. However, there is no penalty for failure or reward for success (outside of being employed). Firing an entire development team is typically not an option, nor is granting the entire team a ridiculous bonus. As a result, most software development organizations blunder forward, moving any missed functionality or nonfunctional bits of software into the next iteration or sprint.

Sprints do not align with the needs of the business. Maybe there is a sprint to build a feature for the next big upcoming trade show, but this is not the norm.

If a release fails, developers don't lose money

Instead of rolling into the next iteration with the same development staff that missed the last iteration, the Six Week Cycle builds in rewards for success. If everything on the cycle commitment is met, then the variable compensation portion of salary is paid out. If the development fails to deliver everything on the list, then they forfeit the variable portion of their compensation.

This attracts confident and skilled developers, while rejecting those who would coast "Wally-style" and hide out. For further information on this topic, see the section called "Compensation" on page 79.

WHY WATERFALL PROCESSES OFTEN FAIL

While not practiced anywhere near as often as it used to be (at one time it was the *only* way to build software), it is still done. More importantly, though, its role these days is to provide more of a contrast, a "this-is-NOT-what-we-do" kind of thing. The antipattern with waterfall style development is that there is no visibility into what is getting developed until the end and no end date is set before the work begins.

Waterfalls and crystal balls
A familiar manufacturing model
When thinking about building software, we naturally think about it in terms of building physical products because that is what we are familiar with. We understand, at least on a basic level, the process of building a physical product, such as a home. A customer sits down and defines all the things that the product needs to be able to do. It needs three bedrooms, two baths, and a big enough backyard for the dogs. Then an architect, steeped in arcane craft and armed with impressive tools, sits down and designs a solution that fits those criteria. He comes back with artist renderings, blueprints, and other documents that show that he has a plan that fits all the requirements. Those plans get handed off to craftspeople who understand how to read all those documents and build the house based on them. Finally, we get to walk through our house to make sure he did it right and have him fix any problems. Then the development phase ends and the house goes into maintenance mode, where "all" we have to do is try and keep the place in good repair.

This workflow is an example of a simple waterfall, where work progresses conceptually in an orderly downward flow to achieve the end result. A waterfall process is an orderly progression through various development phases, marking each step from phase to phase with a set of gates. A gate is a checkpoint in the process where the stakeholders in a project review the decisions made in that phase and either challenge those decisions or sign off their agreement with those decisions to enable the project to move forward to the next phase.

Common phases in waterfall methods include:

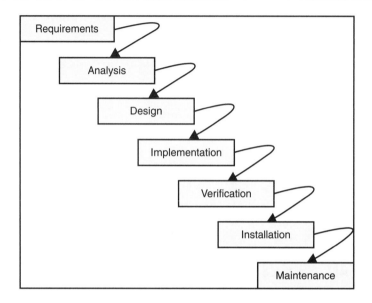

What may not be obvious is that waterfalls and their gates are driven by the *cost of change*.

Going back to the home building example, you know that your architect charges by the hour, so you try to get all your requirements for your house figured out up front. You do not want to have to send him back over and over with all the things that you had not considered. You are going through the analysis and requirements phases, and it is very likely that your architect will want you to sign off on your list in some fashion to commit to your requirements before significant investment is put into design. When designing, the architect has to work out every detail of the building and then bring those designs back to you. At this point, the project must pass another gate, where you are expected to sign off that his design is what you wanted. The reason for completing this step—and going through the gate before entering the construction phase—is because it is expensive to change the design after construction has begun.

For more discussion on this topic, see Chapter 6, "Managing the Cost of Change" on page 89.

Killing your project with process

Let us say that we have built our software product using a waterfall methodology. Somewhere down the road in the process, we find that we need to change what we are planning. Either we have made a mistake or, more positively, we have learned more about what we are building and can improve the solution we are crafting.

I am a waterfall kind of guy.

Development manager/Software director at a large telecom company ~2002

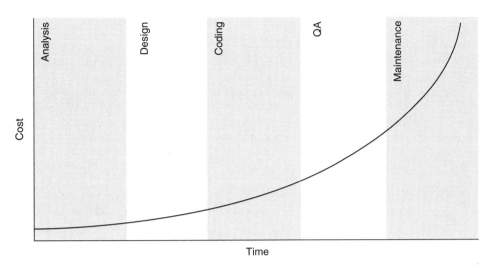

FIGURE 2.1

Cost of change curve.

Here's a quick rough sketch of the cost of that change (Figure 2.1, cost of change curve).

Specific costs of change

The impact to make a simple change in what you are building, by phase:

A New Need Was Discovered during the	Activities	Cost of Change
Analysis Phase	Change the analysis findings.	Five minutes
Requirements Phase	Analyst updates findings and gets stakeholder sign-off. One hour. Requirement engineer updates requirements docs. One hour.	Two man hours
Design Phase	Analyst finds the most recent findings, refamiliarizes himself with them, and since he has since moved on to other things, updates the findings, and sends them to stakeholder to sign off on changes. Two hours. Requirements engineer updates requirements and sends them to stakeholder for sign-off. Two hours. Designer updates design to reflect new requirement and controls impact on the rest of the system. Four hours.	One man day
Implementation Phase	Analyst finds the most recent findings, updates them, and sends them off to stakeholder to sign off on changes. Two hours. Requirements engineer finds the most recent requirements documents, refamiliarizes herself with them, and since she has since moved on to other projects, updates the requirements, and sends them off to the stakeholder for sign-off. Four hours.	One man week

Continued

A New Need Was Discovered during the	Activities	Cost of Change
Verification	Designer reworks completed design to accommodate new needs and attempts to manage the disruption to the rest of the now-implemented design and has changes reviewed. Two days.	Two man weeks
	Developer reworks implementation to reflect new design. Two days.	
	The first analyst is no longer with company, so a new analyst tries to learn the original findings, update them, and get sign-off. One day.	
	Requirements engineer locates and updates requirements and gets approval of changes. One day.	
Maintenance	Designer reworks completed design to accommodate new needs and makes less than ideal decisions to reduce the impact on the completed system. Two days.	Five man weeks
	Developer reworks implementation to reflect new design while trying not to break anything that is already working. Three days.	
	QA rewrites test plans to new requirements and retests the system for that change and unintended side effects of that change. Three days.	
	Analysis performed effectively by support team trying to find clever solutions to work around product's shortcomings. One man week.	
	Requirements require contract negotiation and debate as to whether this change was in the original contract scope while trying to assess if the new requirement is compatible with the existing ones. One man week.	
	Designer struggles to keep a coherent design together while accommodating new needs. One week.	
	Implementer makes questionable decisions trying to keep changes from breaking existing functionality. One week.	
	QA finds that existing functionality was, in fact, broken anyway and sends it back for fixing. One week.	

Reactions to this list

There are generally three reactions to this list:

- One reaction is to think that this example is exaggerated because it is assumed that people who are really good at this will not have these problems.
- The other reaction is the people who have lived it; they realize that these numbers are probably too conservative.
- The third is that they have read Barry Boehm's research back in 1981 and are bored with this conversation.

To get here, we've paid a high cost in terms of overhead, documentation, meetings, and communication in the hope that we can take careful, measured, safe steps toward completing our project and instead we quickly find ourselves in a place where we cannot move at all because it is too expensive. Even worse, the bigger the project, the longer each of those steps becomes and the greater the cost to retrace our steps.

Bad as that is, the alternative is usually worse.

Software reality #1: software changes

Even houses, really, are never finished. We move in and we change the paint colors. We change fixtures, we upgrade windows, we relandscape the property. We might finish a basement or, over time, decide that we need to move a wall or add a room for that nursery we were not expecting. We absorb the cost of change over time when it is worthwhile for us. A fascinating exploration of this process is captured in the book *How Buildings Learn: What Happens after They Are Built*, which caught a lot of attention in software circles because it accurately represents a software life cycle. Why?

A software project has only two states:

- A healthy software project has a perpetual stream of requests for features because people are using it and seeing ways it could make their lives even better.
- A dying software project has no feature requests because people are avoiding using it, working around it, or have found a better option. This is worth noting.

Software that is not changing is dying

This means managing the cost of change means *everything* to the viability of your project.

Waterfall workflows in various incarnations have another criticism to offer. Each step requires you to act with the least information that you will ever have in the software process.

Requirements—At the beginning of your waterfall, you are the least informed about the needs of the project that you will ever be. However, this is the time when you have to make "final" decisions about what the project will end up looking like.

Analysis/Design—At the design phase, you need to create a future code framework, but you do it with only the highest level of details about all the complexities that the code will have to manage. The design is going to be out of date as soon as you start to actually code it.

Implementation—Trying to implement the design that has been provided at this point, the developers have to guess all the details of the kinds of uses that the code will be put to. They will not really know if they covered them all until their code has moved on into the testing phase.

Verification—Only now do we finally have concrete feedback on whether all the previous effort has even come near the target. That is a long time to wait.

Just the first four gates are a long time to wait until a product gets delivered, and you still have to plan for installation and maintenance of your product. Installation itself has to deal with unknowns as you may not have dealt with every combination of browser/operating system/hardware before getting the product into the field. Maintenance is an unknown until the first revision, which is often where you find out that many of the assumptions you made in the implementation phase were very wrong and that it will take more work to tear up the useless infrastructure.

We can fix this process to make decisions when we have *the most information rather than the least*. In the process, we substantially fix the cost of change curve. How? Actually, that topic gets its own chapter. We call it: Chapter 8, "Integrating Automation into Your Development Process" on page 135. But let's see if we can mitigate the risk first.

HIGH VISIBILITY
The business gets regular updates on what development is doing

Instead of waiting until the end—the testing phase—to find out what exactly has been developed, it is better to get visibility into the product at frequent intervals and thereby get the ability to make changes in direction. At least twice a quarter, the major input to the direction is gathered, discussed, and argued and the work defined. Halfway through, a checkpoint exists to see what has been developed thus far in the cycle. Finally at the sign-off, a full demonstration is given where input to future development can again be collected. This feedback loop provides a vibrant method to direct the development of your product quickly.

No ivory tower

Some development organizations work like they have no deadline and the business will continue without them. These high priests of technology sit at their computers cranking out something, but it may or may not be what the business actually needs. We once assumed control over a development organization of highly intelligent and educated individuals. Imagine our shock when one lead developer said: "We don't release software on a schedule, we release it when it is ready." Nothing could be further from the truth of what business needs. Nice for the developers in theory, but deadly for their company in practice.

Meanwhile, the company was struggling to keep up with competition and selling an outdated product. Worse yet, technology had advanced past the initial design parameters of the product and customer support was struggling to keep a product alive. They were using technology that was two revisions behind what customers were downloading and installing on their desktops. This situation was costing the company real dollars while the developers argued over bits and bytes, which source control system to use, or even if source control was really necessary. Each developer had their own sandbox for development "experiments" that would be merged in some future phase when they felt the software was "ready." It seems amazing that a company would allow developers to function this way, but the reality is that many companies are run this way.

Software development cannot be allowed to operate in this ivory tower mode. Companies exist for profit, not a developer's personal research project. Customer frustration was high, and nothing was being done to address any concerns or failures in the product until the next release with an unspecified time frame.

The Six Week Solution allows a balance of reining in development while still providing a defined time for research and experimentation and providing updates to address business and customer needs in a timely manner.

DEATH MARCH

As it applies to software development, a "death march" is a destined-to-fail software project. All of the participants know it is going to fail, all of the stakeholders know it is going to fail, and yet it is kept going. It is kept going by momentum, budgetary laziness, bureaucratic intransigence and the unwillingness of key players—often it only takes one person to raise his or her head from the sand and yell "stop!"—to halt the madness.

A death march story

I once spent three years working 14 hours a day writing a completely new application. It had every feature imaginable. It included every improvement any customer had ever asked for. It was incredibly extensible. It had its own screen layout tool and equation specification language. Etcetera.

All this sounds good right? Maybe not so much, since every requirement up until this point had been specified by one person. Eventually the guy was fired. We were in San Diego and the end users were in Chicago.

If you have been in software development for a while, you can sympathize.

We retooled the product and eventually sent it to beta. But once there, bad things happened. User reaction was "mixed."

There was a long discussion and the overall consensus was that the UI needed a complete rewrite and many of the capabilities would need to be significantly simplified.

I was beyond crushed. Three years of my professional life—to say nothing about $500K worth of corporate development costs—were being washed down the drain.

C programmer (circa 1988)

For a long time creating software was a complex process that used to take years to finish. Then things got *really* complicated.

Sophisticated software development started in the 1960s, when the U.S. space program was funded. DARPA (Defense Advanced Research Projects Agency) got started around then too. Lickliter was dreaming up this small thing called the Internet—the now famous "network of networks."

Developing software for the space program imposed a discipline that is sorely missing in many of today's development environments. For one thing, developers were working under very, very tight deadlines. For another, they had very tight size requirements.

The first computer could only hold 159,744 bits in its core memory. This meant the entire machine could only store 156K (http://www.cedmagic.com/history/project-gemini-computer.html)!

Compare those numbers to software in 2009 where just the core Java Virtual Machine (JVM), which runs Java programs, consumes over 1.5 million bytes of memory; to put it in 1964 terms for comparison to the Gemini guidance computer, that requires over 12 million bits! It was possible to orbit the Earth with 1% of the code required for the JVM alone. It may be fair to point out that the Gemini computer only had to do one thing and didn't have to deal with databases, the Internet, email, IM, encryption, multiple operating systems, and so on, but that one thing was to orbit the Earth and help return a human safely back to Earth.

Now we find ourselves frequently in a death march to produce a product for many reasons, typically to face competition from other companies eager to fill the same niche. It shouldn't be any different from the space race, but it is as there is not *one vendor and one customer* but rather a *multitude of vendors* all competing for the same customers. Getting quality software out the door in a timely fashion is absolutely required, and yet schedules slip and slip again with no usable product to put into the hands of a customer.

Even when you *think* you are sprinting, you are doing a death march because:

- There is no end date
- There is no "good enough" ("this can't be shipped because it is missing feature x")

Instead, the simple answer is to act. Take a critical view of what is done and what is not done. Chances are, the very core bits of functionality are complete and you can start making money off of what is done instead of worrying about what is not done.

Take a step back and objectively evaluate where you are with the product. Are you concerned that no one will like your newest widget because there is a bug in creating a new password? Far too often shops get pulled down by a bug list for items that won't ever make or break a product. Focus on what is important. Once a product is out the door, your priorities will change.

Remember this: you don't have to fix all the bugs, just fix the worst ones so your customer will stay with you until the next release. That's only true if the product works. If your code can't run it for more than a couple of mouse clicks and then it goes boom, you have other problems. Software reflects the group that produced the software; if the company is dysfunctional, then the software is dysfunctional.

MAN IN A ROOM

All too frequently, software teams are carried by the ability and sheer willpower of a single individual or a handful of individuals. Maybe that developer or developers had the original vision or maybe they were simply handy and had the skill to get something done. But eventually they slip or get tripped up over some bug or a feature that was scoped too large. Management is left fretting, wringing their hands worrying if the product will ever ship and the only productive action they have is to push pizza and caffeinated soft drinks under the door and hope that a product somehow miraculously appears on the other side.

All the risk management they learned in MBA school is useless at this point, and no additional resources will make the product get to a releasable point any faster.

The real problem is even larger because software today is simply too big for one person to manage alone. While there may exist an expert on language parsing, compiler writing, middleware, regular expressions, network protocols, operating systems, several different programming languages, and human computer interaction somewhere in the world, chances are you are going to have to hire several people to build everything. A man in a room style of development just isn't going to make the cut and deliver quality software to the marketplace.

On my first lead position, I had a developer who was working on a project alone. I would check in with him from time to time to see how it was going and he would assure me that it was going well. I saw him working late and on weekends, and I knew he was working hard, head down in his office.

He was working hard enough that it slowly started to worry me. I started to dig because progress was not visible in any way on that team. It turns out that he was floundering. Every time he touched the project, it broke.

To protect himself from that, he went to enormous effort not to change anything if he could help it. In the process, he copied and pasted code all over the place with very small tweaks. When the stuff he copied was broken, it was broken in hundreds of copied hiding places.

Every time the project went further south, he worked that much harder to try to fix it. I told him to stop working on it, but he was so overinvested in it that he would sneak around to do it. When the problem finally came to a head, he was working from home on a Saturday night and would not answer his phone. I had to call our IT support emergency line and have them shut off his account access.

He had given it his all, but it broke him. We were eventually able to fix both him and his work, but it was an expensive proposition. We have seen it happen to developers at all skill levels. Coders and caffeine and hard work are not enough of a formula for a successful project.

Senior team lead

THE ROGUE DEVELOPER

Another term for a rogue developer is "cowboy coder." Rogue developers write the code they think needs to be written or the code they feel like writing, but not the code the team has agreed to write. In the Six Week Solution, having such marginable code—regardless of its quality—is a serious problem.

For further discussion about this problem, see the section entitled "The Cowboy Coder" on page 69.

"ARE YOU DONE YET?"

The old-school "Are-you-done-yet? Are-you-done-yet?" approach to software development management drives developers crazy and is responsible for so much bad code.

BUDGET BLACK HOLE

Another problem with software development (and this problem has been carried over to modern Agile methods) is that software development is a black hole when it comes to budgeting effort, resources, and time. Estimates for the level of effort are often too low or shoot for minimal functionality just to get something workable out into production. Money required for hardware resources and individuals required to build the product are too low because developers are eternally optimistic. Given that everything was underestimated, even software shops implementing Agile methodologies are falling short of on-time and on-budget deliveries. There is no reward for hitting everything required for a sprint and no consequences if some requirement was not met during a sprint.

Tuesday/Friday problem

Nonshipping Manager Story

I once worked with a development manager who never shipped anything for her entire tenure with the company. Her whole department was paralyzed with the software being perfect and never buttoned the product up enough to get it to a releasable state. It became a running joke that if asked when something would be done, she would say "Friday" with great authority and when Friday came around and asked again when it would be done the answer was always "Tuesday."

This game went on for months of late nights and weekend work, and there were always very valid sounding technical reasons for another delay. When she was a developer, she was definitely above average but when given the responsibility of delivering an entire product, she crumbled.

Senior developer

The problem was that the goals were never defined for her. She could never say that her team built a feature and it was done, and for the next cycle, they would fix a set of bugs and deliver a new feature or improvement. It was never done, and something else was always coming over the wall from the operations group that was an emergency. Given a framework that outlined the goals, such as the six week cycle, she could have been wildly successful. Instead, her team was left behind in several key technology areas while another team releasing quarterly received raises and primo office spots within the building. Her career and the career of several team members would have been very different had they been set up for success with this process.

Looking back on this experience, it seems like the bleeding would not have been totally stopped in one cycle, but after a few iterations (two or three at most) the worst problems would have been given the focus they required and would have been solved. The team was made up of several bright and motivated developers who would have risen to the challenge. Management never bought into a formal process, and while another group working on a complementary product continued to release on schedule, this team was running in circles chasing bugs that were fixed in one version and broken in another. Additionally, she did not have the tools in place for automating any section of a process and renegade builds were pulled directly from developers' desktop machines to solve the problem of the day in operations. What this development manager, and the team, needed was a measurable structure and a framework to be successful.

For a more detailed discussion of the six week time frame, see the section called "Why Six Weeks?" on page 41.

WHY THE SIX WEEK SOLUTION IS DIFFERENT

Software development processes have focused on the development of software and disregarded the business factors common to a company of any size. The goals of the Six Week Solution are to mesh the needs of the business with software development and produce a process that satisfies the needs of both.

The Six Week Solution strives to break the "analysis paralysis" of heavy processes while producing usable software in a predictable and manageable time. By listening to what the business really needs when writing software, the developers themselves become focused on solving the real problems the company needs to solve. Likewise, with the communication structure in place, the business can understand the unique challenges of software development. As a consequence, the Six Week Solution allows better business planning for new product roll outs, upgrades, and maintenance.

This process is so streamlined that developers don't have to do anything contrary to their nature. And the business has a simple handle on software development that radically reduces the complexity of the issues without necessarily having to understand the intricate nature of software development.

Expectations: What It Means for Software to Succeed

CHAPTER CONTENTS

Agile Development and Business Goals. DOI: 10.1016/B978-0-12-381520-0.00003-5

INTRODUCTION

Sometimes—despite everyone's best efforts to prevent it—software succeeds. This chapter discusses a few definitions of what "successful software" is. Because this topic is discussed extensively throughout the book, we also provide links to more detailed discussions when appropriate.

This chapter discusses briefly what "successful software" means. When appropriate, we provide links to more detailed discussions of these topics throughout the book.

The topics discussed in this chapter are:

- Software Development Sometimes (Accidentally) Succeeds
- Is Aligned with Business Needs
- Manages the Cost of Change
- Is Built in an Automated Way
- Factors Quality into the Core of the Process
- Is *Not* Constantly Being Redeployed
- Progress Is Constantly Being Made
- Delivers Something of Value
- Is Evangelical
- Is Predictable
- Is Both Tactical and Strategic
- Is Game Changing
- Allows Management to Stay Informed
- Is Measurable

SOFTWARE DEVELOPMENT SOMETIMES (ACCIDENTALLY) SUCCEEDS

Sometimes, software accidentally falls into succeeding. The software might have been "bad," but the need was so great that early adopters were willing to look the other way because they couldn't get the answer they needed with any other product. Sales went off the charts for the "wrong" reasons.

In other cases, the problem space was small enough that the project could be managed and delivered with quality. Other cases of accidental success stem from one or two exceptional people driving the dream into reality.

Mostly, though, software fails. Either it fails outright and the project is canceled or it fails to really meet the demands that it had intended to address. (For details about failures, including some real-world stories, see Chapter 2, "The Problem," on page 11.)

IS ALIGNED WITH BUSINESS NEEDS

While it sounds obvious, software development is seldom aligned directly with the needs of the business. When the Six Week Solution is explained to nontechnical people, they inevitably ask "Isn't *all* software development aligned with the needs of the business?"

No, it is not. There are plenty of reasons ("excuses") why this is not the case but regardless, the major point is: the Six Week Solution is designed to specifically align the development organization with the rest of the business.

MANAGES THE COST OF CHANGE

With the focus on functional software at all times that many software development processes pitch, you might be led to believe that you have quality code at all times. Frequently, the converse is true and in the rush to get something working quickly, a lot of cake was left around the oven. The problem is that there never is time allocated to officially go back and clean up the mess that was left behind in the rush to get something functional out the door. The garbage sits for a while, and everybody on the team has moved on to other features and after a couple of months there is no one who really knows why that particular code is there, but they are too scared to touch it for fear of breaking the build or destroying something critical.

Some methodologies—and the Six Week Solution is one of them—consciously work to leave code in a state that can be modified quickly.

This process decision is possible because of the metrics used in the Six Week Solution and is discussed in depth in Chapter 8, "Integrating Automation into Your Development Process" on page 135.

IS BUILT IN AN AUTOMATED WAY

One of the concepts built into the Six Week Solution is managing the quality of code through automation. Sometimes there may be a lone individual in a software shop concerned about the quality of the code, and maybe it's more than one developer, but rarely if ever does management ever peek into the code to see if it is quality code or endless cut/paste and tweak programming. This negligent approach to managing software projects exists for a variety of reasons, including the fact that, until recently, tools did not exist that could determine a measurement of code quality correctly.

Like the time frame of six weeks and the bullpen layout of the office, automation and code metrics are core principles in the Six Week Solution that do not exist universally with other methodologies.

Note that the point here is not just automating your build: it is also tracking changes, integrating code metrics, and taking the steps necessary to make this all happen. See the next point about factoring quality in your software.

For detailed information on this topic, see Chapter 8, "Integrating Automation into Your Development Process" on page 135.

FACTORS QUALITY INTO THE CORE OF THE PROCESS

While you cannot determine if you are making progress until you define "quality" and creating that definition is tricky, you must take the concrete step of defining what quality means to your organization. Successful software achieves "quality" by meeting very well-defined goals.

For detailed information on this topic, see the section in Chapter 7, "Assuring Software Quality" on page 117.

IS *NOT* CONSTANTLY BEING REDEPLOYED

Projects need to be completed and software needs to get released. That sounds more obvious than it is. Many projects are never completed and much software is not released, it is simply redeployed endlessly. This problem and others are discussed in Chapter 2, "The Problem: Why Software Projects Fail" on page 11.

PROGRESS IS CONSTANTLY BEING MADE

Every day you have a checkpoint, and you implement techniques such as 4:30 pm fixes, where you deploy nightly to fix the bugs fixed today. Successful software in this competitive marketplace needs that kind of just-in-time development.

For a more detailed discussion of this topic, see Chapter 7, "Assuring Software Quality" on page 117.

DELIVERS SOMETHING OF VALUE

In today's corporate software world, thing change quickly. Software As A Service (SAAS), radically new customer requirements, and different hardware platforms all make writing usable code an enormous challenge. And no one wants that usable code finished in a couple of years, they want it done yesterday.

To compete in this marketplace, you need to have a software development process that you can adapt easily. You need to be able to respond correctly to requirements that are presented this quarter and are needed for the next quarter.

One other point: successful software makes a profit. As discussed in the section called "A Note for Nonprofits" on page 5, "profit" may or may not mean revenue. The important point is that it costs less to make than it earns. This is critical—software is often seen as a necessary monetary black hole. The Six Week Solution process addresses that problem directly and offers a series of options for solving it.

For further details on this topic, see the section "Successful Software Development: Manages the Cost of Change" on page 33.

IS EVANGELICAL

Successful software is something that everyone in the organization is excited about it, something they are willing to tell their friends in other companies about. And the reason this might happen is because your software solves a previously unaddressed but well-known main point.

For detailed information on this topic, see the section called "The Entire Company Must Buy In" on page 58.

IS PREDICTABLE

For a long time in the history of software, no one—not the customer, not the company, not the developers—knew when the next release was coming. This massively unruly time table maintained a level of chaos that is not as common in other industries (to put it diplomatically).

Using the Six Week Solution, usable software is delivered every six weeks. The entire company gets new software on a predictable schedule. Also, they know not only "when" but also "what": they know what is coming and they can perform *their jobs* based on that information.

For further details on this topic, see the following sections: "Why the Six Week Solution is Different" on page 28, "Software Development Sometimes (Accidentally) Succeeds" on page 32, and "True Negotiation" on page 83. Also see Chapter 4, "Overview of the Six Week Solution" on page 37.

IS BOTH TACTICAL AND STRATEGIC

Short-term successes are critical, but long-term goals are also important to meet. Most software written and delivered today address today's issues, but what about issues that everyone knows are coming six months from now? With the Six Week Solution, you can get a quick win today and not ruin your long-term options. It requires a conscious effort built into your process to be able to do both at the same time.

We discuss this topic throughout the book, but one section that provides detail on the subject is "Why Six Weeks?" on page 41.

IS GAME CHANGING

If you see your software as a revenue-generating component and you start seeing how your software development process can be enhanced radically, the idea that you can one day say "no competitor can touch me" becomes possible. Successful software—really, really successful software—should be leading, not following, and it can become a means for companies to gain a step on their competitors.

ALLOWS MANAGEMENT TO STAY INFORMED

Much of software development around the world occurs in a vacuum, with the company's management only finding out as the software is released what is in the latest version of the product. Like many other elements of the corporation, software development should be on the management's radar. Using the Six Week Solution, management is updated constantly about the progress of its software development team.

This point is made throughout the book, but for more detailed information on this topic, see "Why Senior Management Involvement Is Key" on page 60.

IS MEASURABLE

You cannot improve the quality of your code unless you measure it carefully. How many calls your support line gets is a measurement, but one very, very late in the trip from the software shop to the customer's desktop. You need a much more detailed method of evaluating your software long before it leaves the developers' machines.

Using the Six Week Solution, *everything* is measured. Checkpoints are established for you to take your measurements. Also, the process does not allow renegade development.

For detailed information on this topic, see Chapter 7, "Assuring Software Quality" on page 117.

Overview of the Six Week Solution

CHAPTER CONTENTS

Agile Development and Business Goals. DOI: 10.1016/B978-0-12-381520-0.00004-7

INTRODUCTION

We should have written this book years ago. Independently we had worked to ship software in a timely manner, aligned ourselves with the business part of the company, and shipped software frequently—sometimes quarterly, sometimes even weekly. We had worked on automating the build process with checks for unit and integration tests and had a deep desire to automatically validate code for correctness and complexity. When we met, the concepts were not new to anyone; instead, we realized it should all be brought together and formalized. Thus the Six Week Solution idea was born.

One major project that highlighted all the failings of software development occurred at a very successful company in the mid-1980s. The project began with lofty goals of providing what would later be termed as peer-to-peer networking with a protocol that worked across UNIX, DOS, and Macintosh operating systems, including tackling the dreaded UNIX-to-DOS text file compatibility. Even file names were to be mapped between the limited DOS 8.3 character file name standard and the possibly long and case-sensitive naming convention of the Macintosh and UNIX platforms. Print support was to be consistent across all platforms, as was the user interface with a centrally managed security protocol managed on a UNIX machine.

Looking back, this all may seem rather quaint, but in the 1980s it was cutting edge. It was also an enormous failure.

Here was a classic approach of specifying everything before the project began and ignoring what was learned along the way because the file transfer protocol should have been a spin-off product all by itself. Some of the requirements may have been valid, but the need for all the different platforms was never well understood by the development staff. To make matters worse, the operating systems were changing rapidly and the current Windows/286 was incredibly unstable, often throwing a user back to a DOS prompt without warning. There were not enough staff or hardware resources available to hit the window to get the product to market. It was assumed that no software could be released until everything was ready.

1980s Company culture

At the time, the company was all very cutting edge; there was a cafeteria, two volleyball nets, running paths in the office park, and showers in the office buildings. The company was clearly catering to developers, and it should have been a paradise where they could write code, maybe attend a few meetings, work out every day, and still have a life.

Yet on a Monday in November, the entire engineering staff was laid off.

Why did this happen? There was a collection of really smart people working as hard as they could for long hours who couldn't deliver anything and they were never done. All the concepts, development work, solid teams, and money were all thrown to the wind. The need for a rhythm was clear to make the entire process of creating a software product—from conception to delivery—more bearable for everyone. From management to development, there were no visibility or regular checkpoints to keep everyone informed of the needs and progress. The Six Week Solution was created to address classic problems like these.

ADDITIONAL PROBLEMS

Too often, product management lets requirements of a software project change. This was as real a problem in the 1980s as it is today, and with the speed of communication through the Internet, it is a more significant problem now. Software companies exist in a competitive marketplace where new technologies of hardware, software development languages, and operating systems sometimes change drastically within six months. The temptations to chase the newest bright shiny object are enormous and if you don't chase that object, your competitor will introduce even more FUD (Fear, Uncertainty, and Doubt) regarding your company and product into the marketplace.

Product management

Product management must rein in the draw of chasing the latest buzzword, but yet that buzzword must be studied. The time frame of development must be quick, but still allow for significant development to be accomplished with quality. It is not acceptable to have a three month roadmap that is out of date in a month due to an announcement from a competitor. Yearly releases, attractive from the standpoint of not overwhelming a customer, are not acceptable; conversely, releasing every week because the objective of a sprint is met is not acceptable either.

Long- and short-term goals

The balance between achieving a significant amount of work and staying on top of technology is a concern addressed by the Six Week Solution. There has to be the ability to work on long-term goals while still addressing quick wins and the ability to react to a changing marketplace for product management to be successful.

Sales

On the street, sales often has no confidence in which features, bug fixes, or functionality is included in what release and no faith in the delivery date of a release. It is impossible for sales to promise a customer when a bug would be fixed or a new requested feature will be built. Without any knowledge of what was coming when, sales resorts to the only thing they can do: promise the customer anything and everything.

Marketing

Like sales, marketing is also left flapping in the wind with no good information for what to present at the next trade show or to put into a brochure. Typically, no one in the company, even product management, can communicate the state of the software to sales and marketing. Both sales and marketing need feedback loops to know what is happening with the product and to prime the pump of development with new ideas and needs. With emphasis on committing what work is being done in each development cycle, the Six Week Solution seeks to address this problem.

Developers are typically broken into silos, with developers on one part of a large project not communicating with developers in another part of the project. While the separation may be physical or managerial, delays are forced into surprising locations within a project. Any product of significant size must deal with hardware, operating systems, drivers, business logic, and presentation layers. Yet these various technical disciplines are typically separate from one another, allowing what appears to be a small change in a foundation percolating all the way up the technology stack, only to be found at the last possible stage in QA. To address this, the Six Week Solution puts all the technical disciplines in the same physical location (called a "bullpen.")

Developers' common flaws also contribute to failing projects. In a sea of churning requirements thrown up from a stormy marketplace, software developers attempt to remain in an ivory tower on an island with a huge seawall to protect themselves. Developers will sit in meeting rooms with a large white board and many colors of grease pens calmly stroking their beards and softly murmuring about best practices and object-oriented software development. They use words such as "polymorphism," which sound vague and undefined to the rest of the company as if they came from some ancient dead language. Developers sometimes relish the position they are in as the "smart" people, reinforcing this belief with difficult-to-use software when they finally do deliver something. Clearly something needs to break this approach and get the software development resources engaged into the rest of the company; this issue, too is addressed by the approach of the Six Week Solution.

Quality software cannot be built in a day. No amount of crisis management or adding resources will increase the velocity of development or correct the software quality deficit. A cutesy phrase that gets repeated by developers when management attempts to add additional human resources to solve a delivery timeline or quality problem is: "Nine women can't have a baby in a month." It takes what it takes to build quality software and the processes have to be created and the right people in place before the project begins.

Advance planning

Contrary to so many endeavors of creation, such as building a house, software development cannot be *fully* planned out in advance. Attempting to define every requirement, every use case, and every actor who will use the software, every possible machine communication has been tried in the past with only limited success. Shifting market demands and new customer requirements for new industries that sales will inevitably attempt to penetrate require that any software development effort be comfortable with some level of uncertainty. The term coined for attempting to define everything up front is "analysis paralysis." Many consulting dollars have been spent in requirements gathering, but if the concept of the product is not understood at the outset, it is doomed to failure. Requirements simply appear and shift too quickly to gather them all before a single line of code can be written.

It's like building a house, only it is not

Attempting to build software like building a house leads to disaster. When building a house, there are hundreds of years of craft and science built into the process. Blueprints are standard, the framers know which page to look at to find out where the 2 × 4s go, and even the 2 × 4s themselves are standard. Electricians flip the blueprint to the page defining every junction box, outlet, light switch, and panel. Likewise, plumbers have standard fittings and pipe sizes and ways to adapt such as fitting a copper delivery pipe to a sink, which may be independently replaced later.

Software has no such permanent standards that have existed for such a long time and weathered so many storms to find out, by trial and error, what works and what doesn't. In recent years, attempts have been made to standardize at least the plumbing of software where machines must communicate, but even these "standards" are at most decades old (like, for example, technologies such as TCP/IP). Other "standards" have only been around for less than 20 years and while they define the envelope of what is sent, they do not define the contents. Contrast that fact to the existence of different size pipes for natural gas and water and different fittings, which not only define how something is being transported, but also what is being transported inside the pipe. Software has no prior standard for the full stack of an application.

COMPONENTS OF AGILE ALIGNMENT

The Six Week Solution has three core components for aligning your development team to the business's needs and priorities. Those components are:

- Establishing a development rhythm to match your business with the 6 week cycle structure
- Directing cycle development toward key business priorities with the cycle commitment document
- Matching development's motivations to the business with the compensation structure.

Putting the business and the development team in step, targeting the same goals, and with parallel motivations puts the business much more effectively in the driver's seat of your development efforts.

WHY SIX WEEKS?

Everything in life needs a rhythm. We are accustomed to seasons, and the changes nature goes through at each transition point whether the activity is growth, hibernation, reproduction, or survival.

Establishing a rhythm

Once we decided that we needed a rhythm to software development, we needed to find the perfect interval. A week was too short to deliver major functionality; two months seemed too long as the business would still view development as a black hole. And development needed to consider the business thought process of quarters and all the planning that goes into what will happen in what quarter of the year and how that all impacted the bottom line and fiscal calendars.

Business thinks in quarterly periods. The confidence that a marketing or salesperson can show when answering questions in quarters resonates with business. New requests from potential customers should never have to be stretched out more than 11 weeks, and if a piece of functionality needs to be done sooner and the scope fits, there needed to be a mechanism built into the process that allowed, and contained, the inevitable change request.

Overall, the process must be simple and visible, providing the mechanism for communicating the business need to the development shop and provide understanding of what is happening, why it is happening, how it is happening, and who is doing it. The journalism piece of the process has to be built in from the start. It's not simple because there are many moving pieces both human and electronic, but it's also not brain surgery.

After several attempts at finding the perfect rhythm, it was finally clear that six weeks is optimal. Every quarter provides two natural cycles, which provides two chances to get requests into a development cycle with two opportunities for immediate requests in addition to each cycle.

In 12 weeks there are only six major meetings to attend, although there are many other opportunities to influence the outcome and contents of what is developed within a development cycle. Even with two deliverables per quarter, and eight releases in a year, there still is enough padding to give plenty of time for vacations around the Fourth of July and Christmas where the majority of employees will request time off (in the United States). In the end, we selected six weeks as the optimal balance among business needs, the velocity of software development, and the human requirements of some downtime to recharge.

The need for rhythm

Too often a software organization is built around a single long-range goal such as to deliver the next release and planned with some monstrous Gantt chart plotting all the tasks and inter-relations of tasks to complete the next upgrade (in some cases even plotting approved bathroom breaks!) Nothing in nature could survive this level of planning, for eventually something such as a storm, unexpected cold temperatures, or a new mutation of a virus would destroy the plan. Unlike nature, software development has attempted to define everything up front and get it all on a meticulous Gantt chart. Once the chart is created, the death march begins. The first time a milestone is missed:

- The deliverable slips
- Features are removed
- Or worse: someone thinks that they can make up the lost time later!

In the massive Gantt chart approach, there generally is no defined time for research, no intermediate delivery to gauge achievement, no natural point to adjust requirements or direction based on new information, and no time to evaluate changes in technology and the marketplace. If someone actually did plan for all of those checkpoints, when the first slip occurs these checkpoints are the first thing to be removed from the Gantt chart.

One key goal of the six week development cycle is to provide each individual and the team as a whole with a sense of rhythm to the natural alignment of the business functioning on quarters. Additionally, the assessment points built into the cycle provide their own suspense to complete quality features for demonstration and eventual release.

For the following reasons, the six week development cycle is the perfect time frame for a development organization.

Six Week Solution calendar

Six Week Solution Annual Calendar, 2010

JANUARY						
S	M	T	W	T	F	S
					1	2
3	4	5	6	7	8	9
10	11	12	13	14	15	16
17	18	19	20	21	22	23
24	25	26	27	28	29	30/31

Cycle 1

FEBRUARY						
S	M	T	W	T	F	S
	1	2	3	4	5	6
7	8	9	10	11	12	13
14	15	16	17	18	19	20
21	22	23	24	25	26	27
28						

Cycle 2

MARCH						
S	M	T	W	T	F	S
	1	2	3	4	5	6
7	8	9	10	11	12	13
14	15	16	17	18	19	20
21	22	23	24	25	26	27
28	29	30	31			

APRIL						
S	M	T	W	T	F	S
				1	2	3
4	5	6	7	8	9	10
11	12	13	14	15	16	17
18	19	20	21	22	23	24
25	26	27	28	29	30	

Cycle 3

MAY						
S	M	T	W	T	F	S
1/2	3	4	5	6	7	8
9	10	11	12	13	14	15
16	17	18	19	20	21	22
23	24	25	26	27	28	29
30	31					

Cycle 4

JUNE						
S	M	T	W	T	F	S
		1	2	3	4	5
6	7	8	9	10	11	12
13	14	15	16	17	18	19
20	21	22	23	24	25	26
27	28	29	30			

JULY						
S	M	T	W	T	F	S
				1	2	3
4	5	6	7	8	9	10
11	12	13	14	15	16	17
18	19	20	21	22	23	24
25	26	27	28	29	30	31

Cycle 5

AUGUST						
S	M	T	W	T	F	S
1	2	3	4	5	6	7
8	9	10	11	12	13	14
15	16	17	18	19	20	21
22	23	24	25	26	27	28
29	30	31				

Cycle 6

SEPTEMBER						
S	M	T	W	T	F	S
			1	2	3	4
5	6	7	8	9	10	11
12	13	14	15	16	17	18
19	20	21	22	23	24	25
26	27	28	29	30		

OCTOBER						
S	M	T	W	T	F	S
					1	2
3	4	5	6	7	8	9
10	11	12	13	14	15	16
17	18	19	20	21	22	23
24	25	26	27	28	29	30/31

Cycle 7

NOVEMBER						
S	M	T	W	T	F	S
	1	2	3	4	5	6
7	8	9	10	11	12	13
14	15	16	17	18	19	20
21	22	23	24	25	26	27
28	29	30				

Cycle 8

DECEMBER						
S	M	T	W	T	F	S
			1	2	3	4
5	6	7	8	9	10	11
12	13	14	15	16	17	18
19	20	21	22	23	24	25
26	27	28	29	30	31	

FIGURE 4.1

Six Week Solution calendar: the entire year.

Manageable time frame

Six weeks is a short time frame. Tasks must be relatively small and well defined in order for them to be achieved—with the required quality—in six weeks of development time. This time frame enables us to focus on our tasks and give the tasks the attention they require. (For a diagram showing how the Six Week Solution fits into an entire year's calendar, see Figure 4.1.)

Note: We have worked in one environment where releases were done *weekly*. Weekly iterations sound good in theory, but in the real world, weekly product releases are very difficult events for both customers and the company.

Most things can wait

One of our goals is to prevent external interference and distraction from cycle commitments. Although there are always exceptions, most things can wait until the next cycle to be properly prioritized, assigned, and resolved. This also solves the problem of "sea gull management" and "knee-jerk reactions," which both serve to destroy software quality and in the end do nothing to reduce the time required to produce functional software.

Boundary to benchmark progress and make commitments

Much like the corporate world expects results on a quarterly basis, the Six Week Solution gives other groups within the organization a time frame in which to expect results from software development. Cycle commitments are identified at the beginning of a cycle. These commitments let other departments know the focus of software development for the next six weeks. At Mea Culpa, we identify whether we can complete a task in a cycle. Finally, at cycle sign-off, we can address the specific cycle accomplishments.

Two cycles per quarter

A wonderful side effect of the six week cycle is that it fits very nicely within the corporate world expectation of four quarters within a year. There are two cycles per quarter with one extra week to remove most holidays from the cycle rhythm. Two cycles per quarter allow you to define in greater detail and more thoroughly complete tasks for the quarter, in many cases without a great deal of upfront planning attempting to fully define functionality. This timing, along with checkpoints, gets all stakeholders in the overall business and in software development to focus on what is really important and delivering the important functionality on time with high quality.

Opportunity to change direction

Business priorities and technologies change. Six weeks is a good time frame to build checkpoints and possibly change long- or short-term goals if needed. The short time frame allows the freedom to change short-term goals to deal with inadequacies or environmental changes. Checking back every six weeks to identify long-term goals provides the flexibility to change these goals as situations change. (For a diagram showing how the Six Week Solution fits into a single quarter, see Figure 4.2.)

Forcing scope

An enormous hurdle to get over in any software process, especially when creating a better mousetrap, is to move in small, incremental steps. In the process of building software, you simply must be prepared

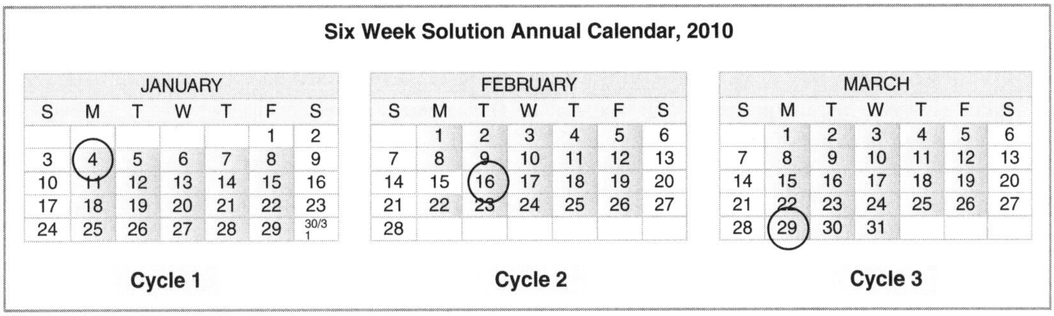

Six Week Solution Annual Calendar, 2010

JANUARY						
S	M	T	W	T	F	S
					1	2
3	(4)	5	6	7	8	9
10	11	12	13	14	15	16
17	18	19	20	21	22	23
24	25	26	27	28	29	30/3 1

Cycle 1

FEBRUARY						
S	M	T	W	T	F	S
	1	2	3	4	5	6
7	8	9	10	11	12	13
14	15	(16)	17	18	19	20
21	22	23	24	25	26	27
28						

Cycle 2

MARCH						
S	M	T	W	T	F	S
	1	2	3	4	5	6
7	8	9	10	11	12	13
14	15	16	17	18	19	20
21	22	23	24	25	26	27
28	(29)	30	31			

Cycle 3

FIGURE 4.2

Six Week Solution Calendar: one quarter.

to throw out a prototype. Instead of starting over from scratch, you must be mentally prepared to force incremental changes. Don't re-create the storage mechanism at the same time you are changing the presentation layer to use a new technology. All structural changes should be made with upstream and downstream systems untouched so that solid testing can be performed. Having a process made up of six week periods forces scope in each cycle to remain at a manageable level.

CYCLE COMMITMENTS

Each cycle revolves around a cycle commitment document. This document is a contract between the business and the development team that specifies the expected deliverables for the development team in the current six week cycle. Collaboration between the business and development to build out the details of these commitments is a key component of the Six Week Solution. Signing this document should be an event, and what keeps it from being an empty ritual comes next.

DEVELOPER COMPENSATION: COD

The cycle document codifies the business's priorities, but it does not yet motivate the developers to focus on it. To create a culture that is focused on satisfying the businesses needs, a crucial part of the Six Week Solution structures part of a developer's pay as a bonus paid at the end of each Six Week cycle. Base salaries are set a bit below competitive wages to align developer's motivations with the business costs of missed commitments. After all, the business is going to make commitments to customers, spend money on marketing, line up resources for rollout and maintenance, and buy hardware for deployment based on the development plans. The pay structure is described in more detail in the Compensation section of Chapter 5 on page 57.

Key elements of the bonus structure include:

• Every member of the development team is eligible for a bonus. (The department has this very cool aspect built into it.)

- Every member of the development team must participate in the bonus program. (The element is a core element of the process, and no one is allowed to skip.)
- Bonuses are paid based upon satisfying every single commitment made to the business for the cycle. (Success means giving the business what they need.)
- Bonuses are paid at the end of each cycle. (They are not paid at the end of the year, but every six weeks.)
- Developers succeed or fail together. (Developers are not allowed to opt out of participation, and this aspect has caused more than one potential hire to back away.)

Provides Motivation

The compensation structure is the glue that keeps the development team in line with the business. While developers are frequently not primarily motivated by money, the compensation factor motivates the team on several key levels.

- It creates a culture where success and failure are fundamentally defined by delivering what was promised, to the business, when promised. It may seem odd, but development teams rarely function that way.
- It also pulls the teams together into tighter units, because the compensation is all or nothing for the team. Either the whole team finishes everything, or nobody gets anything
- Developers are on a dynamic and tightly knit team – not a random collection of individual contributors for perhaps the first time in their careers.
- Developers are acknowledged. Their success is visible in the product, amongst their colleagues at work – and in their paychecks. This is a strong developer motivation.
- Due to the structure of the process, the points of failure are reduced (because other members have strong motivation to be able to pick up the slack). Developers are not working in isolation and have concrete incentive to help each other be successful.

The compensation structure keeps the development team glued to the rest of the business.

SIX WEEK ITERATIONS

The nature of software development has changed: it is no longer possible to take four years to deliver the next upgrade or even produce the initial product. Six months may be a risky time span given the competition you may be facing, so any methodology to reduce the time to market while still delivering quality is a benefit. We know that you have to produce and get profitable quickly and the Six Week Solution is a methodology to get there. (For a diagram showing a single Six Week Solution cycle, see Figure 4.3.)

Breaking your development windows into six week chunks allows quick delivery of new opportunities, fits well with how businesses think and plan, and lets you target changing needs as your product and client base grows. In addition, rewards and penalties are built into the system to ensure that you have a quality product at all times.

By strictly time boxing your investment in software development to six weeks, you enable experimentation and can afford to explore some directions that may turn out to be blind alleys in the long

Six Week Solution Annual Calendar, 2010

	JANUARY					
S	M	T	W	T	F	S
					1	2
3	4	5	6	7	8	9
10	11	12	13	14	15	16
17	18	19	20	21	22	23
24	25	26	27	28	29	30/3 1

	FEBRUARY					
S	M	T	W	T	F	S
	1	2	3	4	5	6
7	8	9	10	11	12	13
14	15	16	17	18	19	20
21	22	23	24	25	26	27
28						

	MARCH					
S	M	T	W	T	F	S
	1	2	3	4	5	6
7	8	9	10	11	12	13
14	15	16	17	18	19	20
21	22	23	24	25	26	27
28	29	30	31			

Cycle 1

| Cycle | Kick Off ◯ | Sign Off ⇨ | Mea Culpa △ | Cycle End ☐ |

FIGURE 4.3

Six Week Solution Calendar: one cycle.

term. It has been a fairly standard thought process in developing software to attack the risky portions of a project early in the development to reduce investment in bad approaches that may not result in a viable product. We embrace that concept and further divide investment into a manageable time frame of six weeks. This time span is long enough to produce a significant amount of work, yet short enough that the investment is not so large that it must be seen through to the end.

The Six Week Solution provides a sharper focus to the development process than even other Agile processes do for several reasons:

- **Transparency:** Explicitly spelling out what will be developed to the entire company increases the focus on the work being performed in development. Checkpoints exist in the method to continue the focus on communication so that there are no surprises.
- **Everyone in the company can understand the cycle:** From the office manager to customer support and sales, everyone in the company will know what is being developed and when it will be available.
- **Rhythm:** If everyone in the company follows this process, everyone naturally falls into the natural rhythm of the process.
- **They should then be able to touch and feel what was made:** At frequent intervals, all interested parties should be able to see and use the software to know what is being constructed.
- **Keeps the development team always focused on business goals:** Developers will wander. The entire Six Week Solution processes is set up to keep them focused and not feel like they are experiencing a death march. Instead, it should feel like a campaign where they are always conquering new territory! Six Weeks is short enough to stay within the short attention spans of developers and minimizes the attraction to the latest bright and shiny object that would otherwise attract their attention. Listing exactly what you need developed keeps them focused on the real business drivers.
- **Skin in the game:** The developers actually have some "skin in the game" as a portion of their compensation depends on delivering all of the items listed on the cycle document. No longer are they willing to fail to start another sprint, but instead they are motivated to complete the cycle commitments and cash a check.

By engaging everyone in the development of a software product, with each individual contributing at his or her highest level, strictly limiting the time spent to create software, changing the physical layout of the office, measuring the quality of the software produced, and rewarding for success, it becomes possible to dig out of the hole that many software projects have dug for themselves.

TIME BOXING DEVELOPMENT: KEY DEADLINES

The Six Week Solution transcends the writing of software, documentation, and meetings and extends into the physical workplace by defining not only how to hire the members of your team, but also how to lay out the office to promote effective software development. The codification of a bullpen area for developers, QA, and technical writing sitting next to one another in an open space leaves the excesses of the 1990s style software development with its ping-pong tables and green rooms in the past where it belongs and moves into development focused on delivering functional and maintainable that delivers high value.

WEEK 1: CYCLE KICKOFF

The big bang of creation for each six week cycle is the kickoff week. This is when all the stakeholders get to express their desires and concerns for the next development cycle. All known feature requests and bug fixes should be expressed and prioritized for cycle kick-off week. Whether strategic or tactical, everything is on the table to be evaluated for inclusion into the cycle.

Optimally, the cycle kick-off meeting is early in the day on Monday morning for the development staff. This forces some preparation by product management in the weeks leading up to cycle kickoff to help "herd the cats" and collect all the input.

The cycle should start with some kind of brain dump by a strong representative of the business. Someone to explain the wins and losses. Explain the features that may or may not exist that would help close more business. It should not be a long discussion but it should certainly bring the development team into the business world for the moment so they have a glimpse of what the challenges may be. The developers will be very interested and they may have some feedback into how the system works today that no one on the business side is aware of.

The interests of everyone should be represented: the simple but hot new presentation that marketing needs, the critical care and feeding feature enhancement that support needs, and the groundwork for the major architecture change that the database developers want. Everyone should be given some time to clarify the reasons for why their top items should be considered. It is important that everyone gets their time; equally important is that their request is treated with respect. You will need a very knowledgeable arbiter for this meeting to ensure that no group's interests or proposal overruns the meeting. There should be enough information at this point to give some initial inclination about whether the request can be considered. Time must be spent prior to the meeting to define the high-level task(s) necessary to complete the goals and hence the groundwork for beginning to scope the time and resources necessary to achieve the goals.

The goal of this meeting is to take the first pass at the things that will be built in this cycle. The meeting should end with everyone having a good idea of what may be possible. There should be a list of research items and follow-up meetings to refine requirements and scope further during the balance of kickoff week.

One other note to both developers and businesspeople: everything you agreed to has been put in writing. Be careful what you agree to at this stage because you will not get to change your mind later.

Sample Kick-Off Items

Revisit charting controls to produce larger screen space for chart
Evaluate <Insert latest data cube technology here>
Define schema for <Insert newest feature here>

Planning week

The planning week is the time when everyone will think about and plan the research and design required to complete the goals. Each person or group will take high-level tasks from the cycle commitment document and break them down into subtasks. At this time, they will identify what other resources are needed to complete the tasks and manage the various dependencies. Each group or person will determine a realistic time estimate to complete each task as well as the goals. In addition to doing a high-level breakdown, all of the dependencies need to be identified and assigned as well. The time estimate will need to fit into the remaining five weeks of the cycle following sign-off.

Large tasks

A critical concept during the planning week is that some tasks are simply too large to fit in six weeks. Fortitude is required to stand up and say, "Dude, that's too much!" followed immediately by, "But here's what we can do quickly, and then we can do this really cool thing!" This kind of feedback is not always easy to hear, when the tasks are of particularly high importance for the business. There is a common pattern for someone in authority to push back and say that it has be done anyway, so work evening and weekends and do whatever it takes. Situations like this have failed before they even kick off. For a number of reasons we will discuss elsewhere, these kinds of efforts destroy software projects, and generally leave both a product and a team that are no longer functional.

A better approach is try to break up the necessary tasks into smaller pieces of functionality, each of which provides deliverable business value. Those pieces then can be prioritized and fit into multiple cycles based on their relative priority. That process feels uncomfortable to many at first, and it is tempting to say the task cannot be broken up, or we cannot live without all of it, but an experienced team almost always can find a way.

You get to play with technology

To developers, this week provides the ability to play with technology and we don't mean the latest real-time strategy game or latest release for the game console du jour. "Playing with technology" at this phase is why lions bring wounded prey home to the kittens to practice killing their own dinner. You play to learn, experiment, and come up with a swift kill. Just as biting a mortally wounded gazelle teaches young lions how they can provide for themselves later, playing with technology allows for a chance to evaluate choices and practice for the best method of working to produce a quality result.

Developers also have the responsibility for tracking down any fuzzy requirements to get more details. Recipients of the product have the responsibility to define any loosely defined requirements to get an honest appraisal of what is being requested. Throwing up requirements consisting of several latest buzzwords strung together because a deal was signed is not a cycle requirement. If you expect honest answers from your software development group, don't ask for fuzzy undefined things such as "what we really need is these data in a Web 2.0 format" and then be upset when that software development group asks: "Which Web 2.0 format?" You need to be able to answer that question because the developers don't know if you are asking for one of many standardized messaging formats or something for pumping messages to Twitterholics. You have the right to know what is being developed and the responsibility to know and understand what you are asking for. Given the right input, you can expect truthful estimates.

Cycle finalization

Before the final document is prepared, the team will gather and make one last pass through the tasks and make sure that everyone is comfortable. This is probably the hardest part of the process. Fairness and full utilization are critical. You want to ensure that the workload is distributed properly over the team. You want to have goals that are achievable but require a stretch. It is very important for the continued survival of this methodology that the business has a feel for the work and believes that the team is pressed. Never should a cycle commitment document be a cakewalk, and neither should it be a death march. Finding the balance is critical.

A document identifying each separate task that makes up the goal and the responsibility for completing that task will be drawn up. At this same time, a document with the identified goals will be written; this is the document we will physically sign, in ink, by our own hands.

Cycle sign-off

At the cycle sign-off meeting, the development organization and the business come together once again to sign the document for the cycle. Each person on the team will sign this document reflecting his or her understanding of the team commitments. This process should be assigned all of the formality of a contract, as that is what it is, a six week agreement between the business and the development organization.

Ideally at this point there are no surprises, but it is a good practice to review all of the items on the document. Make sure that everyone, inside and outside of software development, understands what each item means and the expected scope.

We like to have verbiage at the top and the bottom of the document with the dates of the cycle and the commitment to work as a team.

Sample Top
The staff of ABC herby enters into a mutual agreement to work as a team, support one another, and do everything in their power to successfully complete the following development deliverable in Cycle #1 beginning January 1st and ending February 16th of the year 2010.

Sample Bottom
I firmly understand the scope of these commitments and will do everything in my power to avoid deviation from this scope. Additionally I will do anything I can to support the other members of the ABC team in the completion of their commitments for this cycle.
Signed this day, January 12, 2010

What's in the middle of a cycle commitment document is up to you.

Initially, the line items may be very specific and directly reference the change to be made. This specific approach is useful for new teams or to help new members of existing teams ring the bell of success and have something concrete to point at to mark their contribution to the cycle. The other reason to have specific line items is to help train the wider audience attending cycle meetings for what they can expect to get done in a single development cycle. The specific items may simply reference reports from a bug tracking or ticketing system. Items such as "Fix bug #1245 for Customer XYZ" are perfectly acceptable and still useful even with a mature team.

As the team or team members mature with the process, it is possible to be more open with the commitment, such as "produce a web service to process <something>" because the size of the commitment is well understood by everyone inside and outside of software development. This approach does require other documentation to capture what is being accomplished by this line item, although typically a concept that cannot be defined by a couple of pages is either not well understood or too large for a single developer within the time frame of a single cycle. With everyone's signature on the commitment document, we should now have set our development team in alignment with the current business needs. Knowing that they will be paid out their bonus at the end of the cycle based on satisfying those needs will help keep the development team on track for the next six weeks as they work to satisfy those commitments.

WEEK 3: MEA CULPA

At the midpoint of the cycle, we will have a meeting to review the tasks and goals and talk about our progress. This is the time to address your concerns, remaining dependencies, and loss or addition of resources. We will adjust our goals based on this meeting.

Please note that this is not the opportunity to just replan, but rather acknowledge that as development occurs, we will learn more about what is involved. Sometimes that means making an adjustment to the schedule. In addition, we may have dependencies on items that are outside the software development group's area of responsibility. We may need to adjust our schedule based on an outside group's schedule.

Mea Culpa ("my fault" in Latin) is the opportunity for everyone to do a checkpoint. A straightforward evaluation of the work done to date and work remaining must be performed.

- For the developers, this is an opportunity to influence the future and still deliver quality without a mad scramble at the end of the cycle.
- For the businesspeople, it is an opportunity to listen with open ears to what new requirements may have been discovered.

Gut-check time

Development may come to the table explaining that a task turns out to be too large. They may come with a discovery that there is a better way to proceed that could dramatically change the time required for delivery. If things have exploded, then it's gut-check time. What can be thrown out? Can anything be rescoped or a feature reduced to ensure delivery? These questions are hard, and many times participants (software development included!) are not willing to remove an item from the list. It is important to understand that taking an item off the list isn't throwing it away for all time, because it can come back in the very next cycle.

Business may come with a critical item that needs to be addressed. If the schedule was set up where it should be, with a bit of a stretch to accomplish all the goals, then it is again gut-check time. Just like exploding requirements, something has to give. The same questions have to be answered.

Regardless of where a change in scope comes from, there are only a few choices for the outcome. If too much work was assigned and something didn't get done or the quality of the work that was done is garbage, it will need to be revisited (almost always more expensive than doing it right the first time) in a later cycle.

Another reason for a change at Mea Culpa is finding out that some technology that looked awesome in the first week of planning turned out to be a dud when the amount of data exceeded its design limits. This could be performance, space, or maybe the amount of code required to work around the limitation. Maybe it's a combination of all three. Maybe the licensing of the component prohibits modification. Regardless, it takes guts to throw out work and go another path. Here is where it becomes important that *when you slip, don't fall*. Is there another path or alternate technology that would solve the problem? Either you must find a way around the blocking factor, throw out the code, and go another route or you will be forced to push a rope uphill. Is it worth dragging an albatross around your neck for what could be years when you could go another route in the next six week cycle? Making the difficult call to remove or redirect a line item, while upsetting in the short term, can save millions of dollars and thousands of man hours in the future.

Other Mea Culpa issues

Other conditions can cause a radical shift at Mea Culpa. External factors play a large role when an expected partnership agreement did not close or a business is realigned. Here again, the scope may change radically and require a real investment of time to accurately scope what is now required.

For these and many other reasons, the Mea Culpa meeting is scheduled for a Monday. This is chosen for cases where any realignment of direction cannot be decided within the confines of what typically is an hour-long meeting. Performing this meeting Monday morning gives time to regroup and come up with a plan for execution.

Remember that the meaning of Mea Culpa is "my fault" or, in the vernacular of the early 21st century, "my bad." Simply put, "oops"; if you are going to "oops" something, do it early and communicate. What you want is for Mea Culpa not to turn into "mea *maxima* culpa."

WEEK 6: TESTING

It goes without saying that this process cannot work without a good testing discipline. By the final week of the cycle, you should be feature complete and 100% in test mode. QA has been side by side with the developers all along, which is the main reason why QA also sits in the bullpen so that they know what to expect and, in a mature team, should have been entering bugs as soon as the feature was ready. This week should be like finals week in college; a good student already knows the material and therefore the last week should be a blast, not a long series of all-nighters! But all too often, individuals haven't worked to complete functionality before the final week and it can be a difficult experience. Your goal is to minimize the trauma to the workplace and be 'feature complete' before Monday of the last week of a development cycle.

Cycle sign-off

The final meeting is the sign-off meeting. This should be all high fives and "when can we have that in production?" Schedule this meeting at 2 pm in the afternoon and present all the new bright shiny features, bug fixes, minor modifications, and other improvements to the interested representatives outside of development. Have fun, show off, and go home ready to come back on Monday and start it all over again.

At this point the product is complete and deployable. Development should be done.

It takes a team: no one can win alone

The sign-off meeting is a great opportunity to let your team shine and point out individual contributors and what they accomplished. While a team lead may be performing the presentation, it is important to say "Mikey built feature XYZ and wants to show some unexpected neat things" and then turn the presentation over to them for five minutes. It's also a good opportunity to point out heroic efforts and folks who pitched in to help others. Use this sign-off meeting to inform the rest of the company and to point out publicly the value that individual developers are producing.

There is no "I" in "team"

Sure, it only matters for the bonus that everything on the cycle document was completed. And you want every member of each bullpen to have the feeling that "we did it." Maybe someone hit a home run or stole a base at a critical moment, but it is the *team* that won. Everybody had to do their job to get to the goal. This should also be a big moment for the development team, because at this point, they should know whether or not they are getting paid their bonus for their efforts this cycle. If they are, then the combined motivations of delivering on what they know the business needed, and seeing the additional money in their bank account will reinforce the alignment of their efforts. If they did not make it, or they "missed" as we often say, it is a harder day, but that also reinforces the importance of the commitments they make.

STEERING WITH BUSINESS GOALS

All of this process is structured to allow us to deliver what the business needs early and often. There are a number of benefits to that, but the most important thing is the opportunity to maximize the return on investment in the project. Whether it is a commercially released product, an internal IT project, or even a nonprofit, the project exists to produce value, which is simple and measured easily in a commercial product in the form of sales.

For an internal IT project, the goal is often to provide value that allows us to reduce spending taking place on another business solution. Even in a nonprofit, a development project is still a value-added proposition. For a business to maximize the value of their project, they need to target the most valuable functionality first and ship it early. Commonly, projects deliver a big bang at the end of a roadmap that has a complete feature set. However, if the most valuable pieces of that feature set are completed halfway through the roadmap, then waiting for the rest is throwing away the value you could be getting from those features in the interim. In addition, you lose not only the value that could be gained with the extra time, but also the possible advantage of having reinvested those gains early. In other words, you lose both the early money and the time value of that money. In the six week solution, you are getting deliveries of features every six weeks and they should not be of requirements, documents, or risk assessments but always be business identified most valuable features possible.

Avoiding obstacles

In a nine month long project, not only have you gotten four software deliveries six months into your project, but you have *four meaningful feedback loops*. (Actually, you have more, but we will talk about that further in Chapter 6, "Managing the Cost of Change" on page 89.) Those feedback loops give you the opportunity to see that development is going in the right direction by getting your hands on their product. Then you can correct mistakes, change development direction based on new information or changing business needs, and revise business plans based on actual progress made.

Feedback loops are crucial to software development. Occasionally criticized as "Ready, Fire, Aim!" approaches, iterative development realizes that it is aiming for a moving target. The farther in the future a plan is set, the lower the certainty that the goal is correct or will still even be relevant by the time we get there. Waterfall projects are dependent on a fixed, predefined goal. Iterative projects give frequent opportunities to reassess the progress and goals of the project and adapt to change, both to maximize the value of the project or to stop it all together when it has ceased to make sense. This high-level feedback loop allows for the most dramatic changes of direction as needed by business priorities, but making feedback loops as small as possible protects a project from wasted investments by allowing the development to be redirected away from erroneous or obsolete efforts as soon as the very first moment it becomes obvious that those efforts are fruitless. A healthy development project has feedback loops taking place from the scale of moment-to-moment coding decisions to daily team tactical decisions, all the way up to iteration planning, with quite a few in between.

Delayed decision making

With regular iterations and checkpoints, we are given the ability to push off making decisions until the last responsible moment. If you are like us, you hear a voice in the back of your head telling you that it is a bad idea to put off your responsibilities. However, as discussed in the section entitled "Waterfalls and Crystal Balls" on page 19, we are often forced by software processes to make decisions when we are the least prepared to do so. Delaying decisions allows us to wait until we are as educated on the project as we can be and are as informed on the state of shifting conditions as we can be.

The key phrase in that sentence was "until the last responsible moment." When is that moment? Well, naturally, it depends on the decision being made. If an architecture decision is going to impact the funding necessary to acquire needed hardware, obviously that would need to be made farther in advance so that the funding, or the hardware, could be acquired. If the decision is whether feature A or feature B will be included in the next release, it is often very helpful to delay right up to the start of an iteration. An example of the value of that could be that between the time that the need for the features becomes apparent and the time they make it to the front of the development queue, the marketing department has been to several industry conventions and has seen that feature A is becoming much of an industry-expected feature than we would have guessed, so it has become more of a priority than feature B.

The challenge for the business

One of the wonderful advantages of this process is that short deliveries of high value make it very easy and desirable to hit business tactical goals. For example, a big sale would close if only we had feature x, so we get that on the next cycle and win the deal. One of the significant disadvantages is that large, less iterative projects are forced to evaluate very carefully what their long-term strategic goals are in advance and target those. A Six Week Solution team should have those goals defined, but can easily limp along without them and never accomplish those strategic items if the business yields to the temptation to continuously target small-scale tactical goals for cycle commitments. Unfortunately, this is a problem we cannot solve for you in these pages. Prioritizing investment in a project between short- and long-term goals is a broader business problem all of its own.

Hitting a wall

Software projects in general do not have a high success rate and are subject to a marvelously wide array of technology risks, political risks, and marketplace changes. (This concept is discussed in more detail in Chapter 2, "The Problem: Why Software Projects Fail" on page 11.)

A common question to ask yourself is "What are we doing to manage the risks in our project?" A common solution is to prioritize our work according to what seems riskiest first. Unfortunately, that assumes that you know and can fix those risks, which is rarely the case. Instead, in pursuing the highest value return we can for each cycle, we address two scenarios of unexpected failures:

- One is, that in the course of a cycle, when a risk is hit that causes that cycle to fail, we can throw away *only six weeks' worth of work* and continue in a different direction in the next cycle.
- In the other scenario, we hit a problem that prevents further development on the project from proceeding. For example, we discover that the processing we need to do on some data cannot be done mathematically within an acceptable amount of time. Then, we can cancel the project at the next cycle end.

Because we have built the most valuable features we can all along, we end with the most valuable work we could have done to show for the project. If we had spent our time chasing risks or, worse, just analyzing and documenting, we would have been very likely to end the project with nothing but paper to show for the investment.

When to quit

Programmers solve problems and build tools. That is what they do, and given a cool problem and time to work on it, they will keep building solutions indefinitely. Very likely they will be very cool and powerful tools, but for you, there is a very simple question: "Are these problems the right ones to solve?" Every development cycle that your company goes through costs your company a measurable amount of money. Very likely, it is a significant amount of money. At some point, possibly long before the developers have provided all the value they hope to, the return on the project will stop being worth the investment you are putting into it. At that point, spiral life cycles allow you to have a frequent, fixed point to close the project down, with all the value of the software developed to date available to continue to provide value to your business.

A feature that works, performs its function in a reasonable amount of time, and is of the quality level expected in the marketplace is worth far more than something that might be really cool someday in the future but you don't know when. Sometimes developers, even great ones, have trouble letting go of the software because there is just one more cool feature that could go into it and it will just take a few more days/weeks/months/whatever. "A bird in the hand is worth more than two in the bush." The six week cycle works against developer release constipation by requiring that something useful be bundled up and delivered every six weeks while still allowing future work on the "next really cool thing."

I worked on a project where the product manager would never let anything out the door. She had us completely rewrite working features eight times and it was still never perfect enough to ship. She had us spend three months trying to get the exact perfect shade of blue gradient on some box drawings that she wanted. The project floundered for two years until the company was acquired and the project was cancelled for not making any money. Last I had heard, no customers ever saw the product.

Java developer

The Solution's Critical Pieces

CHAPTER CONTENTS

Agile Development and Business Goals. DOI: 10.1016/B978-0-12-381520-0.00005-9

INTRODUCTION

Team sports provide excellent metaphors for business, and baseball, with its emphasis on team play, seasons, trades, playoffs, tradition, and even designated hitters, provides many colorful analogies. Seeing the Six Week Solution through the eyes of baseball emphasizes team play and helps understand the process better. Everybody has strengths and weaknesses, and it is understood that not every player on the field is the big hitting outfielder, not every player is a utility infielder, not every player is the closer, and not everyone in uniform can be the on-field manager.

Running with this analogy, when you implement the Six Week Solution, you'll need both position players and general athletes. The on-field manager is the architect and bullpen lead, able to make changes to the lineup and assign tasks to people without consulting management. Above the field manager is the general manager, who can deal with the personnel issues, budgets, and trades. Everybody, from the player to the general manager, must contribute to the success of the team to win the big game.

THE BIG GAME

The big game in software development is delivering your product to market, having success, and getting to do it all over again, either as the next step in evolving your product or as an entirely new product. Having successful seasons is the goal in baseball, and having successful releases of a product is the goal of software development.

The general manager sets the tone for the season. He must hire and trade to get the players on the right team. He will deal with contract negotiations. In the Six Week Solution, this means making the final hiring and firing decisions, handling all personnel issues, moving resources around in different bullpens, and reaching out to external resources when something is blocking progress. The general manager is the final arbitrator of every bullpen's cycle commitment documents. Finally, like the general manager in baseball, this person is responsible for communicating upward and outward when things change, including articulating the "what and why" at Mea Culpa.

Each field manager has to keep an eye on the progress of every player on the team and decide the lineup for each game. The bullpen lead—we call them architects—must know what every developer is doing and monitors the progress of each developer. The metaphor of a game could be: each item on the cycle commitment document is like a play, and just like the field manager, the architect must assess all of the circumstances and set the focus for each day's development work.

Every player on the baseball team must continually contribute at the highest level they can, and likewise each developer, regardless of specific role, must be contributing their best every day. It helps to understand the position each developer is playing; maybe they are a graphical user interface (GUI) developer in your platform of choice, maybe they focus on the database, maybe they are specific to one programming language, or maybe—in the best case—they can jump into all of the technologies in play and be competent if not exceptional.

Every person on the team, from top to bottom, must play their role at the highest level they can. Each season is a development cycle, and there are chances to change your position every cycle. In this chapter, the outline is given for the entire team of developers to succeed; all the critical pieces you need to get into place are detailed.

THE ENTIRE COMPANY MUST BUY IN

Before anything happens, there must be buy in from the top. Buy in is required from senior management because this is a change in philosophy that involves critical issues like compensation and the physical layout of the office. Technology suggested for use in the Six Week Solution is available, most of the software we suggest is free, and typically buying a few more machines to perform automation is not the blocking factor. Making the sale up the chain is detailed further in Chapter 11, "Transitioning to the Six Week Solution" on page 203.

Hybrid won't work

While pieces of the Six Week Solution are tempting to integrate into your development efforts, the holistic approach to development extends past just installing an automated build server or writing down what you will accomplish in any time period. Take the entire methodology or risk remaining trapped in a spiral of repeating the same actions over and over. (For further discussions of the spiral trap of development, see the section on "Spiral Development Traps" on page 169.)

Even simple things can derail the company, requiring more meetings for the development staff and other members of the organization to fix issues. An example would be the version number on a release: both development and marketing must be aligned perfectly. The first number of a version must be something driven from marketing so that the whole release plan, including announcements and other material, can be created alongside the software. However, marketing must understand that development needs to stamp the release with something that tracks back into a build and source control. Doing one and ignoring the other will cause a lot of discontent.

Business involvement

Often business sees development as a black box, not as a mechanism to deliver value to the business. The Six Week Solution is designed not only to demystify the process of creating software, but to actively engage business in the process to add value for both parties.

Another challenge is that businesses may think they are too busy to be involved in understanding features that may not reach them for a number of months. You must dispel this attitude and get them involved in the iterative development of the product. You need to get the level of understanding so that they can perceive the progress but, more importantly, so that they can understand the complexity of the task.

In an ideal world, business will come to the cycle kickoff with a passionate desire to have a certain set of features completed in the cycle and will leave cycle sign off with a clear understanding of what will be complete and what will most likely be included in the next cycle.

Business, with the assistance of product managers and marketing, should be the one to make decisions about when a major release should be publicized.

Give business status in meetings to tie cycle to business success

Developers are not in the day-to-day hunt for business. They are not out there in front of the customer. They don't hear feedback from the customer about where the pain points are. When we say pain points, we are not only talking about why the software takes too long to do something, we are talking about how the software *almost* gets them what they need, but if it could just do this one more thing, "think how much more valuable it would be...."

Developers are not at the trade shows, they are not at the dinners with the decision makers. They don't know the promises of the competitors; they don't know the one thing that is preventing the purchase order from being signed.

After the announcement that the product we had spent four years building needed a complete overhaul, I took a two week break. Then I came back with a suggestion. Since the new product was too complex and in reality people just wanted the functionality of the existing product with an easier interface, I said: "Let's just write a wrapper for the Basic so it runs in Visual Basic." Management agreed to try it. It took less than 6 months to go from idea to product, and another few months to button it up. Everyone was a hero.

Senior developer

Guard against external factors

Once the cycle document has been signed, it is critical to let the development team do their work. The rest of the company should leave them to create and try not to bring development into day-to-day issues. Noncritical bugs and feature reviews should be scheduled into the cycle at the beginning. If they are encountered during the cycle, they should be deferred until the next one. Obviously show-stopper bugs or deal-closing issues need to be addressed but these should be the exceptions.

If there is more than minimal interference, the company does not understand the process and it is time to revisit the approach with the management of each group.

Evangelism

Keeping buy in over time requires continual evangelism about what is going on and how it is working together. Because people change positions or leave the company, you must be prepared for a never-ending stream of changes outside of the software development group. The next marketing V.P. will have to be "trained" because their experience might be in the "stomp-and-scream" method of interacting with other departments in the company.

Eleven weeks

Keep driving the point of doing what is right, and doing it when it is needed. Remember: *Any* change to the software, from a small tweak to significant progress on a huge feature, is never more than 11 weeks away. The longest amount of time someone would have to wait for a "critical" enhancement that can be delivered in one cycle (without disrupting the current cycle) is 11 weeks. (This is assuming that you discover the requirement on the Monday after Cycle Sign-Off.)

Why senior management involvement is key

Executive participation elevates the meetings required by the Six Week Solution from mere "meetings" and into the range of a "heartbeat" for a company.

Two things happen when the "big dogs" show up at a meeting:

- First, everybody gets their game face on.
- Second, it shows that this process is important and there is buy in from the top. Anyone on the fence now realizes that this isn't another fad that they need to wait out until things return to "normal."

One other important point about senior management: the reaction of the C-level execs themselves. Their reaction typically swings from "This can't work" when they first hear about the idea to "I've gotta show this to my board!" when they see it implemented. The real-world results are often unlike anything they have ever seen from their software team.

Full cycle business participation

You would never let a carpenter remodel a room without a blueprint. If you do not join development in the discussions for direction, they will focus their efforts where they think it should be. Everything in front of you is black and white. There is no stealth development going on. Don't come back to them two quarters later and say, "Where is feature X?" This process gives you every opportunity to affect the decision process.

Remember that developers have two modes of operation:

- One, where they will engage and truly try to understand your needs
- The other where they have decided that your expectations are unreasonable and will sandbag every estimate.

Obviously you want to keep them in the first mode. You want them engaged and thinking about solutions to the business problems. In order for developers to stay in this mode, it is helpful to understand the inherent makeup of developers.

It is enormously important to get the right people to attend all of the cycle meetings and to keep them engaged at all of them. Of course, "the right people" is a vague term and could easily be argued that it should include anyone being affected by the software being developed. In a software product company, that would be everyone! That is unrealistic, so here are a couple more refined suggestions:

- Your company visionaries should be in attendance for every meeting. If that is your CEO, your hotshot marketing executive, or a particularly farsighted sales representative, they should be there to give the best possible input and feedback into development, as well as being the best informed on changes as they happen.
- The leaders and proxies of other affected business groups should be there too. These are people who can represent the interests of affected teams as well as carry information back to them. Organizations such as marketing, sales, support, and business consulting leap quickly to mind, but it could also be your training group, a users group, or a number of other things.

Delivery channels

One of the most crucial possible bottlenecks for your organization is your delivery channel. To borrow from the lean manufacturing paradigm, the total time from concept to delivery of your product includes many roadblocks aside from "simple" development. One roadblock might be vetting ideas in the business and getting them prioritized on the front end. On the back end, there are a myriad of concerns, such as user documentation, training updates, user acceptance routines, deployment procedures, hardware acquisition, sales and marketing updates, and user's ability to absorb changes.

All of these things impact your end-to-end development time, especially your maintenance burden. While we recommend collocating as much of your business and as many of your stakeholders as you can with your development team, it is particularly important here to consider your training team (if you have one). At the rate of change that your team will be moving at, any slower communications mechanisms than face-to-face definitely restrict the ability of your business to take full advantage of new features by making sure that they get understood by the users quickly.

Number of revisions

One possible "gotcha" of delivering software so often is how many different versions of the software that have to be supported. If your deployment procedure does not keep all of your deployments on the same version, then you have to worry about how you will handle issues in each deployed version.

Hopefully, you are in a situation—a desktop consumer application, for example—where the answer to most problems is something to the effect of "apply the patches." This approach can move an end user up through cycles to one that is being actively maintained. If not, you quickly come to a place where you are trying to juggle creating patches and fixes within *every* cycle that you have deployed, which can bring your development to a halt in sheer duplication of effort. In an enterprise deployment model, you may have a multistage deployment where new cycle changes have to be deployed and tested in a control environment to validate that the upgrade will be successful before the ability of a business to function will be risked on a real upgrade, which definitely slows down the ability of a business to absorb new releases.

In a software-as-a-service model, you have control over your deployments and can keep them all up to date, but in that scenario, you have to worry about whether the changes are dramatic enough to impact your user's experience negatively as they attempt to keep up with the changing product.

The challenge here, though, is to balance taking new releases as often as possible so that feedback can be delivered back into the development process while at the same time managing the ability of your business to absorb those releases.

WORK SPACE
The bullpen

We like each team to be in the "bullpen" (another baseball analogy). The ideal number of work areas will depend on the makeup of your teams and the physical constraints of the building you are in. We prefer 12 but have been successful with nine.

The goal of a bullpen is to create a physical work space where the team cannot help but collaborate. There should be no significant walls or doors. We suggest a circular area with a table in the middle of it. We strongly encourage you to have a conference phone in the middle of the table. If possible, each bullpen should have a drop-down screen and a projector hanging from the ceiling to facilitate team discussions without having to get up and go to another meeting room.

In the perfect configuration you avoid direct external walls (windows), high traffic areas, and other potential disturbances. The perfect bullpens have three solid walls and an office or two, a cry room, and a conference room on the external wall.

It is currently fashionable in society to be very egalitarian in the office. We've even seen offices constructed so that everyone, including management, sits in cubes side by side. In reality, management grabs what should have been a shared meeting room near their cubes and begins camping out in that meeting room, turning it into their offices. It's just human nature and part of the trappings of the job.

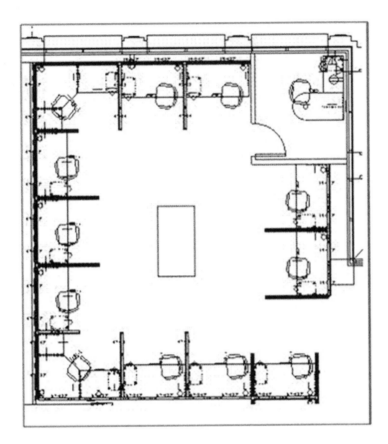

FIGURE 5.1

Who sits where.

Clearly, there will be one or more larger work spaces in the corners of the bullpens. These are naturally the desks for the architects and de facto leaders in technology areas. They are still side by side with the rest of the team members, but they need this space for their work and it helps to reinforce their overall position. (For a look at one potential architecture, see Figure 5.1.)

The general manager needs a space outside of the bullpen to handle personal and personnel issues. Performance evaluations, warnings, phone calls, and salary negotiations should not be handled in the open area of the bullpen. This position needs the office space as it is a tool to do the job they are tasked with.

Bullpen challenges

Before you sit everybody in the bullpen, be sure you have your bullpen leader identified and groomed before you place them in charge of a bullpen. Don't assume you can hire a bullpen lead quickly once all the other developers are in place.

If you do find yourself in a situation where you do not have a natural choice for the bullpen leader, we have had management from above the bullpen sit in the bullpen side by side with the developers. Once an individual is identified as the leader, groom them to take over the responsibilities by letting them take over more responsibility for the cycle documents and running the stand-up meetings. This may take several cycles to get them into the groove, so be ready for the investment. When the time does come to turn over the bullpen, extract the manager.

Multiple bullpen considerations

When growing to multiple bullpens, don't create an A team and a B team. Make the strength roughly equal across all your bullpens. If one team is racing ahead and another is having challenges to meet the cycle commitments, it will demoralize everyone. And don't focus one team solely on new development and another on maintenance.

Even if there is a situation where one team is working on some great new feature, their cycle commitment documents should have items that keep them in sync with the whole product. If you really need to have a team work on maintenance, do not be shy about pointing out the importance of what they are doing and that it really is not just bug fixing but moving the product in a necessary direction.

A job in Chicago was the site of the first Six Week Solution bullpen. There were three of us sitting in the same area. We did all of our development work on Sparc workstations with 19-inch monitors.

We took over a room and got some folding tables. We eventually decided that we all had a very diverse affinity for music. We brought in an old stereo and it became a competition to see who could find the most obscure album that the others had not heard of. We were working 14 hours a day together so it made sense to make the conditions as pleasant and interesting as possible.

Development manager

Don't think this is a democracy

When viewed as a flat hierarchy inside the bullpen, it may be tempting to think that everybody has an equal say in what work needs to get done and how it will be accomplished. Valuing input from every member is a key discipline and must be done without condescension. However, there is a final decision within the bullpens and then there is a final decision above the bullpen leads. Push the decisions down to the bullpen leads and empowering them to make the hard choices they need to make are necessary.

It's not negative to think of the decision making as a "benevolent dictatorship"; it might not be a democracy but the "bullpen-lead-name-ocracy" isn't bad! At the end of the day, the company exists to make money, not pad developers' resumes; sometimes decisions must be made that someone will be unhappy with. The bullpen leads have to be comfortable with this concept.

Another possible problem with the democracy concept is the feeling that because everyone is contributing to the cycle commitments to achieve the bonuses, they should all be paid the same. The simple fact is that not everybody contributes the same amount to the final product. A truly gifted developer can produce 10 times the output of an average developer, with fewer defects and less code. Bullpen leads should have more risk riding on the cycle document, and that risk is materialized in the form of more base salary and more bonus percentage.

Work area

Each individual work area does not need to be extravagant. A six foot work space is sufficient, and we recommend a surface that is three feet deep. This compromise keeps everyone in the open and affords a level of privacy to work uninterrupted at times.

A developer's work area includes a physical desk, but also the hardware necessary to perform the job. Developers love the latest and greatest tools—hardware and software—and having that power at their desktop is, in an important way, a part of their compensation. Developers will have opinions on what processor, how many cores, memory size, and so on, and we agree that they should have the best. Additionally, the advent of dual monitors was incredibly powerful even years ago when one color monitor could be used in conjunction with a "green screen," and with the commonness of dual monitors, each developer should have at least two monitors in work space.

Developers will have opinions about what they want in addition to the machine. We like the developers to have their favorite style and encourage the innovation that may introduce into the bullpens. However, this should be balanced with the need to enable a different developer to sit at their work space and be productive to help facilitate pairing. If a developer likes a track-ball, let them have it, and connect another mouse so that other developers can also use the machine.

The work area, while open to the entire team, is still the individual's space during the work day. Let them hang up anything they want, as long as it is not a clear violation of HR policy. If a good target from the latest trip to the shooting range floats their boat, let them have it. With the type of developers you want to hire, highly individualistic people will be attracted to the position; let them have the space.

Size of teams

In 1920, while writing *Aids to Scoutmastership*, Lord Baden-Powell of Gilwell (who founded the Boy Scout movement) wrote:

"The Patrol System is the one essential feature in which Scout training differs from that of all other organizations, and where the System is properly applied, it is absolutely bound to bring success. It cannot help itself!

The formation of the boys into Patrols of from six to eight and training them as separate units each under its own responsible leader is the key to a good Troop."

Organizations with critical needs to succeed are all organized upon similar lines. The Special Forces of the United States Army are organized into small teams of 12 soldiers for each Operational Detachment Alpha.

While operating in Africa for the British military, Baden-Powell came to realize the ideal team size for efficient operation. He put a practical limit on team size for communication and leadership reasons.

Neither of these highly effective groups has members operating as mere automata; every group member must be contributing at the highest level they can for all to succeed. And yet, flying in the face of these successful organizations, software development routinely brags about the large number of people required to put together some huge piece of software.

For these reasons and many others, the Six Week Solution relies on teams from nine to 12 developers in each bullpen, with one being a team lead. This minimizes meeting time requirements and sizes each bullpen into a square footage that is achievable in most office buildings.

Teams of teams

To grow beyond a single bullpen of nine to 12 developers, it is necessary to split into several bullpens. As projects grow, natural divisions will present themselves and it will feel normal to break into groups focusing on a single technology. Single technology specialist groups are *not* what you need to do, for allowing development to degrade into silos of technology will prohibit sharing of ideas and slow the velocity of change. Find the right mix of skill sets in each bullpen, and remember that you want all of your technologies represented in each bullpen. When splitting into multiple bullpens, remember that it is necessary to keep all disciplines of technology represented.

Software has some fairly natural breaks. Large projects find the need for a persistence layer absolutely necessary, along with a middle tier and a presentation layer. Do not let these perceived divisions of responsibility work to split bullpens. What is necessary is the ability for new features to reach across all technical divisions to drive dreams into reality. The last thing any software development shop needs is to have one level blocked on another and sitting idle.

The bullpen lead becomes extremely important when splitting into multiple bullpens. When first splitting into multiple bullpens, it is a very dangerous time. Feathers will get ruffled, and the shop is growing from a single person driving the team into multiple leaders who may have different approaches, personalities, and backgrounds, which will drive them to choose different paths than the original, single leader.

There are two choices:

- Be every bit the control freak you can be and drive your new teams into the ground mercilessly, pushing your way.
- Loosen your grip a little, like the correct way to hold a golf club or tennis racket. (If you hold it too tight, your swing is not as efficient.)

Baden-Powell had this to say:

The best progress is made in those Troops where power and responsibility are really put into the hands of the Patrol Leaders. This is the Secret of success in Scout Training.

http://www.usscouts.org/history/BPoutlook1.asp

This thought may seem trite in an industry that prides itself in the latest bright, shiny gadget and innovation. However, the problem of communication and leadership is not something specific to software development, nor is software development something so outside the normal parameters of life that it needs its own approach to solve these issues of leadership and communication. The ideas are old and successful, and yet the gap that exists in software development for the application of these concepts is huge.

Pushing the decisions for implementation details to the bullpen leads gives them great power and the smart ones understand the responsibility they have been given for the company, the members of their bullpen, and themselves. If you follow the rules for hiring smart, then the leaders will present themselves and there is no problem handing over the reins of product or feature development to such an individual. (For further details on hiring the right personnel for the Six Week Solution, see the section "Hiring Smart" on page 73.)

In the end, multiple bullpens are the key to long-term success. Having multiple teams addressing different objectives allows you to continue to deliver value today and experiment for the future and longer term value that may not show up for several releases without missing a single release and always showing progress.

PERSONNEL ROLES
Bullpen leads

You must have strong lead developers, which does not mean that they are merely strong developers. These individuals must demonstrate a mastery of developing software as well as an understanding of the business problem. Further, they must be able to communicate to others both in software development and the rest of the company. Finding the whole package in one individual is difficult and rewarding once you identify the correct individual.

Developers

Developers must have a mastery of the technologies they are tasked with and also have an overall view of the industry. You are looking for competent technologists and those who have made a significant impact at previous positions (or, in the case of the recent graduate, have the potential to make an impact).

Developers may be tasked with a specific technology, but they should be aware of the other technologies existing within the bullpen. The GUI developer needs to know at least a little about the middleware and database development. The middleware developer needs to know the needs of the GUI and database developers. The database developer must understand what the middleware can do and how data are getting all the way up to the GUI. This is the reason we suggest that all the technology in use within your development is tested quickly during the interview, at least in the free word association section of the interview.

To a developer, however, the Six Week Solution methodology will be different from what they have seen before. Developers need to stop trying to build the best mousetrap in the world and instead embrace the iterative nature of the process. Developers may have to come back and rework something, but they may also make a discovery that warrants a rework. Yes you want to build the best product that you can, but you also need to reduce the work to six week (or smaller) chunks.

The time frame is a challenge for some developers. They will resist breaking work up into measurable pieces of work simply because they haven't been tasked to take apart the process of software development in this manner. If they feel strongly that they can't release any piece of software until it is 100% feature complete, then they will not be successful in the Six Week Solution.

Developers must remember that every six week cycle is a new contract, and if they really hate what they are working on, wait six weeks and most likely it will change!

I was in a contract position as a senior developer with a large telecom company. After only a month on the job, I was asked to take the team lead position for eight projects. I asked that two specific gentlemen be removed from the team and that I did not even require a backfill.

The first was "the professor." He was the self-proclaimed Java expert. He taught Java at the local community college at night. While I am sure he knew the syntax and structure of the language, he knew nothing of creating working software. All theory and no actual practice.

The other gentleman that I did not want on the team was the "patent holder." His cube was adorned with all the awards and the patents he had written on behalf of the company. He could talk your ear off but he could not create anything. Again, all very fine theory and no actual practice.

Project team lead

Developer motivations

We are going to let you in on a little secret that catches a surprising number of businesspeople off guard. It is particularly surprising when you consider some of the core premises of this process. In reality, money is not a primary developer motivation. Most of them wrote software when no one was paying and would continue to do so if no one was paying. Now that does not mean that developers will build what YOU want for free. What it does do is beg the question, what DOES motivate developers?

Pride

Probably the number one motivation of a developer is pride. They take pride in being smart folks, they take pride is solving tough problems, and they take pride in building something of quality and value.

Toys

In close second for motivations are *toys*. Despite the stereotypes—no, we do not mean Nerf guns and light sabers (although they like those too)—we mean powerful development tools and languages that are enjoyable to work with. Libraries and integrated development environments (IDEs), high-end hardware, powerful third-party components, or even particularly interesting designs and strategies for solving problems.

Money

Probably somewhere around third here, we find money as a motivator, which initially might seem like it undermines the effectiveness of the compensation structure of the Six Week Solution, and for a few people, this is true. But generally, the compensation structure aligns nicely with the motivations of developers who will make things happen for your business.

- Pride motivation # 1: Compensation is an immediate acknowledgment of the accomplishment of the team.
- Pride motivation # 2: Most developers will move heaven and earth to avoid being the reason that the team did not achieve its goals because it is an injury to fail to solve the problems, to cost their team their bonus, or just the let down of not having a completed product to show for the cycle's effort.

Also, compensation helps reduce some common problems. For example, because the second motivation is getting to play with fun stuff, it is easy for a developer to get sidetracked on projects that seem interesting to him rather than things that are valuable to the business. The compensation structure helps rein in that tendency because it jeopardizes the success of a developer's whole team very visibly.

In the bonus structure, we encourage finding people who are willing to put their money where their pride is, so to speak, by investing them in both committing to deliverables that are significant to the business and tying measurable impact to following through on those commitments.

However, having a person who is not motivated by the commitments on one of your teams can do a great deal of damage to a team's morale, ability to execute, and their effectiveness for your business. This is therefore something to look for in hiring and to fix as soon as possible for the sake of the team should such a developer join.

The nature of engineers

- Problem solvers
- Like to build stuff
- Use cool tools when building those things

But the most telegenic aspect of no-limit hold'em is that it allows both skilled and unskilled players to go all in— one of our century's favorite verbs—at any point in the hand.

Cowboys Full: The Story of Poker by James McManus

You want developers who are willing to go all in, which may mean working through a weekend, but it may also mean something more mundane, such as adding 10 lines of comments to the code for the next guy.

The cowboy coder

Yee haw, let's write some code! After thinking about the problem about as long as an amateur bull rider lasts on a championship bull, this developer is willing to jump in and just write some code. "Standards be damned, we've got code to write and there is no time for unit tests."

In previous positions, this person has been very successful to the point that they thought he was a god or at least a son of a god and only half human. He cranked code out so fast, and many times it actually worked or at least worked good enough that some other subject was the fire du jour and everybody got distracted. He's gone from that company and is sitting in yours, while they are left with a morass of spaghetti code in several different languages and a couple of stored procedures that every developer is scared to touch so long as they still kind of work; that code is surviving for another day out of fear, not genius.

It might also be the case that the current management just loves this developer. You'll hear comments such as "Ralph has never let me down, he always comes though" from senior people (who should know better) or maybe management thinks this developer has some skill that your team is lacking because he is talking a good game. If that's the case, you have both a cowboy coder problem and a "manage-up" problem to expose the weakness of this developer without damaging the credibility of the senior manager who likes this developer.

Problem is, he's about to wreck havoc on your shop, leaving you with a design debt that will take years to pay down while maintaining the garbage code he left behind. In our experience, the damage done by this kind of coding costs 10 times the amount of time to remove and get right so that it works in all situations and can be called reliable. Problem is that while this in-flight rebuild of an engine is taking place, many times management thinks things are wonderful because there are a few special cases where this wretched code actually works and performs great; the new solution solves several times more customer problems and should expose the cowboy code as a special case optimization, but management doesn't listen, they want it to still run as fast as the special case and handle every other permutation all at the same time.

Further, this personality rarely plays well with others and more often than not is sneaky too, schmoozing with the bosses while simultaneously undermining everyone else on his team. You have a poison player who does not provide long-term value to any team. However, like the football team who picked this poison player up as a free agent, he might just do well enough to get you into the playoffs from his ability alone.

You really only have three options to solve the problem of the cowboy coder:

- You can terminate him.
- Move him to his own area to minimize interactions (also known as "poisonings") of other team members.
- "Keep your friends close and your enemies closer." Move him into a star team where the cowboy coder is either forced to become a team member or will either quit or do something so stupid that you can terminate him.

Another behavior the cowboy coder is famous for is 3 am check-ins. He's stayed up all night hammering out a problem, finally hits upon a solution that works, and checks in a bunch of code. Then, satisfied with his "contribution," doesn't show up at the office until late the next day, if at all. Meanwhile, back at the office, there are several teams in a holding pattern because any variation from the "happy path" that the cowboy coder went down causes everything to break.

It feels good for a short time because it looks like a lot of work is getting done, but the long-term effects of cowboy coding far outweigh any benefits.

Maintain this code

If a rogue developer gets too far off track developing what he thinks is needed (as opposed to what the company needs), his actions get corrected in the Six Week Solution. He will not be rewarded—he will be penalized. He cannot just say "Well, I'll fix it next cycle." Everyone is watching and everyone is accountable. (For more description of this type of coder, see the section entitled "The Rogue Developer" on page 27.)

Quality Assurance

QA resources need to be open to some new concepts. Not that their role changes from other positions that they were successful in, for they still need that twinkle in their eyes when they show the next problem to a developer!

One of the major challenges is stepping up from testing one area of a large package and grasping the whole. There still will be areas of specialization in some projects, but it is necessary to know all the major pieces of the project and how they interrelate.

Like developers, the time frame is a challenge, for how do they certify a release on the last day of the cycle when developers are still making changes? QA will want time—possibly weeks—to let things "settle in" so they can certify the whole. This approach has been tried in iterations of the Six Week Solution and it is a failed approach.

Instead, QA needs to be comfortable with automation and tracking of changes. They must step up and use the automated build server to get the set of changes and, in doing so, will see all the changes made by developers and know where those changes are occurring.

Additionally, QA needs to be comfortable with automation in their work. They need at least some scripting skills in addition to the natural intuitiveness and delight in discovering new bugs. Without QA resources who embrace automation, they are doomed to forever repeat manual regressing tests and will ultimately delay releases.

Documentation

Documentation in the Six Week Solution has a slightly different role than they may have encountered previously. Requirements are quickly defined intentionally, as there is a good chance that they will be revisited in future development cycles.

Some things will be uncomfortable for most technical writers:

- For example, they will be asked to contribute to builds throughout each cycle and be required to use source control to allow the automated builds. This challenge is mitigated by their presence in the daily stand-up meetings so they know the current status and what pieces need to be created for the user guides.
- Technical writers can also help evangelize the process throughout the company; they will be asked for details by marketing and training. (Note that some writers may chafe at this role.)
- Further, it is entirely acceptable that QA opens bugs against the documentation, and the writers are expected to close those bugs in the same manner that a developer closes bugs. (This will be a *very* different experience for some technical writers.)

But technical writers are no different than other active players in this process; it requires a different mindset, a willingness to use your skills in (sometimes) unique ways. For these reasons, the technical writer is an athlete position in the bullpen, able to understand the product, technology, and process of the Six Week Solution. Ideally, they are also taking this knowledge to other parts of the company.

Product management

Product management must have a very strong understanding of both the business needs and the development dependencies of their company. They must be able to articulate guidance in both directions. The perfect individual can understand everything about your technologies; perhaps they have developed sometime in the past. They also can stand in front of a customer and explain the features of the product in great detail. However, it is very hard to find both of these skill sets in the same person. You may need to split the role into two people: one who is developer focused and one who is marketing focused.

The product manager cannot glaze over when you are talking about the details of supporting products. For example, if you use a database, the product manager should have a strong working knowledge of the capabilities of the current database platform and version and other products that can be added on.

The product manager should be the most intimate with the working of the product. They should be the go-to person for verifying that a feature works and finding workarounds. They should be the first person that the developers check with when they have a new feature they want an opinion on.

Ultimately, the product management is a customer proxy. This is especially important when an organization is dispersed geographically and a true on-site customer cannot exist. Additionally, they are the resource that juggles priorities of sales, marketing, product support, stakeholders, and the definitive users.

Strong product management personalities are required to perform defect prioritization. Any defect in your product—and really harmful defects that are only found at least six months after being in production before they are discovered—is a serious concern to the reporter. The reality of the situation is that these must be prioritized. They may be a serious problem that requires an "all hands on deck" approach at the moment, although many are perfectly acceptable to be addressed wholly or partially in a future development cycle. These people may not be the most loved and popular folks in the company, but they have to be strong enough to handle the position they are in, even if it means not being a friend to everybody.

From The Cranky Product Manager (http://www.crankypm.com/2009/11/translation-cranky -product-manager):

What We Say	What We Mean
You should file a customer commitment.	Your feature request is stupid. Please stop pestering me and go away.
It's on the long-term roadmap.	While not stupid, your feature request is such low priority that it's not slated for a release and won't happen within the next three years.
OK, Mr. Customer, I can see why you want that feature. We'll need to take a look at how it fits into our product strategy and roadmap, and it's good to know how important it is to you.	Notice that I did NOT say we'd do this feature. We might NEVER do it. But I want you to feel like Product Management listens to you.
It's currently planned for Release X.XX.	Yeah, everyone is saying this is going to be in Release X.XX, but I won't believe it until it actually ships.
Sounds like you are using the product to solve some really interesting problems. I'd like to learn more about your use cases.	No one else uses this product this way, it is not designed for your purpose, and we don't do any testing for your type of use. Yikes!
This product will help you increase your ROI and decrease your TCO.	I have no freaking clue what the REAL business benefits of my product are, and I'm too lazy to figure it out.

HIRING SMART

Anyone who has been in software development for any period of time can tell you how difficult it is to find and retain good employees. The need for good developers is great. To complicate things, there are a great many charlatans in the industry using the confusion over so many niche technologies and a fragmented technology landscape to survive in the cubicle jungle. There is not a large adoption of code metric tools throughout the industry and, to make matters worse, many front-line managers on up the chain do not have an honest clue about technology. With management unable to tell the difference between HTML and Java, a good segment of the resumes that you receive is nothing but fluff. Wading through what seems like an endless stream of resumes from social networking sites, recruiters, and job postings tire even the experienced software development manager, and sometimes it feels like you just have to hire someone, anyone, who will sit in the chair and at least try to do the job. Separating the signal from all this noise is the challenge you must accept to hire smart.

College graduate

Hiring a college graduate directly from school is very tempting. The entry-level salary may undercut experienced developers by a large margin. The thought of heroic all night coding sessions pulled off by young greenhorns may seem very attractive, and maybe they actually do have the energy to pull a few all nighters. Problem is that most times, this doesn't pay off and let's be honest as the salary expectations of some graduates exceed that of five or 10 year veterans. Yet every once in a while you do find a diamond in the rough so don't eliminate the young graduates for if they have the intelligence and drive they will excel in the environment of the Six Week Solution.

Five to 10 years of experience

Moving along the time line of experience, the five- to 10-year point seems to be when some real energy is being put behind the science and art of the software development craft. At this point in their career, they have become very capable and can usually create new features well. However, the early success they have enjoyed to this point may be a product of solo work and a gun-slinging approach to coding, leading to them not "playing well with others" and having adopted a NIH (Not Invented Here) mentality pushing them to re-create libraries that are readily available and costing you real dollars to maintain this duplicate code.

Initially, they may express a great interest in your technologies and designs, but they can quickly grow bored and wander to find a new gig. This is also a sweet spot for "consulting," as they still have the energy and have a fresh enough skill set that they can take contracting positions and not be (in their view) tied down to one employer. We don't think this is their fault, as the industry waves money in their faces to act exactly as they do and at this age they may not be truly ready to settle down and put the shoulder to the wheel of a larger goal than the next upgrade to an existing Web site. If you have the bandwidth and desire you can certainly try to calm these stallions and mold them into long-term employees, but have your eyes open as this effort may be a waste of energy. While you should not disregard these candidates, you must go into the relationship with your eyes open.

The seasoned developer

Another type of resource you may need to avoid is seasoned developers who are too set in their ways to adapt to this methodology. They may have been at a large corporation or two up to this point in their career and expect a private office and a measured pace to their work. They may not be attracted to the bullpen at all. The thought of putting a portion of compensation at risk may be outright repulsive to them. Further, the thought that the performance of others may impact the amount they see in their paycheck every month will turn them off. This pattern is easy to uncover in a resume; if they somehow do make it to an interview, the questions suggested later in this chapter will uncover the candidate's true motives of just finding another job.

The sweet spot: 10–20 years

The sweet spot for developers in this environment seems to be the 10 to 20 years of experience point. They are hungry enough and still have enough energy to adapt to the challenges of changing technologies and methodologies, yet they are old enough to have experienced many of the mistakes this process is set up to avoid. While they are ready for a steady, but exciting, environment, they have the confidence and experience to "bank on themselves" that they can get the job done. Further, at this point in their career most have realized that they need something different or they will be a cube dweller until they retire. This is the sweet spot, for they get the value proposition and have the ability to thrive in the environment.

Humor

A manager gathers his developers and discusses an embarrassing bug found by a customer. Three developers think they can fix it, but they are in two groups. The first group is composed of two experienced developers and the second is a young gun. Both groups break, with the young kid sitting in front of the computer, immediately banging out some code. The experienced two pair up, grab a laptop and a projector, and start looking at some code on the wall as they inspect the unit tests. Hours pass and finally the young gun comes into the room with the experienced developers and proudly states, "I found the bug!" One of the experienced developers asks a question, "Which one?"

To allow discovery in this process for both you and the prospective employee, we suggest that you either create an employee agreement that allows you to terminate the employee at any time within the first six months or find a good outsourcer with a "try/buy" agreement. The point with both of these approaches is to allow the freedom to say at any point that things are not working out and you need to part ways.

However, both approaches have their own problems.

- Going with the outsourcer to provide contractors works for parting ways, but is difficult as the contractor is not part of the bonus structure through the outsourcer, which makes it difficult or impossible to have the contractor tied to the same compensation structure as the employees.
- The employment agreement route is also not simple, as software developers are not typically compensated in this manner and may be repulsed by the concept. Unless you are above market

for compensation, this may be a very difficult hurdle to overcome in some geographic locations.

Either approach is not easy, but we have had contractors beating down our door to be converted the moment they have reached the six month point begging to be converted!

Team building through hiring

Remember that these nine to 12 people have to sit in a fairly confined space together. While you don't want to create some homogeneous collective, you do need to ensure that these people will get along. To get along in an environment like this you need to be able to take criticism and be able to joke around. We think that it is safe to say that anyone who is overly sensitive, political, or dogmatic will crumble or become rather upset. In our interview process we make a point of saying something politically incorrect between ourselves (but not an HR violation!) just to weigh the reaction of the candidate.

Interviewing

Interviewing is difficult for all involved. For the candidates, they need a job and are nervous to get the job offer. For the interviewer or interviewers, they need to fill a position and, in many cases, fill it quickly with the right individual because the cost is high to hire and getting someone else new up to speed. We have developed a style of interviewing that will probe the knowledge and abilities of the individual while also discovering if the candidate is a fit for the environment.

Start off by putting the candidate at ease, shake hands and maybe joke like: "You found the office, so you're already ahead." They are going to be in a vibrant environment if they pass the interview, and here's an early chance to see if they will fit.

Keep the interview conversational and friendly, for the candidates need to be at ease and if you are working with an outsourcer they may know they are getting into something different and be even more nervous. Be on the lookout throughout the interview to see if they are confident that they can do the job and still be able to work in a team environment. Assertiveness, but not aggressiveness, is a key trait.

Our interview style seeks to find individuals who can handle the scrutiny and openness demanded by the Six Week Solution without conflict. Wallflowers don't survive in the bullpen.

Finally, you're looking for people who can adapt and have the ability to be taught and learn new concepts on their own instead of having an idea and approach so ingrained that they cannot move forward. Technology changes rapidly, and anyone in the bullpen environment needs to be able to embrace and own the changes.

"D-IQ" (Developer IQ)

We have had great success with a standard list of questions. When you start a new product or initiative, spend some time writing down terms and technologies in use to use as possible questions for future candidates.

Say you are building a Web application, circa 2004. You need people who know HTML, JavaScript, browser issues, CSS, and so on. Recruiters are more than willing to throw you resumes of "Web developers" or "Web designers" until you are swimming in resumes. So how do you separate these people technically? Here's an example set of questions:

- What is HTTP?
- What does the clear style in CSS do?
- What is AJAX?
- What is Flash?

All of these are leading questions. Don't accept the first answer to "What is HTTP?" of Hyper Text Transfer Protocol. If they come back with that, ask a follow-up question such as "And what are the messages?" to probe for an answer such as "get and post" to see that they really know what HTTP does. If they answer "That's what I type before the ://www..." then you can end the interview quickly.

A second set of questions can be given as a free word association test. Call it a "Developer Rorschach" test. Just blurt out the technology and ask the candidate to say whatever comes to mind. Here are some examples:

- C++
- Java
- .net
- J2EE
- SOA

Strong, one-word answers show some experience with whatever the technology word means. Be careful with the candidate who gets stuck on one word such as "beautiful" for every answer, for chances are they are trying to snow you. "Sucks" is perfectly acceptable, and you can look back after the list is done and ask why they don't like "technology X." It's a good point to leap off and probe for what they don't know and find the edge of the envelope.

Probing questions

Another technique used in our interviews is a probing question that is open ended and really doesn't have one answer for it could be answered on multiple levels.

Suggested interview strategies

"How does garbage collection work in Java?"

This is a very direct question, and few developers will actually know and understand how it works. Do they come back with "There are many strategies ..." and start enumerating the differences between the Eden space and a full collection or do they just assume that the JVM handles it? If they have no clue, you're done, but if they nail it, then you have to keep working. How much do they know? Can you drill into concurrent garbage collection and the overhead it takes?

Clearly, this question is geared to Java developers, but you can use it regardless of your technology. If you're doing C, drill into how malloc works and get into memory fragmentation after a program has been running for a long time. Maybe you have another technology for delivering Rich Internet Applications through a browser, as it has to have something built in at this point for they must understand that they are not invoking something to explicitly return memory for use elsewhere.

"What did you do at your last job?"

Here you find out if they led, followed, or got out of the way. Leaders will almost always start with "I did ..." type of statements, whereas followers begin with "We ... ." Those that just got out of the way will blink vacantly.

This is a hard question to deliver for two reasons:

- The first in the current collective mindset in the culture, the interviewee may believe it is bad form to start tooting their own horn when they were a member of a group, so it may take some prodding to extract this out of a candidate.
- The second part of this question is the follow-up question of: "If hardware/operating system/etc. changed to what it is today, how would that affect your design or approach to the problem?"

You really have no knowledge of what they were working on, and you are making guesses, but the point is to let them ramble because if they really got into what they were working on, they will come back with all kinds of things and your next difficult task is to get them to leave it behind and answer your next question!

Tour of the physical workplace

The final section of the interview should be a tour of the office, including the layout of the bullpens and the developer workstations. This is also "Interview Part 2" and should be handed off to someone doing the job that the candidate will be tasked with.

There are two objectives with the tour:

- you want them to see the environment that they would be stepping into
- let them ask questions to someone who isn't part of the "official" interview

They can see the open work place; some people will not be comfortable with it and you should know it is okay for them to pass. In fact, you want them to pass at this point—it will save you both headaches later on. They can also ask you questions, which can provide great insight to where they are in their career.

Let the peer be the one to do a final handshake and goodbye. Afterward, include the tour guide in the decision process briefly to gauge if the candidate is interested and what kind of questions they asked the tour guide.

Profiling

There is perhaps a temptation to use psychological profiles to ensure that you have the correct fit for your teams. While this is very appealing in the promise of telling you beforehand whether someone will fit into your organization, it can unfortunately be a legal quagmire to introduce this into your direct hiring. If you can get your contract hiring firm to perform this as part of their identification process, you may be able to realize the benefits without the legal risk.

Things to watch out for

Resume padders

Beware of "resume padders," those whose resumes have every possible technology they have ever heard about and know how to spell listed on their resume. These applicants will list every three-letter acronym they have ever encountered throughout their career. If you see "XML" on a resume, ask them what CDATA really is or why you can't put a ":" character in a tag name; chances are they will crumble and scurry away like a cockroach when you turn on the light. You don't need these folks on your team.

Cool and easy

If you have been around developers for any amount of time, you've heard one say "It was cool and easy." What they really mean is "I just read about this on the Web and wanted to put it into the product because I thought it was cool and didn't interfere with quality time with my girlfriend." Now you have some code following a framework that no one else in your shop is comfortable with and will cost you more to maintain. More frequently, some new dependency has just been introduced into your product that will mean more headaches with licensing and cost you more to upgrade if there are conflicts with other libraries you are using. At a minimum, you now have a piece of code that works differently from everything else you have, which could be wonderful if it is a leap forward and a huge detriment if it is not the direction you need to go.

Work from home

It has become fashionable to allow work from home, and while there may be valid reasons, such as saving money on floor space for developers to work from home, the structure of the Six Week Solution does not allow for this on a regular basis. If someone really needs to work from home in bunny slippers, they are not a candidate for working effectively in the bullpen.

At the same time, being able to allow work from home may occasionally be necessary. Bad weather may mean that people can't get into the office for reasons out of their control; we've seen entire cities shut down by storms so bad that roads were impassable. Additionally, someone may want to put in some time on the weekend or evenings without driving into the office. The ability to connect remotely and take over the desktop workstation should exist, but not be used every day as the sole form of working.

Overbuilder and perfectionist

This is hard to uncover in an interview, and if you don't listen to the warning signs it will cost you in the long run. If they were never happy with previous projects, you need to drill into the reasons why. Was the software really not ready for production or did they want to keep polishing it until it was perfect? Did they ever ship anything? This is important because it is easy to be fooled by someone who wants to do everything "right" and will never let software go to production because there will always be something to fix or make better.

We have been led down the garden path before only to find that the candidate overbuilt the solution to handle every case they could imagine and completely missed the immediate need. Many times, good enough really is good enough until you have time to come back and expand the solution.

This also leads to an attitude similar to riveting instead of screwing something together. Initially, both approaches look similar: something got built and it looks strong enough from the outside. Unless it really is a one-off that can be thrown away, riveting will require much more work to modify in the future versus screws, which can be taken out to reach the guts, fix the problem, and then button up again.

Other considerations

Most developers are attracted to stability. At the same time, many do not view money as the ultimate end, for they instead view money as merely a tool to achieve other things: cars, houses, vacations, hobbies, and game consoles. Their education reinforces these concepts, for they are more likely to be happy knowing that they built their home personal computer to have certain features instead of purchasing one already built with those features.

It is hard for some people to imagine, but engineers *like to work* and even their hobbies are typically work: woodworking, restoring old cars, music, and so on. Sure, some will use money as a tool to purchase vacations, bigger houses, and so on, but most will buy *more tools* to build something else. To summarize: a lot of people might happily point out the features built into their laptop; engineers will happily point out the features *they built* into their laptop.

The problem is that many developers believe they are fine if they are making a market wage instead of pushing the limits on what the market will bear. This is sometimes difficult to reconcile inside the Six Week Solution, as you want developers who are confident and will be willing to "go all in" and gamble.

Many developers will be attracted to the Six Week Solution not because they can push the envelope and make as much money as they possibly can through the bonuses, but rather because they don't want to screw over their team by coding poorly, thereby cutting others out of bonuses. To the engineer with this thought process, the idea that the development cycles will challenge their abilities and give them motivation to improve is attraction enough.

Hiring summary

In the end, you are working to hire the right skills and attitudes that everyone will run on their own and you don't have to constantly babysit them. Even if every single developer isn't the home-run hitter or nine-inning pitcher, they all can contribute to the success at the highest level they can.

COMPENSATION

Developers working in the Six Week Solution are compensated differently, as they have a base pay and bonus structure that requires some considerations throughout the organization. This piece is critical to the success, as it provides the monetary motivation to achieve everything on the cycle commitment document. *When* bonuses are paid is a large part of the motivation and enables you to show that you are serious about success; additionally, bonuses should *not* be tied to company goals. Finally, criteria of a successful cycle must be considered. It is very important to pay the bonus as close to the end of a cycle as possible. Because the development cycle calendar ends in the middle of a month or at the end of a month, the next pay cycle after the cycle end is the target to deliver bonuses.

Bonuses paid on the successful completion of a cycle must not be based on company performance. If you are putting the effort into selecting the correct features to address in each cycle, then you are getting the things your current and future customers need built into the product; it is the responsibility of stakeholders to steer the developers to work on the pieces that are crucial for the company both tactically and strategically.

One trouble area is how to make the call that all the cycle commitments were met. Ideally, on the second Monday of the cycle there would be unit/integration/functional tests all failing for every new feature and on the second to last Friday all the tests pass. Regardless of how you measure that all the commitments were met, we have found that the simplest approach to payout is all or nothing. Do not fiddle with "80%" of commitments and paying 80% of the bonus, it's all or nothing; make it 100%, pass or fail. This is a very simple black and white approach whether the cycle commitments were met or not.

Base pay

To make the bonus important, and to therefore stress the importance of meeting all the cycle commitments, the base pay should not be above market value and, in some cases, may be below market. The base pay should not be so low that people think they will not be able to meet their mortgage, but not above market to keep the focus on meeting the cycle commitments. The total compensation of base pay plus bonus possibilities should exceed the market.

Compensating QA

Compensation of QA is particularly interesting on this topic. They should be seated in the bullpen, pulling with the team to get the product pulled together every cycle. It seems very reasonable to have their cycle compensation be part of the rest of the team's compensation.

However, this method puts them in a conflict of interests. Their job is to give an accurate assessment of the state of the product. However, if that assessment is negative when the end of the cycle comes, then they are taking money out of their own pockets to say so. Not putting QA on a bonus structure means they are not taking money out of their own pocket, but they are still doing that to people who they are working with side by side so the demotivation still exists. Most other compensation options for QA set up a very antagonistic relationship inside the bullpens that diminishes the team's productivity.

In the end, what way to handle this depends on the management style of those running the shop. We encourage keeping QA on the same structure as development. While it can be a challenge to personal integrity, with involved leadership and automation practices in place, it should not be difficult to keep the QA process on track.

Team compensation

It should go without saying that every person in the bullpen is a team that fails or succeeds together. Everyone should depend on one another's talent, skill, experience, and knowledge. Everyone should strive for their personal best and help one another to do the same. Every member on the team should understand that they are all accountable for the success or failure of the bullpen meeting the cycle commitments and ultimately responsible for the company's success; the compensation structure of the Six Week Solution reinforces this concept.

DEVELOPMENT TOOLS

As a rule of thumb, any developer of the same discipline should instantly be able to be productive at another developer's workstation. In order for this to be true, you need to enforce some standards on tools and configuration. Specific tools are discussed in (Chapter 8, "Integrating Automation" on page 135) because you need the right tools to move quickly. This section aims to arm you with the philosophical tools to accomplish success as a critical piece.

You need to avoid competing IDEs. Pick one for each discipline and standardize on it. If someone is religious about using nothing but vi, you probably don't want that person in your shop.

Make sure you have a standard configuration and a standard set of add-ons. Don't let developers install rogue versions of any tool (including new versions of your selected tool). Put one person in charge of the default configuration and make the deployment of a new version or a new configuration part of your cycle commitments; any tool change must be approved by the architect of the bullpen.

Just as important as enforcing the tool, you need to ensure that they are actually using it correctly. We have seen developers who claim to be using a tool only to discover that they are only using it as a text editor. You should train your new developers how the team gets more out of a tool.

Use the Right Tools

One winter we did not properly blow out the sprinkler system between the silcock valve and the backflow preventer. When we turned up the system we had a nice one inch rip in the side of one of the copper pipes. Being the ever-confident do-it-yourselfer, I went to get my blow torch. After spending 15 minutes trying to melt the solder, I called my brother-in-law. He came over with his torch and did the job in 30 seconds.

The wrong tool was $12. The correct tool was $34. Obviously if we added a lot of zeros to these prices, the decision becomes more difficult. But the important point is that the wrong tool can make a job almost impossible.

Software engineer and homeowner

The decision of an IDE is simple, but it has not always been that way. Our favorite IDE is Eclipse; it is the most flexible, extensible open source tool to ever be developed. Eclipse functions the same way on Windows, Mac, and Linux. Eclipse supports almost all programming languages, including Java, C++, Pearl, Python, JavaScript, HTML, and about any other language you can think of. Eclipse has a plug-in architecture that allows you to include many powerful extensions to the environment.

Coding standards

Every developer has a favorite coding standard. Choose one and make it required. In Eclipse you can force the formatting to a standard enforced on saving so developers have no excuse. A common standard makes it much easier for other developers to read.

One of the most important advantages to forcing a standard is when you are attempting to understand the historical changes that have been made. Most difference engines choke at different tabs and bracket locations. Outside of developers, the difference between a few spaces and a tab may seem ridiculous because it may look the same on a printed page, so what are the technical people complaining about? Do they really care that something is indented three or four spaces rather than a tab? The answer is "yes," and experienced developers know that investing in a consistent approach to how indentations are made in code pays back huge dividends the first time they are comparing code that somehow stopped working somewhere along the way. Having this enforced standard saves real dollars in the time it takes to make changes in software.

To avoid holy wars on coding style, you need strong leadership in the bullpen, someone who is able to accept criticism of any style selection, weigh the options, and then enforce it with an iron fist.

Collective code ownership

Collective code ownership means that anyone can jump into the code and make a change. This is not some "code collective" that spreads risk among the developers; instead every developer is empowered to make a change when it needs to be done. This approach is not possible if every developer has their own "style" to the code they are working on and no others dare touch their code.

Automation

This approach cannot work without automation. We feel so strongly that an entire chapter (Chapter 8, "Integrating Automation" on page 135) is devoted to the specifics of automation.

Build

Over time, we have implemented this with both nightly builds and builds on every check-in. We think both systems have their merits at certain times, but as technology has progressed, the viability and value of frequent building becomes more obvious and is our clear recommendation.

Regardless of how frequent a build system you implement, we strongly encourage nightly, or at least weekly, milestone builds with a higher level of integration testing.

Testing

As part of the automated builds there should also be automated tests. These tests should be a combination of the unit tests written by the developers, along with integration tests developed by QA. A build should be considered failed if any test fails, and no failed build should ever be promoted to QA, much less production.

Integration tests may require additional hardware and software than the developer unit tests, for strong unit tests separate data location and storage from processing, but integration testing must consider storage as well as processing. Because additional resources are required to perform automated integration tests, this type of testing may not occur with every build. Even when you have builds kicking off with every check-in, there may still be a need to run integration tests on another schedule.

Testing levels

We feel strongly that testing is a part of the process at all levels. Developers should be comfortable with test-driven development and using unit tests continually as they develop. With automated builds, unit tests are being executed. QA may have a set of integration tests that are executed at regular intervals. Finally, a need exists for acceptance testing.

A special note about acceptance testing is that if everything is done, this should be a slam dunk. If acceptance testing is difficult for the organization, then that is a sign that someone is not following the process and communicating effectively. The problem may be inside the development shop, if developers are not using unit tests or QA has not yet grown to embrace automated integration testing, or it is external and the stakeholders are not expressing the needs correctly.

CYCLE COMMITMENTS

Once over the hurdle of delivering functional and quality software every six weeks, getting the company sold on the approach, and assembling a team or teams that can actually produce code, you still have to decide exactly what code to write!

Product management should have a backlog of feature requests, bug reports, and a roadmap of future direction. Prior to every cycle kickoff, product management has been gathering new inputs, dusting off old requests to see if they are still valuable, and being prepared with input from every stakeholder and user.

Inputs

Once product management has gathered all the inputs from many sources, they should have a large list. If your product is healthy, there may be bug reports but there will also be a huge list of features. Even if the list is mostly bugs, your approach to making decisions will be the same.

To complete cycle goals successfully, we must each determine the required intermediate steps and tasks. During meetings, discuss tasks required to complete the goals and give an estimate of the amount of time needed to achieve each task and goal. In order to address each goal adequately, we will need to identify each specific task and assign responsibility for completion.

Developers have the responsibility to identify all of the areas where you think that the code could be refactored or a new tool might be used to improve the performance, make the software more stable, or even introduce a ground-breaking feature.

Participate in the benefits discussion. During the kickoff week you need to pretend that you are a consultant trying to find the best ways you can to add value to the business. Think about what you can get done in six weeks that will be demonstrable and impactful. If there are 30 different options, don't try to do all of them. Focus on the top five or 10 that prove the functionality and are the most important. Remember what the product is supposed to do. Don't create options that no one will use.

Let management know what you need

For management to address the team's needs adequately, we need to be timely, clear, and up front about what is needed to complete the goals. Without timely communication we cannot make the goals.

True negotiation

In order for this to work, management must truly negotiate. They must ask for more than the development team is willing to give. They must also be willing to give in. If the team honestly does not think that they can deliver X, then there must be a willingness to negotiate for a reduced scope. This methodology works best when management is engaged, pushes for as much as they can get but is realistic about what can be completed. You want every cycle to be a stretch, but you also want the commitment to be something that the team can achieve.

Good commitment definition

Management should be able to define each task clearly. Before sign-off, the manager and the individual should have a clear concise understanding of the task and the work necessary to complete the task.

Coordinate the dependencies

Management should make sure that the tools, equipment, resources, and support needed to complete the tasks and goals of the cycle are provided. The progress of dependency removal should be discussed in Mea Culpa and finally during the Cycle End meeting.

Never commit to delivery of external dependencies

No one should commit to a delivery for a cycle that is dependent on software or hardware that is not yet purchased. It is the job of senior management to ensure that once a decision has been made on a particular software product or a hardware platform, that the execution on delivery is handled in a well-understood and timely fashion.

A difficult area to understand is the definition of "an external dependency." This is when it is necessary to have part of the product driven by a group outside of development or product management. This can take many forms, but is encountered frequently in GUI development. Maybe you have contracted a development effort to an external company to produce or define how your product is visualized. If the external company is not aligned with your development cycles and the planned order of how your software will be delivered, you are inviting disaster. We ourselves have seen this happen, and it takes the form of contractors working up to the wire during the sixth week of the cycle and missing the deliverable. These external resources are not compensated in the same way as your developers, and they have no motivation to exist within your schedule. If you find yourself in this situation, we suggest performance-based contracts with these external vendors.

If you require detailed quotes and cost analysis, those are excellent items to have as cycle deliverables. You must make sure for the development team's sake that you act quickly on that information. You do not want to let that information get stale. You don't want to put your developers in a situation of being hounded by a salesperson trying to close a sale. Do all the research that you need to feel comfortable but don't let the team start the process if you are not prepared to spend the money.

Be honest with your development organization. If you feel that something is too expensive, ask for more details and make a decision. The team will adapt as long as they know what to expect.

Software changes and upgrades

New software is always a disruption. Make sure that a few cycles have been used to research the best solution and then do an informal POC (Proof of Concept). Once a product has been selected, it is imperative that the time frame for the purchase is very well understood and executed.

Hardware changes and upgrades

Typically hardware is not as disruptive as software. If you are replacing existing hardware, you have to anticipate that some data or application is going to be forgotten/missed. If the reason for the replacement is a failure, we would strongly encourage you to do everything you can to make the drives from the old machine available to the replacement. We keep a collection of external USB drive enclosures that support most of the current drive technologies.

Scoping

Once cycle dates have been established, no one should move them. The temptation to extend a few more weeks should be avoided. Like raising children, one of the most important things about managing developers is consistency.

It will be very tempting sometime in the chaos of day-to-day business to try to add something "critical" at Mea Culpa and then extend the cycle a few weeks to get that addition done. *It is critical that you do not attempt this.* If management and sales can manage the expectation of the customer correctly, then there should be no reason that they cannot wait for the next cycle to see the job done correctly.

Perhaps the most important aspect of the not changing the date is the credibility you will gain with both your developers and your customers. Set a schedule, manage expectations properly, and do everything possible not to deviate.

Fixed iteration scope

Getting the big-bang features knocked out early allows for demos to stakeholders outside of development and increases the enthusiasm for the entire product inside and outside of software development. The risky part here is not to commit to radical changes or feature creep within one six week cycle, but rather to dutifully record new ideas and suggestions for input to future cycles. Many times, requirement gathering still doesn't fully conceptualize what the feature will look like until it is delivered. The battle is to stay on target with quality functional software and a list of new enhancements that were never scoped originally.

There was a project at a company that had to be custom developed for every customer they had. It was expensive, repetitive, and error prone and the company almost always lost money on the deal, despite their attempts to adjust pricing models to cover it.

When the big initiative came to rework that piece to solve the problems, I was very excited. We brought in a big name process company that spent a week on-site training us how to go through all of the stages of their development process. With enthusiasm, we started to use those tools on our new project, and started with the attempt to figure out all of the requirements for this application that all of our customers needed, and would need.

We spent months on it, and not one of us felt like we were getting a handle on the goals. The project floundered in analysis paralysis.

Eventually, when we were just about to give up, one of us encountered an Agile method and brought it into the shop. Instead of finishing all of this analysis, we were going to pick a feature that we knew we needed and start developing. We would work very hard on crafting that solution so it would be in good shape to extend when we picked out the next feature.

Then, we started coding. We made more progress in the first month than in the six before it.

In reality, a project like that never ends because new customers wanted new things and rarely the ones we had predicted. It would happen less and less often over time, though, as we learned what the common features were, and we would know we had targeted what the clients did want.

Flex developer

Scope control

It is critical to be vigilant about scope. More deliverables are missed by trying to do too much than because of any other factor. Developers as a species are eternal optimists when it comes to their own work and external pessimists when it comes to the opinions/decisions of management. If you ask for everything under the sun, developers will try to achieve it and most likely fail. If you embrace the iterative nature of the process and ask for small measurable and manageable chunks, everyone will be better served.

This is perhaps the hardest lesson for everyone to learn. There is a true art to understanding and directing the desire to build it all. You don't want to discourage creativity but you also want to enforce the "let's prove it works" with a subset of the features we think we may need. You need everyone, including the customer, to understand that it is far better to have something to use and improve than to hope in vain for everything to be done and perfect the first time.

Negotiate task lengths

Management should assist each person with determining what amount of time should be allocated to each task. Given the natural desire of most developers to overbuild, it is frequently necessary to rein in the scope to something that is achievable in one cycle and a path to create the full vision over several cycles.

Commit to full utilization

In the interest of fairness it is expected that each person will commit to full utilization. If all of your tasks are done, or you are blocked by some other factor, make sure you do something worthwhile with the time. Help another teammate complete commitments. Write unit tests. If you feel like you are in a holding pattern and spend time surfing Facebook, you might as well be painting a target on your back and should be spending time packing your desk because you're not going to be there for the next cycle.

Communicate dependencies

Developers have the responsibility to communicate what they need and why. It would be unreasonable to expect that an integration test be developed to make sure that the latest fire of the day from production could be duplicated by QA if QA doesn't have production size hardware and disk space.

Sample cycle commitment pitfalls

One of the worst and best things about software developers is their utter predictability.

These are some of the traps we have seen in implementing the Six Week Solution that developers attempt to get into cycle commitment documents that you must make judgment calls on:

Trap	Options to Deal with the Trap
"This code must be rewritten. The old design is horrible."	Three options here: **1.** The code was written by someone else and they don't like it. **2.** They don't understand the code. **3.** They did a poor job the first time. Ask for proof, and if they did it poorly, why did you pay the cycle bonus? Sometimes, old brittle code is just that, old and brittle, and you'd do worse than to flush it and start over.
"The new tool will solve all our problems."	This statement might mean: "I just read a blog about this tool and it would be great to have on my resume."
"We can use this new paradigm; it will solve all our problems."	Really, the developer often doesn't really understand what they are asking for and just wants to play with something new.
"We need to use the new library."	Sometimes a new tool is a game changer; there may be some truth in their suggestion, but beware of making this happen if it means changing everything before you can try it.
"The latest version of something is available."	This statement might mean: "We need to upgrade so my resume stays current."
"We need to upgrade to X."	Upgrade if it makes sense, a product is desupported, or the new version has a feature you need.
	At other times, you'll be backed into a corner and must upgrade because your customers are telling you that you have to run on the same platform that their enterprise has standardized upon. What your developers are telling you is true.

Do not deviate from cycle commitments

It is the responsibility of each person to focus their energies in the direction needed in order to better attain the cycle goals. We should each guard against deviation from the commitments and help one another to attain these goals.

After cycle kickoff no one should be experimenting with new technologies unless it has been explicitly called out in the documents.

Developers by nature are tempted to go deeper into a solution than they need to. Don't jeopardize the cycle to build a Better Mouse Trap; make the functions you committed to this cycle work and save that great suggestion for the next cycle. More than once developers have made a solution 10 times more complex than it needs to be. Then when they find that they are buried and cannot complete their deliverable, they either get sloppy or defiant. No task should be insurmountable. The tasks should always be concise and manageable.

Deviation from Scope Story

We once had a developer who was given the opportunity to build something from the ground up and build the foundation for a new product line because this was the second time a customer had asked us to build a similar feature. We really saw a need for a product to address this need anyway and the revenue that could be generated by making the solution a product offering was very attractive.

The developer did sense the urgency and the chance to earn his stripes all at once because, if successful, this effort would produce its own product line. Long-term resources in the bullpen winced at both the opportunity and the risk, but they were all consumed with other tasks. It was a hard situation for everyone, but we thought we had the implementation planned well over several cycles.

The problem was, it was all overwhelming for this developer and he didn't ask for help. He sat in his desk day after day, pounding the keyboard and telling everyone that everything was on track. Demo's even worked on demo size data so there was no reason to really dig deeply into every line of code.

But he made the problem too big. Instead of focusing on a couple of key bits of functionality every week or so, he overarchitected the entire approach. When it came time for deployment, he found himself with a few problems that should have been edge cases and fixed easily but instead was awash with complexity for any future problem he could imagine and the implementation for the initial customer was a disaster. He ended his employment with us and emailed us sarcastically, wishing us well in future work.

Another developer stepped in and in three days had things patched to a level that the customer's problems were solved and in another week had increased performance by several factors. The original developer needed the guts to ask for help and would have found help easily given.

Development manager

Cycle success

It seems so simple and straightforward to say, "Pay the bonuses if the team fulfills their commitments."

In implementation, this actually can be one of the hardest parts. Setting aside for the moment the frustration and disappointment of having to tell a team that just killed themselves trying to meet their goals that they failed, the more difficult question is "When are they *done*?"

Are they done when they say the feature is complete? That obviously is not going to work, as developers are very optimistic about how well their code will work, which is assuming that their incentive for completion does not interfere with an honest evaluation in the first place. Obviously, QA needs to be involved, but still, how do they measure it? Is it done when all bugs are eliminated? Most software would never ship. No, QA should report the status of the product; management should decide what to do with that information.

If you leave the fuzziness of that decision to management, then they have to make an arbitrary decision attempting to weigh the state of the product against the rest of the business forces in play to decide whether the release should ship as it is. Unfortunately, that method removes much of a developer's ability to impact their delivery, as it is measured against factors they cannot affect and frequently are not even aware exist.

The best way to handle this is with test automation. Using an executable requirements framework as discussed in a later section ("Executable Requirements" on page 112) allows us to define success criteria in a concrete, repeatable fashion and end up with a simple indicator. Green bar, everything works; bar of any other color, it fails. This also helps reduce the necessary pain when it is time to inform the team that they have missed the goal. It is less personal, and if your environment is set up right, they knew they had failed before you had to tell them.

Managing the Cost of Change

CHAPTER CONTENTS

Agile Development and Business Goals. DOI: 10.1016/B978-0-12-381520-0.00006-0

INTRODUCTION

Previous chapters discuss the exponentially growing cost of the change curve and its staggering ability to destroy your software project. This chapter outlines strategies on how to tame the curve and maximize the return on your investment into your software project.

There are several primary methods for managing the cost of the change curve. The good news for most executives is that they have direct influence on most of them because they are driven by business-level decisions more than technical ones.

- The first is to use feedback loops to short circuit the curve.
- The second is managing how unknown factors will impact your development process.
- The third is investing in infrastructure to make sure that the current product status is never on your list of unknown variables.
- Finally, we lower the base of the curve by reducing the cost of development across the board.

We will explore each angle of attack in detail.

FLATTENING THE CURVE WITH FEEDBACK LOOPS

A common analogy for software development is the history of warfare. It provides many examples of never-ending swings between the dominance of heavy armor (process) and light, mobile forces (agility).

In software development, we have recently left a time of heavily armored processes that attempted to protect businesses from risks with tools such as gates, contract negotiations, rigorous advanced planning, and high structure practices. That time frame was characterized by large, expensive projects with ponderous and expensive processes, blind pursuit of perceived guarantees such as CMMI certifications, and painful contract negotiations that attempted to constrain every target deliverable.

The current popularity of Agile processes, in contrast, focuses on steady, light, disciplined efforts that enable a business to change directions on a dime to best respond to change such as unexpected opportunities or pitfalls. The challenge of those processes is to recognize change drivers and prioritize accordingly. Like driving a car, if you want to stay on the highway, you can never take your eyes off the road.

Feedback loops are the mechanisms used to identify internal drivers for change in a project and inputs for correcting the course of the project appropriately. Each one provides measurable status on the progress of the project that brings change drivers out as soon as possible. At the same time, it provides a checkpoint where responding to changing factors can be accomplished almost immediately.

Both of these points are crucial in short-circuiting the cost of the change curve. Simply put, the sooner you can make a necessary change, the more of the curve you cut off. So, the sooner we know about internally driven changes, the less expensive it will be; the faster we can respond to needed changes, internal or external, the less expensive it will be. (See Figure 6.1 to see this curve represented in a graph.)

Let's be specific.

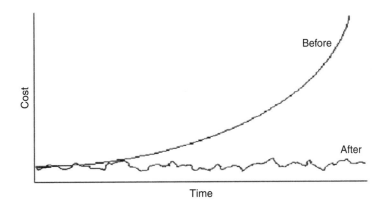

FIGURE 6.1

Before and after managing the cost of change.

Frequent releases (product feedback)

Many businesses consider themselves to be doing pretty well if they release one or two versions of their product a year. Even using the Six Week Solution, it is possible, sometimes even appealing, to release to the customer only a couple of times a year, choosing from the eight releases that come out of the development organization to those one or two releases driven by the strongest customer mandate. Those releases provide a big bang for marketing departments to talk to with all the changes produced in the release. Unfortunately, this common practice is one of the biggest setups for running smack into the wall of the cost of the change curve.

Even when not planning on releasing the product of every development cycle, it is necessary to think of every release as a candidate to be promoted to a customer-facing release. Failure to do so leads to sloppy quality and the bad idea that any problems found could simply be corrected in the next release. Remember, the focus is always forward, and using a six week development cycle to only address bugs is ludicrous when you need to get new functionality out the door.

The risk here is developing a product that failed to fit the customer's needs. Because the industry is effectively developing in isolation for six months to a year, in that environment you will be a long way down the road before your users get the opportunity to see if you correctly understood and served the needs they had for the software. Not only are we wasting significant development investment and losing out on the opportunity costs of working on the right value adding features, but we are also adding impediments to building the right pieces by creating things that will need to be substantially transformed or ripped out to make way for what we actually needed.

Customer is on-site

One tenet of agile development is that the customer is on-site. This rule exists because it is too easy to stray from the original goals, and temptation can take even the most focused player's eyes off the game. This is easy when the product is being developed for internal use, but difficult when you are developing a product for many users outside the walls of the company. A proxy is

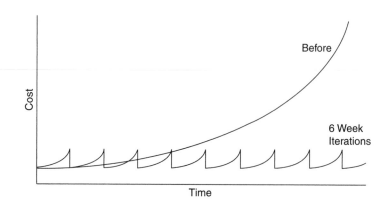

FIGURE 6.2

Idealized six week iteration change curve.

required, either via strong product management—preferred—who actually communicate with customers regularly or by internal users for an external product. Failure to use real users or a proxy for them will destroy a product as surely as poor design. (See Figure 6.2 for an idealized cost of change curve.)

Very Late User Feedback

One project we saw took some initial requirements for crucial, game-changing features from the end user and went off to implement them. When they were delivered, no actual end user feedback was gathered.

In reality, the end users were not sure how to use the features and did not touch them for a year and a half. Sadly, that is a year and a half that the company was getting no value from these high value features. It is also a year and a half of the code base growing around those features and more dependencies forming on the assumptions of the implementation.

Eventually, the end users got brave and started trying to use the features. Suddenly, the needs of the features started appearing. A lot of wrong assumptions about the implementation had to be thrown away and rewritten. That waste could have been headed off by earlier user feedback.

Senior developer

Deploy every release?

Ideally, in the Six Week Cycle, it is best to deploy every release, which means that every six weeks we put a new product in front of users. The frequent response to this is that deployments are considered costly for a variety of reasons. Marketing would rather wait for a "big" new thing to sell. Support and sales do not want to handle the pain of what feels like perpetual upgrades. The training team cannot keep their materials up to date. However, marketing can set up controlled deployments with key customers for feedback, and deployment pains can be addressed in a variety of ways such as development to support auto-updating or other relatively seamless means of transition.

The benefits, though, are substantial. Imagine, for example, that you have a 12 month lead on your competitors in your product domain. Your team goes into an intense development effort to develop the next generation of features to keep that lead. After a year, you roll out your shiny new product for your customers to admire. Unfortunately, your understanding of what your users needed was either slightly off or has failed to keep up as their hopes have changed. Also a problem is that your competitor did not have that problem, and now you are fighting for every inch when you should have been smoothly sailing ahead.

Rule of thumb: Never space your releases out for longer than you can afford to absorb in wasted development time.

Frequent iterations (planning feedback and Mea Culpa)

The next feedback loop is our largest inside of a Six Week Cycle. It is an iteration planning loop and provides the opportunity to steer the cycle to the most successful completion. We recommend weekly or bi-weekly iterations inside of the release cycle for planning purposes. It provides many key opportunities to identify and correct problems inside of the cycle. (See Figure 6.3 for graphs of cycle projections based on weekly velocity.)

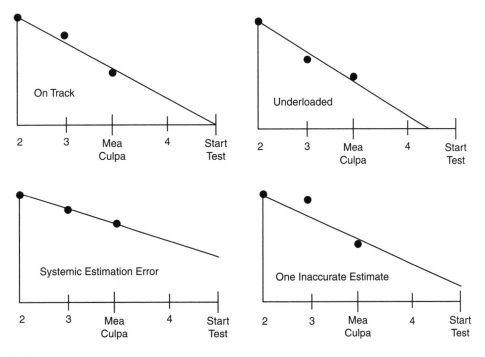

FIGURE 6.3

Cycle projections based on weekly velocity.

If each of the development weeks of the cycle is an independent iteration, then two things become necessary:

- First, a prioritization of the features being requested for the cycle.
- Second, aim to measure delivered features for each of those iterations.

The most important checkpoint in the six week cycle is Mea Culpa, which is the official opportunity to address scope issues within the cycle. With weekly iterations, the team has two data points on the pace of their progress toward meeting their cycle commitments and is able to do a simple extrapolation to see if the cycle is on track or not. This depends on splitting the features down into bite-sized pieces that each delivers business value. It takes a great deal of practice to do this effectively, but the benefits are by far a more predictable and manageable project.

The importance of prioritizing those pieces comes at negotiation time. If the team has done the highest value pieces in the first couple of weeks and finds that they are overscoped for the cycle, negotiating the scope of the cycle becomes much, much easier. Dropping a lower priority feature that may have even been perceived to have "barely" made it into the cycle is much simpler than dropping a highest value feature.

Also, it enables the business to have the most flexibility. Should the business come to Mea Culpa with important items that need to be negotiated into the cycle, they have the least valuable pieces of the cycle remaining for trade, which maximizes their opportunity to get the highest value from a cycle by trading a newly realized, high-value proposition for a lower value, previously committed feature in the cycle. The key here is using measured progress for planning over the frequently wild guesses of most developer estimation techniques. Naturally, the measured pace of the cycle iterations provides great feedback for correctly scoping the next cycle at sign-off. The argument for the accuracy of using last cycle's pace as the most accurate representation of next cycle's likely pace was made by the XP community after its introduction in the book *Planning Extreme Programming* by Kent Beck and Martin Fowler under the name of "Yesterday's Weather."

Other challenges

There are challenges at Mea Culpa. If someone carries into the meeting the expectation that everything is done and it's time to add more work, then those expectations need to be reset. Another trouble spot is failure to understand that something not yet done must be removed to make room for quality in a new request. Even experienced developers and managers can fall into either of these traps. Beware the "Ides of Mea Culpa" and manage it correctly to ensure success and quality.

Frequent status updates (work coordination feedback and the daily stand-up meeting)

With the entire team being responsible for the successful completion of cycle commitments, it is crucial that they effectively coordinate their efforts. Tasks that had been split from features need to be reassembled into finished products. Challenging or risky items need to be watched for problems. Development work in general needs to make the best use of the knowledge and existing tools that can move development forward. The stand-up meeting provides those opportunities. Each developer needs to give reasonable feedback on what they are doing and how it is going so that the team knows how things are progressing and can help things along most effectively. As with any of the feedback loops, these updates should come as often as we can afford to invest in bad work that we must throw away. Along with many other agile processes, the Six Week Solution recommends not going more than a day without coordinating work.

Of special note when planning is a mistake that is made by nearly every developer when first promoted into a team lead position. In the desire to show that they are up to the job, simple features are tackled first from the cycle commitment document. This leads to trouble as more complex items are put off until after Mea Culpa, giving no time to adjust to any problems of scoping. These new team leads need some coaching to help them, and by way of them the entire bullpen, that difficult stuff needs to be tackled first.

There is, however, one exception to tackling the most difficult items first, which is when some feature or change is, for reasons outside of the control of development, going to be released to a customer out of sync with the six week cycle. Typically, this need arises from a failure to manage a customer correctly, but the other case is when dealing with customers who have other rules, such as a holiday lockdown on any new software from Thanksgiving to after New Year's Day. In these cases it is possible to get squeezed into the situation of releasing software out of sync with the six week cycle, and the only way to manage it is to employ version control techniques of branching. Note that this will nearly double the work, as the "back-patched" feature or change must also be ported into the current development, so schedule accordingly. This concept of the multiplier of work is lost on nondevelopers who have no understanding of the process and tools involved so it is up to the manager to be strong and ensure that adequate time is allocated.

Frequent programmer rotation (directional feedback and intraday reviews)

During the course of a single day, it is a good idea to change up the pairs working on particular features. This is an excellent opportunity to avoid "group think" errors that pull a pair into shared errors in thinking that can take development off the tracks. Any experienced programmer can tell you stories about being stuck on some coding task until they went to someone else for help. That person probably did not even contribute to the solution, but just the act of having to describe what is going on in a component to someone else made it obvious what was blocking the efforts and how to fix it. We get these benefits, to a deeper degree, when we change pairs frequently. The process of bringing in another mind and getting their input into a project avoids useless or error-laden development paths, thereby heading off future changes before they happen.

Pairing should extend beyond the producer/consumer model to include others not involved in the task directly. It is easy for two developers, even experienced ones, who are splitting the work for a back end and front end GUI to go down a bad path because of the familiarity with the task (and with each other). Introducing new team members to the development task provides two benefits:

- First, someone outside of the core developers becomes familiar with the inner workings of the code.
- Second, it forces the core developers to "talk to their dog," but it's (hopefully, because you have hired correctly!) an intelligent dog.

The phrase "talk to their dog" comes from the concept of turning away from the computer and explaining what you are writing to your dog. If you can do that, then you really understand what you are doing! Another example is that most people don't really grasp a subject until they have to tutor someone on that subject. The point is to rotate your pairs, and rotate frequently.

Frequent integrations (product progress feedback and automated regression test)

As frequently as we possibly can, we want to take measurably progressed development items and integrate them back into the product for running against an automated regression test suite. This provides us with two protections to avoid setting ourselves up for delayed (and therefore more expensive) changes:

- The first protection is to tell us as soon as possible if we have made a change that broke a previously working feature. The closer we are to a change when we realize it was bad, the more likely that it will be a trivial matter to fix it. After all, the changes we just made are very fresh in our mind, and we know exactly what few things have been changed between the last time that it worked and the time that it broke.
- The second protection the continuous integration gives us is protection against divergent development paths. If programmers are going down mutually incompatible paths, the longer they do so, the more costly and error-prone it becomes to try and reconcile their divergence. With continuous integration, checking in changes almost becomes a race because the last one in has to do the extra work of merging their changes with those that came before. This keeps divergences small and manageable, and subjected to more automated validation.

Frequent testing (task progress feedback and unit tests)

The best practice for that actual, moment-to-moment development of features is generally called Test-Driven Development (TDD). This practice provides feedback on the progress of the task at an amazingly detailed level. We talk more about TDD in this chapter, but in short, the developers are required to write a test that shows that the system is lacking something that they need. This test will fail to pass initially. Then, they develop the code with the goal of making the test pass. Clearly, if that code is bad or they get off track, they have their test to run to show them, and will run it every couple of minutes.

Once they get the test to pass, it is time for them to look at the new code they wrote and clean it up to the best design that covers the needs of that code. Again, they now have the test they just wrote to help them have confidence that they will not break what already works during that restructuring.

The value of this cannot be overstated, as it provides what many have considered to be the Holy Grail of software development.

Now, developers can forever be keeping the internal structure and state of the code in the best, simplest, most adaptable form that they can manage because they can restructure that code at will within the protection of the tests they have written. If they break something, long before it sneaks into production as a regression, even before it gets to QA to find, they have large suites of programmer-level tests that can flag for them that their change to the program structure has broken something and is probably faulty. Because these feedback cycles are so tight, they can frequently avoid tedious time spent in a debugger tracking down the reason why it is bad. Instead, they throw the last few minutes of work away, go back to a system in a known good state, and try again.

Another benefit of TDD and the tools that support TDD is that it separates code into manageable chunks and frequently does not require that the entire product be "stood up" to test a change. Even today most software development is so immature that testing is performed on the entire product instead of components. Other industries figured out that this was bad a very long time ago: imagine if an alternator could not be tested before it was installed into an automobile—disaster! Instead of learning from manufacturing, software development still tries to assemble the entire automobile before finding out that the alternator isn't producing enough amperage. Use TDD and avoid this disaster.

Frequent discussion (concept feedback and pair programming)

Even before writing that first unit test, though, we already have a feedback loop to keep us on track, for when pair programming, a programmer is having his/her ideas and design decisions reviewed on a moment-to-moment basis. If the benefits of this are not immediately obvious, it is easiest to use a counterexample to demonstrate it. Very commonly, especially on waterfall-based projects, code reviews are used as gates to make sure that only good design decisions are allowed into the product. After writing the solution to a current problem, a programmer brings their solution in front of some number of peers to have their conclusions reviewed. Unfortunately, if the solution is bad, we have already wasted some time pursuing it. Also, the developer who is working on it is now invested very personally in their solution and is likely to defend their work rabidly against criticism. Desire to not backtrack or argue with a defensive programmer reduces the feedback into the solution, and it ships with only the most glaring issues challenged. For pair programming, that resistance gets turned on its head. Long before the programmers get invested in a solution, they are already bouncing it off their pair, who can throw their best ideas into the mix before a solution has started to solidify. The pair gets the opportunity to craft the best solution that the two of them together can manage, which is generally far better than either one alone. Having already headed off several possible development dead ends and chosen a better direction, now the pair is ready to start writing tests to demonstrate the new needs of the system.

The Fallacy of "Shortcuts" Story

In one cycle, our team was committed to redesign a crucial piece of functionality to better match the user's expectations. I was carrying the bulk of that effort for the team, and toward the end of the cycle, I was running out of time and had a lot left to do. I ended up working long and late hours alone trying to catch up.

That is where the biggest error happened. Exhausted, at 3 am, I had an idea for an implementation that seemed good. It wasn't. There was no pair programmer to question it. In the effort to go faster, test-driven development got put aside, so there were no unit tests to catch it. The problem only revealed itself intermittently under heavy volume and load so it managed to pass regression testing and was put into production. In production, it occasionally reported bad data. Support took days to prove that the problem existed and to figure out how to reproduce it. Fixing it required a significant effort to rip out and replace all the components related to that bad implementation decision. It took two programmers one week to reimplement, a couple more days for QA to attempt to prove the absence of a bug that would not happen consistently in the first place, and then system downtime for support to deploy the fixes.

The final cost of bypassing the feedback loops and repairing the issue in man hours alone was easily in the tens of thousands of dollars. So many times we know better, but we think we will not get burned when we take shortcuts like this.

The old gaffer in Lord of the Rings *used to say, "Short cuts make long delays."*

Team lead

AVOIDING THE CURVE BY MANAGING THE UNKNOWN

Most traditional development processes are designed around the idea of protecting a project from the unknown. They add various pieces of armor in place around the project, such as contracts, voluminous documentation, and rigorous schedules, in an attempt to prevent anything from derailing the project.

Unfortunately, all of the mechanisms attempting to protect the project from the unknown often hide the risks. Those that do offer some protection are inadequate because many unknowns are inherently built into the task of building software. Many newer development methodologies swing the pendulum in the opposite direction. Because there are so many unknowns, let us focus on being able to meet the unexpected intelligently, leaving room and means to adapt the project to our advantage. The families of methods with this philosophy are called Agile, and by Agile they mean a fairly simple thing: being "Agile" means to always be able to get the most value from your resources as your knowledge changes through the course of the project.

What, exactly, are all these unknowns that we do not know? Let us take a look.

Unknown #1: how do I plan the future?

What I know I don't know

Every financial prospectus discussion starts with the same disclaimer: "Past performance is no indicator of future results." Business in general and technology in particular are extremely volatile fields. Starting a project that will take a year or two with any idea that will still be valuable by the end of the project is frequently riskier than betting in the office football pool. Quite a few things can change your project dramatically.

Market changes

One area of uncertainty is the marketplace. During the course of a project, the world is shifting around it. Market opportunities appear or disappear very quickly. Disappearing opportunities frequently make businesses also disappear. New opportunities frequently only pay off for those who can react to them the fastest. Whether the project is a customer-facing product or an internal IT project, for a Fortune 100 company or a local nonprofit, the needs around your project can turn on a dime.

New creative leaps forward

All the math and engineering trappings of developing software often lead people to miss or forget that software development is very much a creative process. Those game-changing flashes of insight, the "Ah ha!" moments, stubbornly refuse to come on any kind of a schedule, so our plans need to be prepared to capitalize on them whenever they come.

New technological opportunities/threats

Statistics speculate that the technology field changes so fast that it is an entirely new field every seven years. The implications of that statement are relatively clear. Businesses either need to be prepared to take quick advantage of technology changes or to be overtaken by competitors that do. Frustratingly, even the best minds in the field are frequently surprised by which new technologies will completely change the business.

New competitive opportunities/threats

Finally, the battlefield of business competition is frequently unpredictable. With little warning, needs pop up to grab newly available market share or to capitalize on marketing opportunities or to counter competitors' advances.

A simple metaphor

Responding to all of this volatility requires looking at project planning with change as an expected occurrence rather than as something to be avoided at all costs. The project that attempts to protect itself from the forces of change that would invalidate the master plan sometimes digs its heels in most strongly when the plan has become the most obsolete. Effective projects use the feedback loops discussed earlier to run a project like a road trip. The smallest feedback loops keep the car between the lines on the road. Bigger feedback loops drive decisions such as which lane to choose or when to pass, and the biggest feedback loops may change the route or even the destination entirely given live information on things such as road and weather conditions.

Making decisions from unknowns

When planning the project, then, our best opportunities for success are to make decisions when you have the most information possible. Some projects attempt that with exhaustive research and projections and prototypes that attempt to resolve unknowns up front. All of those can be worthwhile tools, but costly and returning little value that can be realized as revenue. Better projects delay decision making until the last responsible moment. At the beginning of the project, if you make all the planning decisions, you will be doing so with the least knowledge you will ever have about the project. By waiting, we get the chance to capitalize on the team's learning. Of course, there are a myriad of reasons why waiting too long can put a project in jeopardy, so the phrase "last *responsible* moment" is key.

Unknown #2: what is needed?

When going into a software project, defining what the project needs to do always seems clear and simple. After all, we have a problem to solve, it is enough of a problem that we are ready to embark on this costly endeavor to fix it, clearly we know what we need, right? Generally, no, not really.

Stage 1—apply knowledge to the problem

We know what our problem is, but we do not know what we need in our solution. We probably have some ideas that may even seem very promising, but until we try to create them, we really know very little about what we want from a solution. Our ideas have many unexpected implications or technical problems that may make them unfeasible. Most commonly, though, we really have very little idea what we want the solution to look like and have to brainstorm and try out a few ideas.

Stage 2—learn from the solution

We have picked a solution to pursue and are learning through the process of implementing it all the implications of our decision that we could never have seen coming. During this process, we are creating tools to suit our domain and realizing they have more applications, integration points, or desirable extensions than we had originally imagined. In essence, our solution is transforming our problem into something new, opening up new opportunities for our business. At the same time, we are learning where our original solution does not fit our problem as well as we originally hoped and probably are having ideas for how we "wish we had done things."

Stage 3—return to stage 1

Many processes believe that this cycle can be circumvented with exhaustive up-front research and design. Generally, that is time spent (a) not producing realizable value for your business and (b) entrenching the team into a solution that resists using what we will learn as we create it. In practice, this cycle will happen anyway. We can inhibit it to fearfully control change or we can utilize it to maximize our value. This process is input into every level of the feedback loop to help planning and implementation of a project be the most effective.

Still, developers are developers, and they will always want to build the neatest new toy they can imagine. That is why we pay them. The next best toy, though, is not always the next highest value item. Planning for this feedback helps keep development prioritized by things that will provide the highest return to the business. Providing value is what keeps a project going long enough for the developers to get to go build all the exciting new toys they imagine, if they just have the patience to wait for the right moment.

Avoid speculative investments

Unfortunately, both for the business and the developers, there is a strong tendency to assume that we can see into the future. A piece of work comes in and we think: "I know I am going to need this later so I will just build it now so I have it." The work could be features that are not needed currently to support the user, design work not needed currently by the existing code, or code not needed currently to pass the tests. You wouldn't build streets for houses that you never plan to build so why put code in your software that you may never need?

This work is often violently defended as necessary "architecture" or "preparation" for future work, and once in a while that is true. Far more often, though, we are gambling. We are gambling that the next features, the next design, or the next piece of work is going to be what we think it is. With all the unknowns discussed here, hopefully it is clear that making this kind of decision on your own is a high-risk gamble. The likelihood is that we are wasting our work on a dead end that will never come to pass.

Even so, though, let us say the idea does work out. We guess what we will need, and six months down the road, we turn out to be right, actually remember what we did, and are able to use it effectively. Does the cost of making the change when we know exceed the cost of doing it early? In simple financial terms, let us say that it will cost us $10,000 in time and labor to make a change today and the same to make the same change in six months. Why on earth should we spend that money now? Even if the gamble is not a large gamble, we lose the time value of that investment for six months of waiting. Once you add in the risk that the investment will not be needed in six months after all, you definitely have a losing proposition.

An even more specific example comes up commonly in software development. Many projects have a great debate about internationalization. It is unquestionably an expensive endeavor, and the assumption is usually that it will be less expensive if we focus on it from the outset. However, what is the trade-off, really? Instead of a big-bang effort that we can clearly monetize when we need it, we make almost invisible payments on every feature we create that pay us nothing until we do actually need it. So is the aggregated total of all of those minutes spent every day on it less than the single large effort later? We are not aware of any good measures on this, but in our experience, the difference seems pretty negligible.

A counterexample to internationalization is security (if your product will need security). Building an application that only exists on one user's workstation may not need much security, as the physical machine location (inside a home, for example) may be enough. However, if your product moves data between businesses, you can be assured that someday a customer will want their data locked down. Wiring in security after the fact is difficult and results in "good enough" solutions that will always be an issue going forward with a security-conscious customer. Better to embed security from the creation to head off these problems later.

The primary lesson here: only build what you need for *today*.

Unknown #3: when will it be done?

A common fear in adaptive project planning is the misconception that there are no hard deadlines from which to make business plans. If the plan is so variable for all of these unknowns, how does the business make a marketing plan, a rollout plan, know when to buy new hardware, or make all those other decisions necessary to roll out the product? In practice, a correctly run project can adapt to feedback as necessary, as well as give better dates to plan with, and earlier feedback when things change.

Estimation vs measurement

Typical estimation processes are barely better than guesswork. We ask questions such as "How long will it take you to implement this?" and believe the answers and use them to build elaborate Gantt charts that should tell us when we are done and justify the work. Supposedly, these charts show us what the impact of every change will be on our milestones. More often, they just tell us how far behind we are and how much we have to work harder to "catch up" because the end date of the chart has been fixed for quite some time. We do not catch up, of course, because other tasks are not shrinking to help, no matter how much overtime we put in. In fact, other tasks seem to consistently run over also. The deadline gets missed, and we try to break the news to those waiting on it that it will be done "soon" and put in more overtime. We just know if we try hard enough we can catch up with just one more week. And one more week. And one more week.

Estimates are flawed, we all know that and we always have, and yet this pattern plays out over and over again. Time boxing works into the six week cycle, and iterations in that cycle enable us to fix dates and vary scope instead. But how do we set that scope without falling into the same trap?

One of the problems with Gantt chart-style planning is that it cannot account for systemic error in estimation—when all estimates failed to account for the hour spent every day on production support, that a particular technology is just slower to work with than was expected, or, as we had happen at one job, the power for the office building would blink out in the middle of work a couple of times a week and send everyone scrambling to try to recover. (See Figure 6.4 for a graph of systemic estimation errors.)

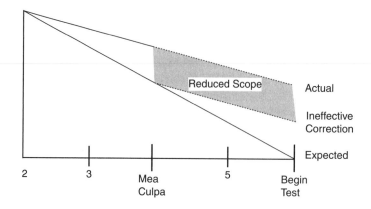

FIGURE 6.4

Systemic estimation errors.

The alternative is a rather tricky proposition of *measuring effort rather than time*. In essence, if we estimate the amount of work it takes to get a task done, then we can measure how much work we get done in a time box. This gives us a velocity that shows us how fast we are going based on measurements rather than guesswork.

To measure work, however, we must create a scale. When we measure the size of an object, we measure in inches or centimeters, but we only know how big those measurements are because we have a reference for them, a ruler or tape measure that allows those scales to be reproduced consistently over and over again.

There are many strategies that have been created for this, but in essence, they revolve around comparing tasks to each other. If we start saying that a task is a "1" and another task is about twice as much work, so it is a "2," then what those numbers represent is far less important than that they be repeatable. So, all tasks after that can be measured to say: "This task is about as much work as that task that we said was a 1, so this is a 1." Generally, a scale that has a unit of work be about what we could accomplish on a really good day and keeping tasks broken up to five or less of those seems to provide the most repeatable numbers.

Of course, that does not eliminate the problem of the estimates being flawed, but it does give us some more mechanisms for coping with the errors.

Planning for error

With a measured velocity in a fixed time window, and a measured unit of work, we now have simple tools that handle many variations for us. Let's take the example of systemic error given earlier. Let's say that progress on our work is just progressing *slower* than our optimistic initial estimates. You initially had 300 pts worth of work to accomplish in the next four cycles. However, you're finding that the teams are only able to finish 65 pts per cycle. You not only can plan for what will be done at the end of those four cycles, but you have a much more accurate idea of when they would be able to finish the work than just hoping it can be crammed into one more week. You know that it will probably take one more whole cycle to finish the workload and can plan accordingly.

This also allows you to accommodate the inevitable intermittent estimation errors when either the better or the worse of those happens. For example, if you had six cycles in a row where your team accomplished 60 pts of work and then one cycle where they accomplished 80 pts, how do you think you should plan for the eighth cycle? Well, unless you know that the change is repeatable, you know that the team is most likely going to accomplish around 60 pts of work again this time.

Measuring velocity gives another indicator of project health. If it is changing steadily without obvious external reasons, such as adding resources, then something is wrong.

Velocity that is always increasing probably means that the team is afraid and is padding their estimates every cycle. Velocity that is always decreasing probably means that the code base has quality issues that need to be addressed.

Unknown #4: when is it done?

Software is always plagued by defining *doneness*.

Is software done when the customer has everything they want? If the customer has stopped asking for things, the software really is finished, it is dying because it no longer offers the user anything they want.

An old adage for this is that if software has no bugs or feature requests, it has no users.

Is it done when all defects are gone? In most shops, that is a distant goal, and the product has value that can be and needs to be realized long before we can get there.

The Six Week Solution, like other time-boxed processes, adds to this difficulty because being done has to be measured so precisely. At the end of the cycle, the work stops regardless and the question becomes are we done? Do we get paid? That problem has two parts that need emphasis.

Always done

To be able to fit into the six week cycle, to have QA not be in a constant state of backlog, and to have sound deliveries, the team needs to learn to work toward a state of always done. That means, at all times, keeping the system in the best functioning way possible and ready to ship, which is a point of contention for many developers who have never learned to work in a highly incremental fashion, but a necessary skill, that reduces the risk of wrong or destabilizing development paths and maximizes the ability of the business to collect their return on investment. Most coarsely, if we come to the end of a cycle with a destabilized product because we have incomplete tasks, we have done worse than miss the cycle commitments. We have not delivered *anything* because they cannot take the product as it is and gain value from what was completed in the cycle. The feedback loops we discussed in general and test-driven development in particular help the developers always know that they have the system in a good state.

Executable requirements

At a higher level, we need another tool that both tells us that we are still in a good state and answers the other crucial doneness question, which is: "Did we deliver what we committed to?" That tool is executable requirements.

Executable requirements are a systematic way of expressing requirements as software, as running, self-validating tests. Another layer of test-driven development, the tests let the developers know when they have completed their goals. They are never out of date because they are run against the product constantly. They are rarely vague because we see exactly their intent in action. They also protect us from regressions, from unintentional losses of existing functionality.

These tools are still emerging and are primarily QA-centric, but the goal of them is to be friendly enough that an educated business representative could express and input their requirements directly into the requirements system and see the requirements turn green when the feature is added to pass the test correctly.

It is also especially nice to arrange the tests such that the company financier can just log into a page in the requirements system and see a green bar showing complete or a red bar showing not complete. Ambiguity is a concern when people's compensation rides on the answer.

Unknown #5: how do we not block ourselves?

In order to manage a project of any scale, many tasks must be progressing at the same time. These tasks can often undermine or invalidate each other in surprising ways. Many developers have discovered to their dismay that they had months of work ahead of them when they tried to bring separate tasks together and found that these tasks could not coexist. The more a project scales, the more parallel tasks are taking place and the bigger that risk gets. (To see this divergence represented graphically, see Figure 6.5.)

The tool for avoiding these unexpected roadblocks and increasing our ability to scale is continuous integration.

Continuous integration

Ever work on a document, such as a Word document (or, hey, even a software development process book) with multiple people? One enormous challenge is how to not step all over each other. If two

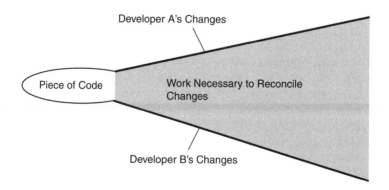

FIGURE 6.5

Divergent development branches.

people take the document and make changes to an area and then put the document back, what usually happens is that the last one to put changes in writes over the changes of the other, which are lost then.

Developers use version control products to help make sure that concurrent changes are not lost and provide some tooling that makes combining those changes easier but that pushes out the problem, it does not remove it. The bigger, higher impact, and more intricate the changes are to be merged together are, the more the tooling fails, the more manual the effort gets, and the more risk there is of introducing errors. If the changes are enough in conflict, merging may not even be possible, and one set of changes can still get thrown away.

This dilemma is often described with the analogy that "nine women cannot have a baby in one month," saying that breaking up a job across multiple developers does not speed some projects along because their work breaks when put together like this.

The solution is continuous integration, and it involves two pieces:

- The first piece is to shrink the changes as much as possible. With the tooling available, merges become relatively trivial if they can be kept very small, which requires developers to develop the skill to break their work down into very small, safe pieces that can be implemented and checked into version control. These check-ins should be once a day at the longest interval and as often as every few minutes with masters of this skill. Then, developers never have an unmanageable merge with their peers and realize it very quickly if concurrent changes are going in conflicting directions.
- The other piece is our favorite song, automation. When merges and check-ins occur, automation should be in place to run unit tests against it immediately and integration tests against the product as a whole as soon as practical. This helps provide developers with feedback as soon as possible that they are continuing to stay on a stable path. Again, quicker feedback makes for less expensive corrections.

Unknown #6: what will implementation require?

In software development, as with so many other things, the devil is in the details. When planning and designing solutions, the following military cliché so often applies: "Battle plans never survive the first few minutes of battle." The full needs of a solution are often surprising, from an algorithm that runs exponentially longer as data volume increases to hardware limitations, such as the inability to move large amounts of data around fast enough, to "merely" discovering an unexpectedly large number of cases that require special handling, to the common realization that the users have themselves forgotten how many details are involved in an activity being automated. These are the kinds of often unpleasant surprises that simply cannot be discovered by any analysis or foresight but only by actually attempting to implement a solution. Again, tight feedback loops inform the business quickly of the impact to plan and allow for adaptation.

Unknown #7: what was broken in the process?

Changing software is a risk. Any change, however new and seemingly isolated from the rest of the application, runs the risk of introducing problems into the software. Hopefully soon after, but sooner or later, we have to come back and spend time to fix those problems. Well-designed software makes it easier to reduce the scope of areas impacted by a change. Good feedback loops inform us sooner and make it less expensive and easier to find and fix those problems. Good, fast feedback loops depend on good, fast automation.

Black box: the sacred cow of QA

Classically trained quality assurance professionals have a very simple—and understandable—view of testing. Quite simply, they should not require any understanding of the implementation of the application. They should be able to drive all testing through the system from end to end in the exact fashion that the end users will. The point of this ideal is as clear as it is desirable. If I make any assumptions about the implementation of the product, the tests are only as useful as the assumptions are accurate, which makes for incomplete testing. If I test the application any way that differs from the way that the users do it means that I am leaving the possibility of defects in the control paths through the system that the users use, whereas I, the tester, did not. This view is often referred to as black box testing, meaning that I just use the box, I cannot see what goes on inside it to make it work. Manual testing, with sufficient time and support, can get very close to this goal, although it is extremely costly in manpower, time, and sometimes hardware. To make that more manageable, of course, we look to automation. Unfortunately, some things are very difficult to automate testing on.

Graphical User Interfaces in particular pose certain challenges. Point and click tooling records the actual actions of an end user, such as what they type and where on the screen they click, and then plays it back, checking for expected responses from the application. This method is very fragile and can quickly become more expensive than manual testing itself just trying to keep all of the tests running when very minor application changes can break the tests by the hundreds for every time the GUI changes just slightly, running the risk of breaking a recorded test.

Other tools take information about how the components of the UI are built to make the actions and expected behaviors more robust. Note that we are already breaking open the black box, creating tests that have knowledge of the structure of the applications. However, these are better tools for UI testing, but they are frequently very slow because, in computer terms, user interfaces only have to take things at the incredibly slow pace that users can produce them. These tools are great for UIs, but if you have a large enterprise application that processes huge chunks of data, passing them through many moving parts, and you have to validate every possible scenario for all those components through the UI, your tests will quickly be far too slow to be usable. For large applications, the tests may take several multiples of time longer than building the software, which puts this form of automation always in a catch-up mode.

Complex interactions between multiple systems or that depend on inputs or outputs from external systems are just a couple more of the many cases that resist efficient end-to-end automation. In an approach of concurrently operating systems, where communication order and race conditions exist, software may pass the scripted tests perfectly, only to fail epically in production.

However, if we can test 98% of the solution more reliably, consistently, and, most of all, less costly by breaking this assumption, is the 2% left over worth the difference in cost or can the 2% be covered manually as before, but now at a tiny fraction of the overall cost?

Grey box testing: automation over perfection

The opposite of black box testing is called, predictably, white box testing and stresses the product's individual components with full knowledge of the inner workings of the product. Developer tests such as unit tests are a good example of that. Somewhere in between the two is a compromise that gives us our 98% solution mentioned earlier, and because it is between the two, it is sometimes predictably called grey box testing.

Grey box testing takes advantage of some knowledge of the internal workings of the system to make intelligent trade-offs between completeness of testing and manageable test automation.

Grey box testing requires two things to be successful, one that makes some managers and QA engineers uncomfortable and one that makes some developers uncomfortable.

The first is that grey box testing requires careful, constant evaluations to make good decisions on how far to pull open the box to create tests. Opening the box not often enough makes tests difficult to maintain in the face of the rate of development change. Opening the box too much means that defects sneak past the tests more easily and accrue all of the costs we have been discussing. There is no autopilot to testing here.

The second need of grey box testing is designing an application to be testable, which seems like a commonsense statement, but testability is rarely considered an important driver in product design. However, the need to create good interfaces and provide good structural information to tools also pays off here, like it does at the unit test level. It creates an architecture that has fewer problems between components because the communication between those components has a clearer structure. It gives us better entry points for future product features, such as enabling new UIs to be layers on existing business logic or opening up application programming interfaces to business partners. This is the same pattern that we have been talking about with regard to test-driven development reapplied at a higher level to lead a product to a better architecture.

Unknown #8: will the product be maintainable in the face of change?

This is an unknown that developers worry about a lot. When the requirements of the business need the product to change its behavior to go in a new direction, will the product be able to handle those changes? For most projects, the answer is "no." It can go for a bit, with many Band-Aids being placed over many problem areas, but a dramatic change for the application is the beginning of a slow and painful end to a project.

It grows more and more expensive to change with more and more defects as the original architecture crumbles beneath the changing requirements until eventually the design debt is so large that the project is declared bankrupt and a "rewrite" is planned. Rewrites always sound good, initially, because the pain of the old system has gotten to the point where we will often do anything to get away from it. Because we know so much more about the needs of the system, surely we can create a better design now. Unfortunately, it is hard to overestimate the amount of knowledge that has now been embedded in the tangled jungle of the old product. So many special cases, subtle business rules, and important features have been written into it that a rewrite will always cost a project in terms of lost functionality. In the meantime, the rewrite is always trying to play catch up to the original project, which is also usually moving forward until the new system has caught the old one and we are ready to throw the switch to change over, only to discover that a new set of problems has been created. The chase to catch up takes far longer than we expected in the processes.

So many good software applications have never recovered from this scenario, but it can be avoided.

Refactoring

Refactoring has become a somewhat abused term, so let us be clear on our definition by going back to the guy who wrote the book on the subject. Martin Fowler calls refactoring "changing the structure of existing code without changing its behavior." It is not a rewrite, throwing code away, or adding new features. It is restructuring the code so that its current design always reflects the needs of the current functionality of the application. The changes should be small, covered with tests to validate that the behavior is unchanged, and gradual. The activity is often invisible from the outside of the project, and the business value of the time spent is hard to measure. However, not taking the time to refactor code when it needs to change has, on occasion, been compared to a surgeon who does not take the time to wash his hands before going into surgery. To say it another way, many consider it such a harmful lack of professionalism that it is outright criminal.

Refactoring is essentially managing design debt and is also one of the easiest things to lose sight of when using the Six Week Solution. Because the external indicators of design problems are subtle to measure when pressed to hit cycle commitments, it is hard for developers to continue spending time on this activity if they fear it will cost them their income.

The subtle influences of culture and paired programming are crucial to an environment that is passionate enough about quality that they cannot leave messes in their code.

LOWERING THE CURVE BY INCREASING PRODUCTIVITY

We have talked about feedback loops that inform us of issues as fast as possible, before they can grow. We have talked about the unknowns that face a software project and how to manage them. Both of these things pull the exponential cost of the change curve down to something more manageable. What we have not yet talked about is how to move the curve down the axis across the board. In short, we have not talked about how to keep writing even initial software as inexpensive as possible. We want to minimize all of the forces that slow down development across the board. These elements have a system impact on the progress of your project and therefore a much magnified payoff when we invest in improving them.

PROVIDING EFFECTIVE TOOLS

The tools provided for the development team can have a huge impact on the speed at which they develop software. In many ways, providing the right tools for maximizing development is blindingly obvious. It is no surprise that powerful tools should help a team be much more effective. However, many projects pick their tooling for a variety of odd reasons unrelated to effectiveness:

- Sometimes developers' pride in their skills will encourage them to stay with known but weaker tools.
- Sometimes, powerful tools are more costly, and someone with control of the purse strings does not want to pay for them.
- Sometimes, very powerful tools are forced on a team that are far more burden than help in terms of efficiency of use, learning curve, setup, or maintenance.

In today's marketplace, you have your pick of a wide variety of free tools courtesy of the open source community, some of which are truly marvelous. After all, they are generally tools made for developers by developers who are passionate about creating effective tooling. These projects are sometimes a bit quirky and support is generally light, but for the right tool, they can provide huge benefits for your projects.

Also available are a large number of commercial tools. They range from the horribly bloated and usually overpriced to the very small and surprisingly inexpensive. We have seen many teams handed a bloated, expensive source control system that drags whole teams back by adding overhead and extra steps to every moment-to-moment code change. As a result, some teams have stopped budgeting for tools like this in favor of any open source solution.

That is unfortunate because many of these tools are more stable and better featured as they have to vie for a commercial market share. They frequently provide huge returns on the investment in them. As an extreme example, a $60/seat differencing tool can frequently change developer hours hunting through test data into literal seconds. Selecting (and sometimes spending money) for the right tools is an important and careful dance for any development team.

LANGUAGES AND TOOLING

Development languages are fundamental, having huge impacts on the effectiveness of a development team. Technology decisions are made for reasons of pride, comfort, chasing buzzwords, or on the word of various trade magazines. The effects of those decisions are broad and subtle.

Pace of tools

Many languages require developers to touch two or three different areas to make simple changes, significantly slowing the development pace. Many require developers to spend much of their time managing resources such as memory where other languages can effectively take care of it automatically for them. Some are just more expressive or concise than others, making development go faster. Developers who are fond of the harder languages frequently take great pride in their languages, declaring with certainty that their lower level approach will outperform the competition.

Assuming that was true, is the difference worth the relative development costs? In general, it is not. Good design outperforms technology choices the vast majority of the time, which alone can erase the benefit of a language standing on the optimizations of its compiler and lead development into an interpreted language.

Tools

Another subtle impact of language selection is the tooling that the language provides. Some languages focused on simplicity when they were designed. Some languages focused on allowing the programmer huge latitude in development needs, at the expense of simplicity. In practice, very little ability differs either way, but languages with simpler designs allow for tooling to be built around them. Some languages struggle to even compile, whereas others have the ability to automate some bug detection or even safe automated code refactoring to take common tasks that eat developer hours down to mere keystrokes and milliseconds.

BUY, DON'T BUILD

Thirty years ago, Fred Brooks included in the book *The Mythical Man Month* a legendary essay entitled "No Silver Bullet." In it he states that the essential difficulty with building software was that building software was complex and that no magic technology would make that problem go away. His observations have stood the test of time, and when he issued his 25th anniversary edition, he added a retrospective of the game-changing things that impacted his original conclusions.

While the majority of his conclusions are still true, one thing made a big difference in development costs: the availability of premade software components. They still do not take the complexity out of building software, but frequently they provide shortcuts around common problems to leave us free to focus on our principal problem. Unfortunately, most of those problems are well understood and lead programmers to want to write their own solutions. It is an easy pattern to see, it allows the programmers to play with fun problems in a relatively known and comfortable domain rather than the frustration and risk of the unknown. The unknown, however, is where money is made, and "rolling our own" is where money is wasted. Avoid it where possible.

On one project we inherited, the original developers spent a lot of effort producing their own database. While on the surface it appeared that they had used a prebuilt component, they really had taken open source from another language and translated it to the language in use for the product. This led to a nonstandard approach to nearly everything in the product, and many of the nonstandard approaches were specifically implemented to get around the translated open source, which resulted in thousands of lines of code to maintain. A better approach would have been to select a commercial off-the-shelf product or an open source project with a good velocity (releases, committers, users, etc.) that talent familiar with the package could be procured directly from the street instead of weeks and months of insufficient training and experience to make changes. What appeared on the surface as a good idea instead cost the company more to maintain than straight out purchasing a license for a product.

EFFECTIVE COMMUNICATION

Communication is a primary system drag on a development team. Waiting for hours for phone calls or emails to be returned to be able to move forward on a system can make your team's productivity many times slower than it should be. Even when developers switch to something else and then switch back, they have lost valuable momentum and possibly halved their productivity. Techies worry about communication in terms of bandwidth ("How fast can I pour communication through this channel?") and latency ("How long does it take to get a message across?").

In human terms, bandwidth looks like this: let's say that we are trying to discuss what an important new feature in the product needs to look like.

	Bandwidth	Latency	Total Time
Email	Written word only, very slow drawing with patience. One hour for write-up. Reasonable to assume three follow-up email questions required.	Estimate 1 hour between emails.	6 hours
Face to Face	Word, gesture, drawing, props, takes 10 minutes to explain. Assume 15 clarifying questions.	Seconds	30 minutes

If we use these concepts to evaluate our communications, then we can effectively leverage our tools to minimize this overhead to our development process. The example here illustrates why bullpens are such an essential part of the Six Week Solution, but colocation goes beyond the development team.

Colocation

To maximize the effectiveness of communicating with the development team, putting QA and programmers in the same space is critical. However, those people also need to communicate deeply with support, sales, and the business to make sure they are building solutions that address the needs of the business. It is difficult to overstate how much more effective the team and product are when they have physical access to other parts of the business. The ability to directly see the support team's pain points or the value proposition that the business is pursuing is almost impossible to fully re-create by remote means. Many businesses limp along like this, managing communication failures as they arise, but it is costly.

IM

Obviously, face to face is our preferred way to communicate, but a couple of other techniques facilitate certain types of communications greatly. Instant messenger services are one of those tools that have many advantages:

- For one, latency (that was time to get your message through, remember?) is milliseconds, at least when the other party is actually available.
- Because both people have all of their digital resources available, communicating extremely technical details is often as easy as cut and paste.
- The cost of switching your attention between one computer-based task to an instant message is very low.
- If the other person is not available, they have, in effect, a note left on their desk to see when they return.
- Most importantly, it is generally free so it only costs creating the convention around signing on.
- As a side note, some managers like to use the tool to watch people's comings and goings by seeing when they log on and off. We do not recommend that. It is easy to subvert and causes the team's attitude toward the tool to shift away from using it to become more efficient to a tool for CYA.

Documentation

Documentation is obviously an important aspect of communication, but it can be such a burden or benefit to a project that it merits its own section. Views on documentation range from the dramatic examples common in defense contracting where the documents for projects are many times larger than the actual product work itself to commercial products where documentation is essentially nonexistent. It is important to evaluate the purpose of documents to decide whether they add value to your project because they certainly add cost and sometimes can misdirect a project.

Writing documentation for a project in day-to-day language is a very difficult endeavor. Capturing all of the important information is usually done in an attempt to make a sweeping effort and much is missed. Even if it is made a daily discipline of a team to document what they need, normal language is extremely imprecise. The best formed grammar can still have multiple interpretations.

Tests as documentation

One of the most precise ways that we have available to describe the intended behavior of a system is tests, particularly automated ones. We have two forms of testing as documentation to explore, and they serve the purpose of covering two different documentation needs. One form of testing, sometimes used as customer acceptance testing, is called "executable requirements." The other is unit testing and describes how the design of the code currently functions.

Executable requirements

Executable requirements, in short, are tests that describe the expected behavior of a system. They are less ambiguous than pages of documentation because they have to be constructed and tooled to explicitly show exactly what behavior is expected. In essence, it is documentation by example. Executable requirements are also far more maintainable than exhaustive requirement documentation because they are run regularly and, when they no longer reflect reality, show up as broken tests to be updated or removed if they are no longer applicable. We discuss tools that enable this kind of documentation/testing in Chapter 8, "Integrating Automation into Your Development Process" on page 135.

Unit tests

Unit tests are tests developed by programmers around individual pieces of code as they are developing them. These tests serve both the purpose of ensuring that the code works as needed and the purpose of documenting the intentions of that code for the next people who touch it. Again, this documentation is far more precise than a design document, now having to meet the stringent requirements of the programming language for clarity. Also, this documentation is always up to date if running the tests is built into your automation because the tests start breaking as soon as they fall out of date. It is worthwhile to point out that simply the act of writing these tests in a maintainable fashion also drives better design in the code of the product itself.

Code as documentation

There is another key programmatic documentation discipline that is hard to overvalue. That discipline is to write *self-explanatory code*. This should not be mistaken for adding piles and piles of comments into code, where they still are constantly out of date and regularly misleading. Rather, this is prioritizing communication when writing new code. All the programmers on a team (presumably) speak the programming language they are working in. That language provides them with the opportunity to communicate with extreme clarity and precision with that structure by putting effort into good naming of components, creating components with clear and succinct purposes, and keeping them simple enough to understand. The amount of detail that any given day of coding requires is such that most busy programmers are lucky to remember what they wrote for more than a couple of weeks. This kind of self-documenting code is a huge time-saver and gain in efficiency for anyone who needs to be in that code later, including the original author!

Tools as communication

Sometimes, pictures speak louder than words. Whole structures such as the Unified Modeling Language (UML) exist to give common visual vocabulary for people to communicate in that fashion. It is common practice to create design diagrams for this purpose and keep them around to explain the design of a piece of a project. Of course, the inevitable life cycle of these documents is that they become out of date by the minute. Some projects actively spend much of their development time trying to keep these documents up to date, thereby slowing down the document's decay. Others do not even bother and just know that the documents are always out of date. Either way, the documents become less and less useful and more and more misleading until they are entirely useless and are abandoned.

For far less overhead than the writing and maintenance of these kinds of design documents, we can replace them with a wide array of reverse engineering tools. These tools serve a dual purpose of being structured drawing tools for creating the kind of pictures that we have been talking about, as well as mining existing code bases for their structure and attempting to create these drawings automatically. It is a quick effort to reverse engineer a piece of code, tweak the resulting picture for clarity, and use it for a communication need. After that (ready?), *throw it away!* Why? Because storing, finding, and maintaining that diagram cost more than re-creating it. Using an old version that is no longer accurate can easily derail future efforts. Consider these artifacts communication aids rather than documents for an archive. Only polish them as much as is necessary for the current need, use them, and then let them go.

Documentation archives
Don't.

Documentation archives, really
No, really, we mean it. Don't do it. You can cut your team's productivity by 90% or worse with documentation overhead. Do not create documents that do not have clear and immediate business value.

Wiki

Okay, so here is your documentation archive. This is one occasion where we highly recommend one technology, which is called a "wiki." A wiki could be considered a social media, a "Web 2.0" tool. In essence, it is a Web site where all the users have built-in, dirt-simple tools for editing the content. It is, really, too dynamic to be called an archive and too casual to be considered real documentation. It is, in effect, a giant, organized, searchable, developer scratch pad to throw down tidbits of information that they do not believe should be lost. Tool or technology tricks, development conventions, end-of-life schedules, time of requests if desirable – it can give a home to any kind of information that could take up a piece of paper somewhere, but doesn't need to. It is the least burdensome way of giving your team to communicate that keeps their communications indefinitely and universally available.

Sustainable pace

There is a very crucial aspect to lightening the load of your team that will keep your project humming along for a long while. It is almost entirely in the control of upper management and it is shockingly unpopular. The XP community calls this a "sustainable pace." The idea is simple, but the discipline of it is very hard. Quite simply, a development team cannot maintain their peak productivity indefinitely, any more than a horse can run at top speed all day. Given the right motivations, the periods of sprinting can be pushed and extended, but not forever. The ideal goal for a development team over time is to find a pace that is not peak output, but *sustainable* output. A sustainable pace of work is a level of effort that the team can reproduce again and again consistently and reliably. A pace like that does not burn out your team, nor does it leave them lounging around. They work hard, they go home to their families, and are able to rest and return to do it again.

It is a frustrating fact of developing software that it is an entirely mental effort. If it was entirely physical, like the early forest logging efforts, it would be far more obvious when fatigue has set in. Initially, there are errors in judgment. Accidents begin to happen, such as people making mistakes with tools that injure people and/or productivity. This can continue as long as the losses are "acceptable," until people just start giving out. They cannot even pick up their tools any more. They are done.

The same things happen in the mental effort of building software. As people get tired, they start making mistakes. Their judgment is no longer sharp, they are too tired to follow essential disciplines, and they make messy, error-prone code. We have already written many times about the costs of bad quality code. Those mistakes compound on themselves, making progress ever slower and more difficult. Frequently, the programmers are trying so hard to dig their way out that they work hard and harder, with less and less effectiveness, just trying to reverse the idea. Eventually, the programmers start to break. Some stare blankly at their screen, trying to force themselves to continue. Some get sick. Some have violent outbursts. Conflicts in the team escalate. Eventually, they either make so many errors in judgment that they have to be let go or blow up and walk out. Sometimes, they just do not come back on Monday morning and you do not hear from them again.

We have spent weeks, and sometimes months, trying to rectify decisions that were made in a sleep-deprived haze at 3 am or made by a soon-to-be-dad furiously coding under pressure in the waiting room while his wife was in labor. (No, we are not kidding: we have seen it more than once.) Or a number of other situations that can be summed up simply:

Programmers need to be at their peak mental acuity or they can do far more harm than good.

Another recipe for bad code is to deploy untested software (but you have all your tests under automation, so that doesn't happen, right?) on Friday at 4:30 pm. Naturally, things fall over almost immediately, and suddenly we have a development crisis to get things back on track. Programmers are getting called in when they are already tired to try to put things back together, and they come up with whatever piece of junk might get them back to their families soonest. Wait, all of your business-people are also there to make sure that it does what they needed, right? There is no end to this story that is not only very expensive for the business, but very hard for business morale.

Finding a sustainable pace is not a license to not work hard, but is the recognition that fatigue is the enemy of good software. Ideally, the developers are starting to wear out on Friday afternoon, just in time to go home, rest up, and start again on Monday.

Quality again

We've beaten this to death, but one of the most crucial factors in keeping the cost of development down is keeping the quality of your code as high as possible. The most obvious drag of poor quality is the time spent fixing old stuff rather than creating new stuff. Also, a clean design makes it simple to add in new functionality, whereas a messy design will drag down every effort that it touches.

Obviously that reduces your team's pace, but it also makes it more difficult to plan. Measuring the velocity of your team can enable you to account for some of it on average, but deviations from the average velocity will be more dramatic spikes and dips due to forces that are nearly invisible at a planning level.

Pair programming makes it all go smoother

When it comes to process, we are happy when we have metrics that tell us the impact of our efforts. We talk elsewhere about the metrics around the practice of pair programming, but it is hard to measure all of the ways that pair programming can move your project forward.

On a recent project, we had to do a performance review for a programmer who we will call "Jerry." Jerry had been spending most of his time pairing, which can be a challenging exercise until one grows comfortable with it, but this case was particularly so because the project had not been very long lived, and due to project constraints, Jerry was almost always paired up with Gerald. The project was moving along at a reasonable pace.

So the question is: "How much was the programmer in question contributing to moving that project forward? Was the other programmer carrying him or was he carrying most of the load?"

It's hard to measure. That was specific to that situation, but the other advantages of pairing are hard to measure too. In that situation, Jerry was an advocate for test-driven development, where Gerald was pretty new to it. It was possible to measure Gerald's increase in skill level to a weak degree by seeing that the number of unit tests that Gerald wrote on his own started going up. The code quality metrics did not show a dramatic change in either developer's code quality, but those metrics are still somewhat limited in what they can tell us.

Other things we cannot measure are how much having a pair kept the energy in the project running high or how much they were able to help keep each other on task.

However, in our experience, pair programming speeds your project along by keeping the team well trained on the code base, the tools, the techniques, increasing quality of the code due to instant review of each coding decision, keeping energy and momentum going, and keeping work on track.

GAUGING PERFORMANCE WITH PAIRS

To gauge an individual programmer's performance, triangulation is key. What should jump out is what kind of difference a programmer makes to an effort.

For example, say a pair is cruising along on a task and then one of the programmers trades out for another. The task takes off, bogs down, or just keeps going. What can be inferred about the programmer who left? The one who traded in? The one who stayed the whole time? Obviously, there are many possibilities due to types of tasks, individual technical strengths, and personality matches. A single instance is far too little information from which to draw conclusions, but watching these for patterns can reveal a lot over time.

Taking on responsibilities over assigning work

Speaking of practices with subtle impact, here is another that will make your project run smoother:

Allow your team members to sign up for their own work.

No, we are not saying that they get to *make up* their tasks (although that can surprise you from time to time). Presumably, the tasks are already set. The cycle commitments have been established. Now the team has to somehow pull them off. Let the developers pick the tasks that they want to take responsibility for. Almost always, they will juggle things the way you would have anyway. They know their areas of strength. However, whether the task distribution is what you intended or not, you will get far more investment in seeing the tasks through to completion if they have taken those responsibilities on themselves rather than having them handed to ("forced upon") them.

It is a matter of intrinsic motivations. Developers are intrinsically motivated by their pride in their work and by their distrust of authority. Taking on their own projects serves both motivations. Assignments conflict with both motivations, offering replacements that are weak and extrinsic, such as fear of authority.

Leaving programmers room to problem solve

Whether it is a coding problem, an office layout problem, or a process problem, programmers are fundamentally problem solvers. They are the people who get called when x is not working and others are looking for ideas. Effective companies take deep advantage of this by leaving their teams a lot of room to solve their problems. Make the problem visible, make the priorities clear, and then let them do what they do. Imposing solutions whenever it can be avoided is not using your resources to best advantage and deprives your team and business of important opportunities for advancement.

Assuring Software Quality

7

CHAPTER CONTENTS

Agile Development and Business Goals. DOI: 10.1016/B978-0-12-381520-0.00007-2

INTRODUCTION

Software that functions as it should, every time, in every situation, is boring (and, of course, unheard of). Some people might use the term "reliable" for software that functions every time. But really what we want is boring, so boring in fact that you don't stay up at night wondering if things are processing correctly. You don't have to think about changing your work habits around the cases where features do not quite flow right. In fact, you want to be able to not think about your software at all.

If a tool has to do a job, then it should do a job every time in the exact same way. A firearm must go bang every time the trigger is pulled and send a bullet down range at high velocity to perform its work. If there is no concern that the firearm will do its function properly, then there is no need to be concerned about failure to feed a round or concern over pulling the trigger and nothing happening; there is no drama and that is often a very good thing. Firearms that are reliable are respected. Put aside any feelings you have of the tool itself and consider the AK-47 as designed by Mikhail Kalashnikov as a machine. It's a harsh example, but it makes the point.

The AK-47 has two moving parts: a piston/carrier assembly thrown rearward by expanding gasses and a bolt that rotates in a channel to chamber and extract a round. That's it; just two parts and it works every time. Users of this point-and-click interface are not worried about it doing anything other than the intended job. It's a simple machine, has minimal controls, and new users can be trained very quickly. Replacing the words "soldiers" with "users" makes the discussion sound like software instead of a firearm.

Why is this tool more successful than others? The answer is because it started with the design. The original design was so simple that development and QA were simple. It was also simple to manufacture, could be built with less tooling than other designs, and used stamped and bent steel instead of cast or machined steel for many parts. Everything in the design was focused on simplicity. And all the work of development led to a tool that could do its job in harsh environments under stress, every time.

Software, however, is complex. It has many moving parts, at least conceptually. It has to deal with networks, security, operating systems, different CPUs, and—most importantly and often most frustratingly—users, which means that the design must start with simplicity at its core. Starting there leads to testability and overall quality in the software product.

Tell your developers to build software as if Mikhail Kalashnikov built software. Make things simple and small with a minimum of moving parts. Don't couple things together that don't need to be involved with each other. Make reliable and boring software.

But sometimes you think you can't be simple. The need is complex, the market opportunity you have to get something out the door is short, and you don't feel you have enough staff to pull everything off with high quality. Unfortunately, the cost of that trade-off is not always obvious. Almost always, your project health depends on your ability to manage scope instead. If something doesn't have to be built, don't build it. Build as little as possible, and build it with quality. (See the section entitled "Buy, Don't Build" on page 110 for more detail.)

Ask yourself, "is this necessary?"

Peter Deng, product manager at Facebook

THE VALUE OF QUALITY

Quality is a difficult thing to measure. The value of adding or removing a feature from a product can be estimated with marketing studies, customer surveys, or similar mechanisms to attempt to measure the change in valuation. Some aspects of quality could be measured with market studies or customer surveys to see how changes in the external impressions of the product impact the perceived value of the product. These types of things rarely happen, though. Other aspects of measuring the value of quality are harder yet. What is even more frustrating is that the less obvious and measurable aspects of quality have the biggest impact on the success of your project.

The obvious aspect of quality is what we call external quality. This really boils down to what your end users would say when they are sitting on their therapist's couch and are asked "How does this product make you feel?" It is defined by features that users expect and do not have or did not expect and are excited to have, as well as errors, bugs, and various usability issues. It really boils down to if a user considers a product to be worth the effort.

In calculating its value, external quality is best described as a multiplier of the monetary value of a feature.

Value of a Feature = Feature External Quality ∗ Innate Feature Market Value

---

In other words, if we develop a feature that we estimate has a $1000 minimum market value, and assuming a 1–100 scale of software quality, that feature's value could vary from the minimum $1000 with poor external quality to $100,000 with an outstanding external quality.

Internal quality, however, is demonstrably an *exponent* on the development costs of your project.

Development Costs = Feature Complexity $^{\text{Internal Lack of Quality}}$

So, for example, let's say that we have a fairly simple feature in a new project. Because we have no low-quality code involved, the cost of the feature development is related directly to its own complexity. This will get done pretty fast. However, let us take that same feature and add it to an existing project. For every part of that project, it has to worry about its own complexity and the complexity of the features it touches. In a well-structured project, that will be only a small portion of the whole. In a badly structured project, every piece of the new feature has to manage its complexity ∗ [times] the complexity of each other feature it touches whether it should have to or not ∗ [times] the complexity unnecessarily added by the bad code structure. The more complex the new feature, presumably the more other features it will touch, which keeps the cost going up roughly exponentially.

The next question is: "Which factor has a stronger impact of the overall software life cycle?" Let us start with the following simple equation:

Feature Development Costs = Initial Development Costs + Bug Fixes + Future Maintenance and Enhancement Costs

---

That does not look too scary, right? No multipliers, after all, so everything should go up pretty proportionately. Well, initial development costs, while notoriously difficult to estimate, are generally manageable. Subsequent changes of any kind, however, are affected dramatically by the quality of the code written. A slightly more concrete example will make the internal quality exponential equation a little more clear. In well-structured code, a simple bug fix could take a development hour (see the waterfall discussion "Why Waterfall Processes Often Fail" on page 19 to see how even that number can explode with hidden costs). In poorly structured code, that same bug fix could cost you a week. That's a factor of 40× on a small change!

It gets worse. That same factor keeps compounding, but the reason for it is really that the code structure makes it hard to change. That same factor continues to apply to *any* kind of change in that code, bug fixes and maintenance, as new feature development. Depending on how isolated that feature's code has been kept from the rest of the product, you could be adding that cost of change multiplier to the development of *every* feature that you do going forward.

For example:

- **Feature A** was developed poorly, the code is hard to change. It was developed such that it touches 10% of the current project. Now, we need to add Features B–F.

As a simple average, we could say that:

- **Feature B** Development Costs = Feature B Direct Costs + 10% Likely Overlap with Feature A * Feature A Maintenance Costs

The term for the bad code from Feature A in our product is *Design Debt*. Like most debt, it doesn't really hurt until payments come due. In this case, in the form of an *interest* payment of 10% Likely Overlaps with Feature A * Feature A Maintenance Costs.

Let's assume that we are developing B–F in alphabetical order, and we did not learn from our mistakes in A, so we create equally bad code when developing Feature B. Development teams that are consistently creating more design debt have *Design Deficit*.

The cost of that deficit is shown like compounding interest in developing Feature C:

Feature C Development Costs = Feature C Direct Costs + 10% Likely Overlap with Feature A * Feature A Maintenance Costs + 10% Likely Overlap with B * Feature B Maintenance Costs

---

As you can see, over time the costs of future changes, be they new feature development or simple bug fixes, grow exponentially as code quality is allowed to be poor. Compound interest is great for our retirement accounts, but not great for our development budgets.

Debt management strategies

If we have some poor-quality code in our project:

- we have to pay extra to change it any time we work on something that touches it and
- the number of things that touch it is, in itself, one of the measures for how bad the code is. Bad code touches everything and is itself hard to change.

Having bad code in our project is like having credit card debt. We can handle it in several ways.

Design debt strategy #1: ignore it

How fast would your family go bankrupt if you steadily accrued debt and made no payments on it as compounded on itself every six weeks? Naturally, that depends on how much debt you accrue in each cycle, but optimistically, we'd give you two years, and pessimistically, six months. The same is true for your development project.

Design debt strategy #2: pay interest

Every time that we touch the code, we will simply absorb the extra cost of development in our current development effort. Development will slow down and costs go up by some factor, but we believe it is affordable for whatever reason.

Feature Cost = New Development Costs + Code Maintenance Costs * Bad Code Interest

Design debt strategy #3: pay off anything that might accrue interest

We want to have our entire budget available to us at all times, so we pay off our debt wherever we see it.

Development Costs = New Development Costs + Preemptive Code Structure Improvements

Unfortunately, which debts are going to cost your business are not always obvious to your programmers. A piece of code may be poorly structured, but if it works and is rarely touched, you are wasting time to fix it. No interest payments are going out so why spend money on it? If you have a debt that is not charging you interest and may never come due, why pay it?

Design debt strategy #4: pay off highest interest debts when bills come in

When a product change is going to accrue interest payments by touching poorly structured code, in the Six Week Solution we fix the structure immediately rather than "paying the minimum payment" to maintain it. Because we are already making changes in that area, the probability is that there will be more, so let's clean it up now. That gives us a flat cost model:

Feature Cost = New Development Costs + Bad Code Balance

This gives us the most manageable and predictable model for managing existing design debt. The programmers' mantra should be simple:

Always Leave the Code Cleaner Than You Found It!

How much cleaner? Well, that depends on how big a payment you want to make, but as a general rule, some proportion of the size of the current development effort seems appropriate. If the change I am currently making is an eight hour change, then two to four hours of paying down debt seems proportionate. This really is a judgment call and is dependent on having people of good judgment leading development. A highly connected piece of code is going to charge interest more often and may be worth paying more on. A fairly isolated piece probably deserves a little less attention.

How to select where to stop cleaning up code is difficult. When fixing a bug, it makes sense to look around, as typically you'll find more bugs as problems cluster together. If real problems are found, fix them now and don't wait for a customer to find them. Also, the code is fresh in your head at that moment. Following practices outlined earlier in this chapter, the developer should have created a new unit test or enhanced the existing unit tests so it is safer to fix additional problems at this time than waiting for later.

Other times, it is a code interface that is just clunky. Here is a judgment call, as the number of touch points must be considered. Is it invoked in just a few locations and a refactoring is safe or is it used in hundreds of locations and the testing burden would be too much to accept at this time? It is a soft and fuzzy line that is not always clear. Strive to always leave the code cleaner, but do not fall for the temptation to re-create everything.

Design debt strategy #5: ensure yourself against possible changes

There is another aspect of managing design debt that is more proactive than the preceding discussions and is, in some ways, harder to handle properly. That is the idea that we design the code in advance to accommodate changes that we anticipate. This could be considered similar to buying insurance. We accept a known cost in the form of currently unneeded design and development effort in an attempt to mitigate the risk of the cost of future change. Developers are particularly prone to this kind of effort and, in fact, have generally been trained to think that way by waterfall-style project planning. We have talked elsewhere about crystal ball project planning, and yet we so often fall into the trap of thinking we are smart enough to know what we will need to do next and when.

Let us be extra clear:

99.9% of the time, this idea (falling into the trap of thinking we are smart enough to know what we will need to do next and when) is a bad idea.

The reasons are simple:

- Design in anticipation is rarely cheaper to add now than it would be later, especially in clean code.
- If the cost is the same now or later, we are losing out in opportunity cost the features that we could have built instead that we could get value from now.
- Our expectations for both future needs and the timing of those needs are rarely right. Therefore, the investment is rarely realized anyway.

If we stay with the insurance metaphor, it is occasionally important. Each of them has a time when you need to worry about it. Health insurance coverage is often proportionate to your general health. Life insurance is important if you have more financial obligations than means in the event of your death. Home owners insurance is necessary to cover your mortgage debt. Then there are the product extended warrantees you could buy on your television, your tires, your appliances, your bed mattress, your carpet installation, your shop tools, your furniture, your car, and so on that are almost always a bad idea since the very product is stacked to cost more than your odds of a failure. Too often, businesses build their products like they need to buy every possible kind of insurance they can. Unfortunately, they often find that all they have in the end is insurance against a lot of change that never comes.

Build only what you need now. Build it well and it will handle changes as needed.

EXTERNAL SOFTWARE QUALITY

External quality is simply how good your software seems to the end user. Much of that is based on feel, but in good engineering fashion, there are rough metrics for each of these also.

Three questions that describe external software quality are:

- "Do I like the product features?"
- "Do I like using the product?"
- "Does the product feel reliable?"

These are pretty touchy-feely kinds of questions, which all really mean "Do I feel good about this product?" That is sometimes a very difficult and uncomfortable standard for the supposedly logical programmers to try to meet, so let us break it down a bit more.

I was once assigned to rewrite a central engine for an off-the-shelf product. This feature was both the product's best selling point and its biggest headache, because the technical problem was fairly nasty. They had rewritten it three times before, and still did not feel it was something that would hold up for them.

The team did not use anything remotely like the Six Week Solution, I was literally the man in the room, alone, barely even seeing others over the water cooler for six months. When it was time for me to deliver, I did a review of the design for this "difficult, problem feature." The manager looked at the work and said, "That is simple. What took you six months?" My response was "It took me six months to make it that simple, so it would hold up unlike the last three attempts." And it did hold up.

Senior developer

Feature set

The Kano model was created in the 1980s by Professor Noriaki Kano to classify different types of features. It is particularly helpful in prioritization and breaks features down into the following categories:

- Features that attract users to a product.
- Features that display whether the perception of value is proportionate to the investment. In other words, the more you do with the feature, the more users like it.
- Features that users require to be present to consider the product viable.

- Features that users do not care about one way or another.
- Features that users want to go away. (Anybody remember Clippy?)

Tools like these are great to help product managers prioritize your feature backlog.

Usability

The things that make a software product feel usable to the end user go through different phases as they grow in familiarity with the product. When they first see it, perhaps in a sales pitch, they are looking for it to appear "intuitive." Whether or not they can learn their way around the product gives them their crucial first impression of the product's quality. For occasional users, they may never form an impression beyond that.

For regular users, they move quickly to measuring based on how easy it is for them to perform their most common operations. Cumbersome wizards and lengthy workflows that helped them learn their way around quickly start to feel like an impediment as they need to accomplish things quickly and easily as part of their daily operations.

For power users who will be using the product regularly throughout their day, even short workflows will begin to be frustrating if the product cannot respond as fast as they can move from one task to the next. Responding to their requests does not always mean that the product can keep up with them, but it does at least provide them an interface that does not make them feel like their day is spent waiting on the computer to catch up.

Finally, for all groups of users, they need reasonable avoidance and management of their mistakes. Products that easily let them take negative workflows, and do not allow them ways to recover from those workflows, will quickly frustrate all but the most advanced users. Everyone makes mistakes, but nobody likes feeling like the computer is going to punish them for it.

Reliability

A user's impression of the reliability of a product is surprisingly subjective. Measuring something like a system's 99.9999% uptime (the amount of time that a system is up without crashing or needing to be taken down for maintenance) seems like it would well reflect a product's reliability. However, just as a person will decide that an electronics product is "cheap" because they do not like the plastic from which it was made, a software product's reliability is measured by more subjective standards. A user's perception of a product's reliability can sometimes be stated as "Do I trust this product to work?"

For instance, a product that reports errors back to the user is rarely considered reliable. Those errors could be handled flawlessly internally, maintain a consistent and stable state of data and execution, and be prepared to move forward with any other task flawlessly, but if it does all this and still tells the user that there was an error, it breaks the user's trust.

Likewise, the behavior of the product during use needs to be consistent with the user's expectation. A perfectly logical user interface that appears to work differently than another, similar-seeming part of the product will produce discomfort in the user that disturbs trust of the product. Also, a part of the product that behaves one way in one case and another way in another situation may do so for perfectly valid business rules, but it must work very hard to convince a user that it is not being "flaky."

While looking at product behavior, blind alleys of use cases also disturb a user's trust of the product. These things often happen when buttons or menu options exist with the expectation that they are placeholders for future functionality. If users seem to have a feature available to them and find that using it does nothing, they begin to question which features will and will not work. Obviously that is a big break in the user's trust of the system.

INTERNAL SOFTWARE QUALITY

The external quality of your software is very visible to anyone who talks to the users or works with the software themselves. However, the health and long-term viability of your software project depend more on the geek stuff, the black magic, the quality of the internal structure of the product, all that "stuff we pay geeks to worry about." You do not have to be a programmer to keep an eye on that, you just need to know some software fundamentals that will affect your overall project and know what cues to look for that will tell you when trouble is brewing.

In an early team, I had inherited a custom project that was a disaster of design debt. The code was in such bad shape, the customer was afraid to ask for bug fixes, because they already knew that any code changes would add more problems than it would fix. Unfortunately, the bugs that it had were bad, and could not be worked around.

Naturally, we were on the verge of losing the customer. Actually, they were looking for someone to outsource the work to so that they could get around us working on our own product!

It is tempting at times like this to just rewrite, which is one way of saying we are declaring design bankruptcy. Unfortunately, in all the mess that was in that product is an awful lot of knowledge about all the little quirks that the features needed, and it is hard to truly appreciate how expensive relearning all of those details can be.

Instead, I sat down with the client to talk about a strategy for digging out. Obviously, trust was deeply broken and had to be rebuilt, starting with telling the truth. Yes, it was a mess, and likely, fixing it was going to feel like it was getting worse for a little bit. Our strategy was to start putting automated tests around the product for each feature we needed to restructure. We would miss details, for a while, but every time we did, when the client complained that something broken made it through, we would get that covered so it would never happen again. With those tests in place, we could start to restructure the design to pay down that debt.

It was rocky at first—a lot of things broke. Those broken things taught us what tests to write, which we did, and fixed, and kept going. As the tests grew, the programmers and the client slowly started to trust them. The team started having safety to go after design problems because they could trust the tests to tell them about problems. In the end, the product was solid, and the customer was starting to move work from their other departments to us to work on.

Senior programmer

Software fundamentals

What makes building software different from building anything else is that it is easy to change. If you build a house and then decide you do not like the shape, you have a big investment ahead of you. (See the section called "It's Like Building a House, Only It Is Not" on page 41.) If you design a stereo, you better make very sure you have what you want laid out before it goes through the manufacturing process or you will have a huge investment in an inadequate product.

However, most people do not bat an eyelash at suggesting major changes to software. Instinctively, they feel like they should be able to move large pieces around with a minimum of effort.

The thing is, those instincts are right, that is how software *should* work. Software really should be "soft." Unfortunately, poor code can make the idea of moving your kitchen to a different part of the house seem easy. Worse, poor code is far easier and faster to write, requires far less discipline from a programmer, and initially, from the outside, can look like wonderful productivity.

So what makes code good?

Error-free execution

Obviously, good code should enable the external quality measures already discussed. In other words, it should do what the user expects and not error out. That is the simplest measure of code quality, which is very important. Many, many *star* programmers have made a name and career on doing exactly this, and doing it very fast. What could look better from a business perspective? The equation seems simple.

Feature Net Value = What People Will Pay for the Feature − Feature Development Costs

---

People will pay more for an error-free feature, and if the developer time spent is only the time in the initial development, then the conclusions are simple. The real cost of the feature, however, is a slippery thing.

Cost of Feature = Initial Development Time + Cost of Bug Fixes + Added Impediments to Future Development

---

Flexible code structure

Defining good code structure is actually very hard, other than to say that it needs to be changeable. So, instead, let's look at what makes code hard to change.

Duplication

If your code does that same thing in more than one place, and possibly more than one way, then you have the burden of having to do twice the work (or 10 times or more) when you need to improve, extend, or change that piece of code. A bug in one place gets fixed in one place and is left in the rest to jump up at you later. The programmer's axiom here is: "Don't Repeat Yourself."

Complexity

If a particular piece of code is allowed to get very complex, it makes it hard to change. After all, before you change it, you need to understand every twist and turn of the code to make sure that you understand the impact of every change. It also makes it easy for errors to hide. Which error is easier to spot?

$3 + 4 = 8$ *or* $18 + 84 + 95 + 13 + 3 + 123 = 337$

Good code works very hard to stay as simple as possible. The good old K.I.S.S. principle applies here too.

Coupling

Any particular piece of code depends on other pieces of code to work. In good code, they do not have to know *why* they work, only how to use them. The more that code A has to know about code B, the more code A has to change whenever code B changes. That is called coupling, which should be minimized as much as possible.

Dependency

Related to coupling is dependency. In the previous example, code A is dependent on code B. Dependencies always need to be managed with the goals of:

- reducing the number of them
- making sure they point in the right direction

For example, the general structure of your program should not have to change because some small detail changes. The impact of that change is too expensive. Rather, details should be independently changeable and should be dependent on the needs of the overall program structure. Dependencies should flow from the most general to the most specific pieces.

Expressive code

Another cost of change is knowledge transfer. For a variety of reasons, such as illness, new resources, and overall development pace, it is important for a programmer to be able to get into an unfamiliar piece of code and be able to understand it quickly. Several strategies have been tried over time and all of them require effort on the part of the original programmer.

Documents and diagrams

Create external documents that explain what was going on in the code. These can be made very expressive, but can also become very expensive and are inherent duplication. Any change to the code now also has to be updated in the documentation. Even tools that promise to reverse engineer the diagrams from the code are always out of date with the latest changes to the code base.

Comments

Adding comments in code is essentially moving the external document internally. You lose the ability to add diagrams, in general, but presumably, it is easier to maintain documentation if you only have to make changes in one place by modifying the comment with the code. In practice, this has the same problem that external documents do, which is that programmers frequently overlook updating them, so they start to quickly become misleading.

While there is a case to maintain method header comments, as these are used by automatic documentation generation tools (such as javadoc), the internal comments are typically excuses and apologies in code. The developer comments a line with "multiplying x times y" is essentially useless and brings a question of whether the developer knew what he was doing in the first place. Other comments are generally deciphered as "I just couldn't think of a better way to do this right now" type of comments and again are useless.

Code

The last option is to make the code itself as expressive as possible. There is no duplication, so that problem is solved, but it means that the programmer now has a new measure for good code that he has to emphasize beyond just getting the code working. This can be a hard thing to convince them to do, and tools in the continuous integration part of the process that produce a metric on source code are great to help get developers convinced.

SYMPTOMS OF DESIGN ROT

Here are some simple, external symptoms of a project that will warn you when your design is rotting even without having to be in the code yourself.

Constant open heart surgery

Ever been on a project where it seems like everything you ask for seems to require moving mountains? The product needs to present data sorted by a different column or some similarly trivial-seeming request, but apparently it requires changing half the product. Worse yet, it does not appear to just be programmer pessimism—it is really taking forever to accomplish and is affecting everything! If this happens on occasion, there were probably just some bad assumptions made in the system's design, but if this is the story of your project's life, you are probably struggling with design rot.

Keeping an eye on the coupling and complexity of code in the system is a great way to alert that there is design rot and gives an early heads up that some area of the code will need a real investment to get into a maintainable shape.

Groundhog day

Say one part of the system needs a change, so it gets implemented. Suddenly, that breaks another part of the system. When that gets fixed, something else pops up. Fixing that breaks the first change. Change requests just keep getting reopened or, possibly, you asked for a change and got it. In fact, it is likely that it was even painless and simple. Unfortunately, it only affected one small area of the product. Now you have to ask for the same change again for this part over here. And over here. And over there. If either of these kinds of déjà vu are your regular companions, it's time to sound the design rot alarm.

Four-letter features

You have an area of your product that has become a cuss word around your development shop. The bugs seem to be endless, and so does the programmer complaining. Many studies have shown that bugs seem to stick together. Generally, this shows that the design in that area is failing.

Single-use tools

The system had a new feature, a new problem, a new challenge to solve. Let's take an example: your Web application needs to present a user with a very long list of options to choose from and it needs to be done in a relatively bandwidth-efficient and user-responsive fashion. So, value paging or searching or autocompletion or something similar was implemented to solve that problem on the worst offender. Now, you need to do the same thing somewhere else, but it seems like that will take as long or longer than fixing the problem the first time. Warning sounded, and the iceberg is much bigger than expected; fix this or you will sink the ship.

Lipstick on a pig

When new change requests come in, the discussions around it are mostly concerned with how the team needs to "hack" this request in. A hack, by definition, is a change that degrades the design around it. Other common descriptions for this scenario emphasize working around problems, forcing things to work, or otherwise embellishing useless artifacts. This is putting lipstick on a pig, dressing something up to sell it and not caring about the consequences.

Fear of the future

When the change requests get to the team, and the droning on about how hard it will be starts, you notice that none of the things they are talking about seems relevant to the actual delivered product. They are "laying the groundwork" for future needs that have not happened yet, but somehow, you are already paying for them. Did you mean to buy insurance?

Fortress of solitude

Somewhere in your application is a desert. None of the programmers wants to go there because they seem to think that death is waiting for them. They do not know how it works. Everybody who has tried seems to have failed. Maybe you still have the original implementer. Maybe he is the only one willing to go into the desert to make changes. Maybe even he is scared of it. Either way, the rule to live by it this:

If it requires only the best and brightest programmers to understand your software, you don't have quality software.

Does your product really have pieces that only a few understand? Are these pieces necessary or are they a product of rapid development? There may be a case that the code is an implementation of some mathematic problem that only a few have the background to understand, but more often than not it is merely poorly written code or a difficult concept that needs to be designed and structured differently.

QUALITY AND SOFTWARE CRAFTSMANSHIP

The Agile software movement has spent a great deal of energy around trying to make the software industry grow up to the maturity of its much older siblings. Frustratingly, that process begs the ongoing question:

What family does the software development activity belong to? Is it a mathematical discipline? A scientific pursuit? An engineering discipline?

The engineering view and verbiage are common, and we even fall into using it in this book. However, the conclusion of many Agile practitioners is that software development is a craft, such as carpentry, writing, furniture building, or automotive repair. This view was explored in wonderful detail by Pete McBreen in 2003 in his book *Software Craftsmanship: A New Imperative*. The idea has received a lot of attention in the software development community as it reflects so many aspects of the field that always had to exist in near resistance to the software engineering culture in order to make projects be successful. More recently, in 2009, thousands of software developers signed the online Manifesto for Software Craftsmanship (http://manifesto.softwarecraftsmanship.org/) in support of this paradigm shift. Finding people with these values towards software development means finding people who understand the impact that quality has on a project. These are the kind of people you want on your projects.

Marks of a craftsman

If you are looking to have a bit of fine woodworking done, you want to know something about the craftsman who will be doing it. It is, after all, a large investment in a product that you will not see until it is done. To be able to do quality work, craftsmen have disciplines to which they adhere. This is not the same as having a formula that they follow in their work. In fact, masters are likely to depart entirely from known formulas. They know they can do this not due to conceit or recklessness, but because they know through experience that they can rely on their skills and disciplines to manage and adapt through unknown areas of a project. Those disciplines are things such as keeping their work area clean so that no wood chips can damage surfaces and storing their finishes upside down so that a skin does not form on the top that will contaminate their final product. They keep their tools very sharp so that they can handle what is needed from them and keep them well organized so that their tools are at hand when they need them. There are hundreds more examples, with each little discipline adding to the craft of the master.

Similarly, they rely on their skill know-how to strategize their paths forward. A novice woodworker cutting a joint might attempt to cut all the pieces to the right size right away and then be frustrated by a loose fit. A master would know they can make the pieces slightly bigger than they need because they know they can shave a little off by hand quickly and cleanly to make a perfect fit. The key here is skills, not knowledge. A well-studied novice might know that the second way is better, but not have the practice and ability to do it that way because they cannot make those small adjustments effectively.

If software is a craft, then there are similar marks of a software craftsman's work to learn, to practice, and to cue in to. Few, if any, craftsmen become a master in every area, but sadly, many software developers fail to ever become masters of any.

Note: In the use of the term "craftsman," we are in no way intending to exclude the many outstanding female programmers we have met over the years. However, we find terms such as "craftsperson" or "craftswoman" to be cumbersome and intend our use of "craftsman" in the same sense that the word "actor" has come to mean both male and female actors.

Managing complexity

Managing the complexity inside of software is a developer's primary responsibility, and how they go about it is essential. The progress from a novice to a master on this topic is generally marked as the slow decrease in a programmer's reliance on their own cleverness. A brilliant programmer often relies on their own cleverness to attempt to hold as many of the details of a programming solution in their head as they can and keep them organized in there. This is marked at a code level by large, highly interdependent components of code. When one change affects another area, the programmer just knows this because they are holding all those details in their head and adjust things accordingly. This is a novice method of working.

However brilliant the programmers are, they will eventually be unable to hold everything in their head anymore. As they learn, they are forced to break their solutions up so that they do not exceed what they can hold in their head at one time. As they gain mastery, they will hopefully learn that, even when they can hold everything together in their head, the more they do, the more room for error they make. A master breaks the pieces up into as small and simple pieces as possible so that developers can actually gauge all of the impacts of change at a glance.

Code cleanliness

Complexity goes hand in hand with the question of what good code looks like. Spending the time to keep code as clean as possible is important and is a skill that takes practice. We have seen many novice programmers who have been encouraged to clean up their code as much as they can spend days on just that because they have not yet created the skills and habits that make it quick and painless.

Frustratingly, that is part of the process of becoming a good developer and is hard to shortcut. Some of our discussion that follows on peer input helps on this. Initially, though, a programmer considers code good if it works. At this stage, their idea of "works" is evolving to encompass what "works" means. Does it work if you only use it exactly right? Does it work for all normal cases? Unusual cases? "Feel" solid for the user?

The next step down the road of clean code is the realization that almost everything we write is going to have to change at some point. While developers are growing through this, they are struggling with questions of how to best enable that change. When should they structure code in anticipation of changes and how do they do that? It is easy for a lot of time to get spent in anticipation of changes that never come at this stage.

Finally, as they are learning how to structure code simply so that it has no extra pieces but is simple enough to extend later, the masters are worrying about how their code communicates. As the best, most precise documentation of the behavior of the system, the code needs to express not only to other programmers what is going on, but also to the initial one, who looks at an awful lot of code and is likely to be relearning this like a stranger only weeks after writing it in the first place.

SIZE OF WORK PIECES

One practice leads to another, and the previous one leads directly into discussing how we attack our programming problems. A new programmer generally just dives right in and tries to do everything at once. Progress is hard to gauge because everything will get done all at once. Design is hard to make clean because they are trying to juggle every responsibility of the code at the same time. We have worked in shops where developers are left in this mode for months while the business just hopes that they will have something good at the end.

In the meantime, the developer is frequently drowning in keeping things straight. At the same time, if their work impacts anyone else's code, which it almost always will in one degree or another, then their code is becoming more different than the other programmers' code daily. In the end, all their pieces have to go in with everyone else's pieces, and they take generally about half again as long as it took them to reconcile all the divergences. Simply stated, the less time that you can make a meaningful change in and get it integrated, the more of a master you are in this area. Masters can take a complex problem, pick a small central piece, pick a crucial step, write it, validate it, and check it in to source control and do that every few minutes. They make the thinnest possible end to end linkages they can, then begin to expand them, and do it all in very small, easily digested pieces. Common comments, such as "six weeks is not enough time to get the really big jobs done," show a lack of mastery in this area.

Of course, it is fun to kick over the pile of blocks and start over, but businesses cannot make money off it in the meantime. A mature team can and should check their changes constantly *and* have their product working at all times in the process.

UNIT TESTING

Testing is obviously key for developers. After all, how can they say that their work is done if they have not run it to see? Well, sadly, we have seen many programmers do just that, so maybe that is the start of this discipline. Hopefully they progress past it quickly to an almost equally novice approach of at least running their work and seeing if it acts as expected before calling it done. If not, the QA folks will certainly express their feelings on the subject.

One step better than that is to use a tool such as junit, nunit, or rspec to begin validating the proper execution of individual components of their code. Those tests usually attempt to test a whole module at once, against a bunch of difference cases, and are often riddled with external dependencies that make them hard for anyone but their creator to use. They break easily and require a fair amount of upkeep, but at least they exist and are repeatable. Better than that are smaller tests that test one thing so its failure actually tells you what code broke and do it without external dependencies so they are less fragile, have less maintenance, and are run more easily by others on the team. That is a huge step forward. It is still painful, though, because creating these tests involves navigating a bunch of interconnected components in a complex setup before we even get to test anything.

This occurs because the components are still too interdependent. Mastery of this discipline writes the unit tests first, which clarifies the goals of the code first and forces reducing those interdependencies that make setups complex. This is the test-driven development cycle, which, simply stated, writes a test, writes the code to pass the test, and then, with the test there to make sure you do not break anything, restructures the code until it is simple and clean.

Peer input

Back on the subject of programmers' cleverness, or at least their own perception of it, we have the discipline of having our work reviewed. When a programmer is still leaning on their own cleverness, they are not likely to seek other opinions of their work. The pride of a craftsman is a tricky thing. It is important for them to take pride their work, but if that pride means resisting feedback because it wounds the ego, then it is a problem.

Hopefully, the desire to make the best work they can should drive a craftsman to have another set of eyes check their work for problems before they occur. Sometimes, that kind of review is imposed externally on a team in the form of design or code review sessions, which devolve quickly into thesis defense as the present defends their decisions and resists changing code that, in their estimation, is finished and behind them. This is likely to find and fix major problems, but skip many minor ones and opportunities to simply improve the code structure.

The best practice is to program in teams of two. These pairs get their ideas vetted immediately while they are more malleable, making for the best-quality final product. This step is hard because not only does it take adjustment of pride, work habits, and overcoming often introverted temperaments, but it also meets often real (although sometimes just perceived) resistance from management due to the assumption that two people are being paid to do one person's job.

Controlled experiments on pair programming have shown a huge increase in code quality and a drop in the defect rate of two programmers working together over two working independently. This improvement dwarfs what turns out to be only a slight (10%) decrease in productivity of the pair over separate developers (Williams, L., Kessler, R. R., Cunningham, W., and Jeffries, R., *Strengthening the Case for Pair-Programming*, IEEE Software, Vol. 17, No., 4, pp. 19–25, July/Aug 2000. January 2009 update: IEEE Software 25th Anniversary Top Pick Paper; on the list of most-cited IEEE software articles for a 25-year period).

And what is good, Phaedrus,
And what is not good—
Need we ask anyone to tell us these things?

Robert M. Pirsig (*Zen and the Art of Motorcycle Maintenance:
***An Inquiry into Values*)**

Integrating Automation into Your Development Process

CHAPTER CONTENTS

Agile Development and Business Goals. DOI: 10.1016/B978-0-12-381520-0.00008-4

INTRODUCTION

If we believed promises made in the 1950s, we'd have jet cars and all our redundant work would be automated by now, leaving people free to concentrate on the real work of thinking. It hasn't happened yet.

Software Configuration Management positions still exist in the software development industry, and while those employees use tools to track changes, their work has not been automated. It is not a surprise to find a master spreadsheet maintained by hand to track changes or scripts run by hand to pull a list of check-ins from source control. With a manual approach, because it is overwhelming to track which unit tests have succeeded or failed, the focus is typically on larger integration testing, which is done manually by a QA resource.

Build master positions still exist as caretakers of a single point of failure in the form of a "pristine" build machine, hidden behind physically locked doors under the guise of security. Sometimes this setup is even promoted to the level of a selling point for some development shops, touting the level of physical security they feel they need to justify why the build is still on a single machine behind a locked door. Further, the magical build machine is behind a second firewall inside the office and no one can touch this machine but the build master. The question should be asked: what does this mystical build master do when there is no build to produce?

Manual code reviews are still scheduled and, if they are taken seriously, require an investment to prepare for the meetings. This requires time from both the reviewer(s) and the "review-ee" to inspect code and enumerate questions and suggestions all prior to the review. Then the actual meeting takes place and, without serious preparation, degrades quickly to the placement of curly braces or maybe a more modern argument of ternary statements vs if statements. Instead of moving toward best development solutions, the developers instead represent the defense of their work before a firing squad of their peers. Everybody leaves a code review feeling smart or beaten down, depending on your role, but rarely are changes made unless there is an individual responsible for driving the changes. Best-case downstream effects are that more builds are produced, which causes more work by QA resources that are already overloaded by the large integration tests for which they are responsible.

QA resources and code reviews are absolute necessities for any company serious about producing quality software, and both are wasted on endlessly going through empty motions. Many software shops are trapped by the processes they have and need something to kick them into a different mode of operation, but there always is another crisis or a pressing customer need that is a bigger priority. Some are blissfully unaware that there is a different approach because what they are doing is how things have always been done; plus they've been told they are "agile" now and feel the improved communication is solving these problems.

"Agile" itself has many different meanings when applied to build processes. To most, the ability to produce a build, including building an update to a previous release, is proof positive that they are an agile company. Some invest in serious Capability Maturity Model (CMM) training and implementation, hoping to get the certificate that shows they are level 2 and have a repeatable process and they think that too is agile, yet most are more concerned with certification than any agile process. Both trains of thought strive to produce agile-ness to some degree, and even with scrum meetings happening daily or even several times a day, the main process of building software proceeds along as it always has and no one dares touch the high priest's make file. Sure, the make file runs by itself, it's automated to some level, but there is still an individual responsible for pushing the big red make buttons, and everybody holds their breath collectively while the build runs, hoping their latest check-in won't break the build.

Maybe the "real" automation approach is in place because the software shop has a resource who has mastered cron. To the awe of their fellow employees, they edit the crontab with vi. All hail the new king of the shop, and every eight/four/two/one hour the build kicks off. Automation has been achieved, and the shop feels one step closer to the creator of the universe. They think life is good because the build is automated.

But is the build really automated? Look deep into the question and the answer is profoundly no. Either an individual pushed the big red make button or a cron job did, but the process is the same. It is necessary to look into the physical world for a metaphor to outline the build process instead of the neatly organized artificial world of the office lit by fluorescent lighting. In the physical world, nothing happens until an event occurs; a butterfly flaps its wings in South Africa and it rains on cornfields in Iowa. It's chaos in action.

Weather is chaos, and what neatly organized chaos it is! In Colorado, it can rain in the summer and snow in the winter without any person pushing a button. We don't know exactly when it will rain or snow, or sometimes both in the same day interspaced with 70 degree weather, but we can count on snow sometime in January, maybe. That maybe is enough to plan and predict. You know you'll need a snow shovel at some point in the winter, but not the exact day you'll need it.

We may not know exactly when a developer is going to make some rain (check-in code), but we know what to do when code is checked in; kick off a build! The action drives the reaction, not the clock. Developers understand (or should understand) event-oriented programming, they get notified of an event and must do something to react to that event. The butterfly flapping its wings is the event of checking in, and the rain on the cornfields of Iowa is the build kicking off.

Instead of software development being its own beast inside a business, it should follow standard business practices. It has been said that nothing happens until someone sells something; the only difference with software development is that something has been checked in, not sold. Where a salesman may take an order for a custom door, then that request gets translated into a work order for the factory floor, the door is built, tagged, loaded on a truck, and then delivered; software builds should be not different in that a check-in kicks off a build (work order), the build assembles the artifact (factory floor), the artifact is bundled up (tagged and loaded on a truck), and finally the artifact is placed in a directory somewhere (delivered). Instead of being some magical event to build software, it should follow a form that people understand by being automated.

The well-automated build does many things; it is not only a build producing an artifact of an .exe or .war file. The unit tests are run. The code is analyzed. Reports are produced. Emails are sent. Documentation is produced. All because someone made a change and checked something into source control. Those analyses give almost immediate feedback to the specific changes just made, making it quick and easy for the developers to react to that feedback. Now automation has been achieved.

Why should we take on such an expensive project such as automating builds? It pays for itself with quality checks, feedback loops, and project status, ensuring that the project is always moving forward, enabling change with confidence, and assuring that you are keeping your house clean.

In a field filled with world class automators, whose very job it is to create tools that automate tasks and solutions for others, a staggering number of tasks are commonly done very manually or not at all, including documentation, testing at every level, measuring test completeness, artifact versioning, defect detection, and code-quality analysis.

As an industry producing software, automation does not universally exist.

CONTINUOUS INTEGRATION

The concept of continuous integration has been around for quite a while now. There are many tools to provide continuous integration and, surprisingly, some even work together. Any investment in continuous integration will pay off, but it requires discipline that few developers, QA resources, or management actually have at the start of the process. The challenge is to train the development staff and QA how to use continuous integration to work smarter, not harder.

There is much interest in continuous integration, and many organizations are implementing continuous integration tools as part of their move to agile development. Difficulty surrounds this move because not only do developers have to change some working habits, but there typically is a large investment required to match the capabilities of the tool to the organization itself and for that reason alone it is daunting.

At one level, a developer refreshing the code base frequently to catch all the changes from the rest of the team and coding and running unit tests is integrating continually. This works fine for small projects or in small teams, but when the number of moving pieces exceeds some level or the number of developers is increased, this approach does not scale. The approach of desktop continuous integration leads to the infamous "works on my machine" immaturity of developers and organizations as a whole. For a developer, unit tests are developed that are not meant to be run in an automated fashion. For an organization, it leads to small deployment configuration changes that crash unexpectedly and a need for more expensive tools to measure memory usage or performance. In the beginning, desktop continuous integration works, but it fails with time.

Stepping up to the next level begins to introduce two new concepts, for typically a build server does not provide unit testing automatically. Therefore, the need for a build server must be recognized and then the maturity to conceive unit tests to execute with each new build must be constructed. Once the automated build server is in place and unit tests are executing, everybody is happy again. Now code is checked out to a clean build server environment, compilation happens, unit tests are executed, and finally some reporting is provided and the overall productivity will increase. There are measurable gains at this level, and the quality of the product will demonstrate the emphasis on unit testing.

However, a few new problems are introduced when introducing a time-based build automation server. While the builds are running on a regular schedule, and typically at night because that is the most comfortable time, as the thinking is that it doesn't impact the workday, now every morning is spent resolving build problems and test failures from the previous night's build. This work to solve any build problems occurs on every individual developer workstation where each developer checks in new revisions to solve the problem on their own desktop machines. This process is made more difficult because the developers have moved on to new and different work items, and the context of the change made yesterday has been lost. Now each developer is individually paying the cost to dig back into the work of yesterday, remembering all the changes made the night before, and trying to identify what areas might be problematic. Everybody, developers and QA, eagerly await the next nightly build.

With nightly builds, QA is generally happy, for they can come into work in the morning, pull the build from last night, and begin testing all the fixes. Eventually, however, comes the day where last night's build fails and it takes several days to resolve the problem or problems while QA sits idly or continues ahead on a previous build that is even further out of the developer consciousness. The concept of nightly builds works for a while, with a small team, but eventually as more resources are added, the rate of changes made in a day exceeds the capability of the team to deal with the complexity and it reaches unmanageable levels.

When all the resources are in the office, fixing a build problem is difficult enough. Managing a situation where developers are checking out on their own schedules and one has a newer (or older) revision of a shared piece of code and they are arguing over which developer has the real revision that should be used should be accompanied by the sound of money blowing out the window. Yet these ridiculous situations are tolerated in many companies. Managing a situation where the build is broken and one of the developers in conflict just left yesterday for a three week vacation to the Canadian Rockies to get himself "centered" again and nobody knows the password to his machine to get the file he forgot to check in or find out exactly what version of a file he was using is a serious problem.

Clearly, a different approach is needed. Builds must be frequent, but not necessarily nightly. The time that builds take needs to be managed aggressively to minimize the time between check-in and feedback from the build process, until we have just minutes to wait. Frequent builds keep the developers on target, yanking them back to the code they just checked in quickly before they have time to get excited about the next new feature and lose the enthusiasm for what they are working on now.

To some, Nirvana has been achieved. Builds are kicking off with every check-in (after a reasonable delay to catch all the files in a check-in set), machines are humming, disks are spinning, the end product artifacts are being produced, and finally the clouds have parted and the angels are singing.

Except in QA, who look like they were just sucker punched and then tackled by a professional football team.

QA doesn't need every build!

It's easy to pick on developers for a lack of discipline in writing their code. There is almost a badge of honor to have "your own" coding style among many other stereotypical quirks of developers. And there is no argument that many developers need to raise the bar in their work.

However, QA is nearly as bad if not worse. The typical QA person is tracking things with spreadsheets and some bug-tracking system, which to the outside observer looks very organized and methodical; clearly these are detailed-oriented people who thrive on minutiae. But there is a flaw when they are thrown into a software shop that is performing continuous integration and the velocity of change accelerates and many builds are produced in a single day; they want to test every build.

This attitude is driven by history. When a build server tracking changes does not exist, a QA resource is at the mercy of developers to assure them that nothing else changed except the lines of code absolutely necessary to correct the defect. The problem is even developers know that statement is a lie, for of course they just made a little tweak over there, which shouldn't affect anything. Most developers could stand being tortured and still wouldn't admit that their changes might have had unexpected side effects. QA, being mercifully spared the requirement of fluency with the source control system, has no idea where to start to compare the changes and typically does not know the programming language anyway.

Quality assurance has to get comfortable using tools in addition to the bug-tracking software and spreadsheets they are comfortable with. Source control is their biggest weapon in the war against developers making "unauthorized" changes. A build server that lists every change since the last build should use the source control to assemble that list. With those concepts, QA is armed with the tools necessary to take a build when necessary and not look at every build.

Of course this need cycles right around to developers who now must enter comments into check-ins that can be deciphered by others, which includes those who have never held a 20-sided die in their hands or have never compiled the lasted Linux distro themselves. To do that, QA needs support from management to help the developers help themselves and realize that the comments for check-ins have to be improved. This small change pays off when QA realize that they can trust the build server, the comments, and the list of changes. Now QA is free to take a build when necessary and not start every day from the ground up reassembling data, installing the product, and just getting to the large integration tests before it's time to go home.

Continuous integration provides high visibility without a lot of work

When continuous integration is in place and the build is performing as it should and produces not only target artifacts, but also reports and documentation, then the entire company is affected positively. Just as the developers had to step up their game to pay attention to a different set of details and enter good check-in comments, the company must be trained to use the product of all this investment.

The next layer to accept the change provided by continuous integration is support. This may be direct front-line customer support or a technical support supplied as a back office function. Once support begins to trust the product of the automated builds and sees the value of tracking every change made to the code base no matter how small, the velocity of problems being solved increases. This is good for support because they know exactly what was done and how it affects a customer; it's even better for development because they are hearing feedback on the value of what is being produced. Managed correctly, this feedback loop increases and developers begin pouring more details into changes, which makes support jobs easier and another level of happiness has been achieved.

There are investments to get to this level in addition to the build server. The build server must also be tied to some ability to browse the source control repository. No doubt about it, the fact that anyone in the company can see the code will strike fear into the guts of developers when they first realize what is happening. As in any evolutionary process, the strong survive and the weak disappear. Some developers will choose to leave, which is exactly what should happen because they have been surpassed by a process with more capabilities.

Some of the strongest developers are also the exact same developers who regularly break the build, which on the surface seems counterintuitive. When first beginning the automated build process it is a new discipline that must be learned, as even extremely talented developers have not typically been challenged in this manner. Over time, the "oops" check-in diminishes and instead what happens is that something new is introduced that breaks the build, not because a couple of source code files were not checked in but rather that there were unintended side effects of the change that broke something else that the developer was not aware of at the time of the creation of that new feature. This type of break, when unit tests fail, is wonderful, as everyone is alerted in short order and the problem gets hammered out quickly into a form that all can live with.

Alternately, there is another kind of developer who is not yet grasping the magnitude of a broken build. Maybe they like to check in once "everything is done" and resist continuous integration with passive inaction. They gleefully check in a whole section of code, forgetting to merge the changes that have taken place since their last source code update; worse yet, they'll go out for a long lunch or leave at the end of the day without knowing if their changes were successful or not. Developers behaving in this way need help to overcome this behavior. Unfortunately, much of the time this is a bit like telling kids "you can play video games after you finish your homework." There is a level of maturity expected to be an effective developer on a team producing quality code at a fast rate.

This ability of the build server to track all changes and publish these changes to a wide audience on demand is crucial to providing increased communications without a large investment. Sure, developers have to step up comments when making changes, but managers must ask themselves which is more efficient, a developer spending a couple of minutes entering a good descriptive comment or having meetings with many resources throughout the company? To the manager whose life is divided into near one hour chunks of meetings, the answer is not always clear, for meetings are the tool to get things done. These managers must realize that a developer's work is not divided into one hour units.

Developers must also grasp the importance of check-in comments. Once they do, the signs are easy, as you'll see more thought put into the comments and the growth from "changed a few things" to "fixed the bug causing X, changed foo.java, version 1.18." The first comment is brief and the developer hasn't had to maintain several versions in the field or hasn't grasped the value of check-in comments and is willing to flail around working to fix the next bug. The latter comes from an experienced developer who doesn't want to waste time trying to remember what they were doing three months ago and instead leaves a trail to lead to the change quickly.

Small investments in documentation pay back big dividends.

Problems with visibility

The phrase "You can take a horse to water, but you can't make him drink" is well known, which will happen when introducing a build server that produces documentation and tracks changes. There is an ingrained resistance to accepting what comes from a software development shop regarding any list of changes that companies and individuals have learned over years of half-truths from development about what really changed. Further, in a nit-picking list with extreme detail, there is so much noise for tiny things that an end user would never realize and has no way to tell if something changed that people outside of development glaze over when presented with such a list. In the end, even if the list is readily available, most people throughout the company will never look at such a list, and fewer still would be able to make sense of such a list.

Even without understanding every tiny thing that changed, the existence of such a list should be well known and understood throughout the organization. Typically, the rallying cry for a User Acceptance Testing (UAT) phase of a project is that the users, internal and external, do not know exactly what changed and will not invest any time in reading release notes to find out. They would rather get in and use the software to find out for themselves and report anything they do not like or are not comfortable with at the point of UAT. So the problem really isn't the list itself or the build server, but rather twofold in that users will not trust the list from development due to past experience and users will not invest time in deciphering the documentation they do get.

Both the developers and the users are wrong. Developers are not writing comments when they check in changes that any reasonable human outside of software development would understand, and users have no need to understand what was changed at such a granular level. While it may be true that someday software developers will become a distinct subspecies of the human race through inbreeding and natural selection, the split is huge between developers and users regarding change documentation.

Both sides have to change to actually use the documentation being produced from the build server. Developers have to write comments that humans can understand. Users, and this audience is internal users, need to also step up their game to actually access build server documentation and filter out trivial nits and be able to focus on the impactful (to them) changes within the software. The development group or the internal users cannot change their behavior quickly, and it will take some investment of time to remove infrastructure comments from valuable comments that are useful to users.

Even when recognizing the need to produce a list of changes and using the build server to produce the list, do not be surprised when internal users do not read the list. Only constant and unrelenting pressure will help drive the usage of any change list.

Of the two groups, developers are easier to educate and change once they begin seeing the value that good comments have from the support team. Internal users will resist any change in behavior simply because they have never had to inspect such a list before and feel it is outside of their job responsibilities to do so. Until buy-in from all levels happens, be prepared to produce watered down lists of changes and continue to take baby steps to influence other departments throughout the company.

BUILD PROCESS

Before a change in the build process can be entertained in an organization, a fundamental hurdle has to be overcome. This hurdle is the decision to accelerate the build process from a periodic or nightly build to more frequent builds. Simply moving the nightly build to run at noon isn't enough nor is running build every hour. The answer is that builds run with every check in of code. Every change in the code base produces every artifact dependent on that piece of code, every time it is modified.

The build process itself is straightforward. The steps are to check out code from source control, retrieve libraries, compile the code, run unit tests, run integration tests, produce code metrics, report code coverage, and finally assemble into the deployment image.

No additional builds run if the same artifact is currently being built. The reason is clear once a large shop in using continuous integration builds, for so many check-ins are performed during the day (another developer discipline, not waiting until they have a lot of code to check in) that kicking a full build with all the tests and metrics quickly becomes unfeasible, for builds would stack up and the really necessary builds would never be completed.

Unit tests are typically simple enough that they do not need hardware resources outside of the hardware to actually run the build. However, integration tests will require outside resources such as a Web service or a database. Both types of automated testing are necessary and valuable, as it affects the overall quality of the software being produced. Creating them does require buy in from management that does not consider developer time to be wasted on them, as well as a financial investment, to provide computing resources for their use.

Metrics on code are simply automated code reviews, performing analysis at a level of detail that is hard to do manually. These ensure that standards within the code are met in ways that a "code style" never would and leaves manual reviews to consider higher level design concerns. Amazing enough, many bugs are patterns of code that can be detected by a machine. Some, especially issues stemming from concurrency, would be nearly impossible for a human to locate in a large code base. These simple scans lift an organization out of problems that appear on the surface to only be reproducible in production. The first bug found with code metrics could pay for the entire effort. Softer rules show probabilities of areas where problems may lay otherwise undetected long before they fail in production.

Producing reports to highlight code coverage by tests provides insight on weak sections of code. Typically, the sections of code that are breaking, and therefore costing money to support, are the same sections that don't have coverage by unit testing. The typical resistance from a developer is that writing the tests would be "hard"; the problem with this mindset is that it is difficult to survive as a company without these tests. Proper unit testing requires improved design skills and work habits and may require training or even an investment in time for outside coaching to help grow these areas in the development team.

Finally, the artifact is produced. This may be a simple jar or dll resource or an entire .exe or war file. Help is linked into the artifact, and the artifact is posted to a shared location for distribution.

Two important notes are that the artifact produced for QA is exactly the same as what would go to a customer and if any step along the way fails, or exceeds a threshold, the entire build fails and the artifact is not produced.

METRICS

In anything at all, perfection is finally attained not when there is no longer anything to add, but when there is no longer anything to take away.

Antoine de Saint Exupéry, writer and aviator

Metrics can be as simple as measuring the adherence to a code format standard or deeper into code scanning for concurrency problems. Both have merit and both serve to perform automated code reviews. The benefit is that it provides concrete and impersonal measures rather than frequently stylistic, ego-oriented feedback of peer reviews. The best metric packages will function in both the build process and on the desktop, which include integration with the development environment.

Stupid coder tricks

One direction of metrics is to avoid "stupid coder tricks." Imagine pseudo code where a procedure is defined as:

```
void method setAMember(String input)
{
   input += "Value: " + input;
   memberString = input;
}
```

This doesn't look like much of a problem at first glance, and in some languages this would be totally functional.

Now imagine a line of code that invokes the aforementioned method:

```
Object.setAMember("My value");
```

And still the problem is not immediately apparent. The problem is a violation of modifying the parameter in many languages, as the parameter is not an "in–out" parameter; worse yet, in some languages this could actually clobber the stack. Unless a detailed evaluation of every line is performed in a code review, this would never be found—while a machine scanning the code finds this pattern every time.

Other stupid coder tricks, such as simple copy and paste, are even harder to find. Buried within millions of lines of code could be two sections of code that are very similar. Originally, with a deadline breathing down the developer's neck, the developer copied a functional section of code and pasted it elsewhere, maybe modifying a variable or two along the way. It worked, and everybody moved onto the next crisis of the day and time passed. Later, a bug was found in one of the copied bits of code and it was corrected quickly. Later still, the same problem was found in a different part of the product and it was also corrected. Twice the cost, two times the failures; it is hoped both were found in a QA phase and did not fail for a customer.

Some "copy–paste detection" is required. The hard part of finding these issues is that a string compared for lines of code is not sufficient. The scan must tokenize code and compare the tokens, not individual lines. Once this gets implemented, not only will code produced from cut and paste be found, but also similar code developed independently by multiple developers. Don't Repeat Yourself (D.R.Y.) is a central design principle. Ultimately, this leads to a smaller and more robust code base with fewer issues, for common code is factored out into shared modules, which are better tested and perform better.

Unused code

Removing unused code seems simple enough; if it's not referenced, then it is not needed in the build and does not need to eat up development resources to keep its state in step with a changing system. Two dynamics come into play with unused code. First, the developer is reluctant to remove the dead code for the reason that it might be used again someday. Second, on large projects it is difficult to tell when the caller stops using exposed methods in a dependent project.

Developers want to keep every line of code every written, and for that reason they may merely comment out code instead of deleting it, which is a very cowardly act that most developers will do by default unless someone or something is checking on them. They know from experience that the next manager will want something fast and if they can hack what already works they can meet the deadline. This is a horrible thought process and does not rely on tools that they should be using fluently. Source control is the answer, and becoming comfortable with source control tools is required, for lacking trust of source control is a sign of immaturity in a developer. Developers have to get over the hurdle that the tip revision of the source code tree is the ultimate truth and instead embrace that the tip revision is merely the current state of the software. Discipline must evolve to leave enough documentation with every check-in that comparisons of changes are possible quickly. Tools exist to point out unused code, such as methods that are no longer called, variables that are assigned but never used, or even simple things such as unused imported references become a developer's ally, allowing the code to remain as lithe as possible at all times. Trust that source control has all previous versions and proceed with confidence.

Where developers scanning for dead code fail is when a library exposes methods that are no longer used by any piece of code higher up the dependency chain. Dead code can be hidden by many levels of calls, all appearing on the surface as very important to the overall functionality but ultimately never used. This code rot is disturbing, for it highlights a communication problem. It is totally explainable because everyone is running as fast as they can and the feeling is that it's really not that important in the long run. But what happens more often is that the dead code has been superseded with a new approach or library and the bloated code lies like a beached whale until a new developer discovers it and begins using it again and now there are two branches, both wound tightly into the product, that do the same thing in different ways. Automated scans for unused code don't have the same limitation and will discover invocation chains that a human would miss.

Scanning for unused code helps keep your code base tight and helps remove any investment in maintaining dead code. Further, it provides you with one more tool to realize that development work is not done when there is nothing left to add, but rather complete when there is nothing left to take away.

Cyclomatic complexity

This metric is crucial to quality and is often overlooked. The standard developer response is that code is optimal and complexity doesn't matter. Imagine code that has existed for years, with many developers all contributing to it and managers pushing for one more feature. Each developer had their own style and each used different structures and approaches to the code. Everybody thought it was great, and it did function, but now one more bug has been found and it falls on a new developer to fix, as it has been a while since anyone has touched it and the current manager just wants it done right now.

Cyclomatic complexity measures the number of paths through a section of code. When a development shop begins using cyclomatic complexity as a measurement of code quality, a lot of code will be flagged as too complex; most of these are easy enough to fix. Initial resistance falls away when weeks and months have passed and a developer goes back to fix a bug or add a new feature. It's easier to fix or add new functionality and the light comes on and they "get it," finally. But once the easy wins are done, a new pattern emerges. The bug reports and the complexity start to align, the bugs are in the complex code, and every time a bug gets fixed, one or more bugs pop up.

Cyclomatic complexity isn't a measurement of hard code. It's not flagging a complex algorithm. Cyclomatic complexity is flagging poorly conceived and written code.

With a language such as Java with garbage collection, addressing cyclomatic complexity frequently produces a side benefit of managing memory consumption much better for variables that are tightly scoped. Instead of memory being consumed for long sections of code, they are allocated, used, and freed within the scope of a single method, allowing that memory to be recycled for the next calculation.

Another resistance to any concern of cyclomatic complexity is an old rule found in experienced programmers, which is that the measure of how big a singular method code can be is driven by the screen size in that a single method should be visible on the screen all at once. It was a good rule when it was conceived, which was sometime in the 1980s or 1990s when the maximum display was 40 lines by 80 characters on a monochrome display. With today's monitors and video cards conspiring together to produce a screen size and fine resolution that would be the envy of any television short of a projection television in the 1980s, this rule falls flat on its face and now works against the developer to produce hideous code. It doesn't mean that a scan for cyclomatic complexity will catch every section of code that is too big or too complex, but forces a realization that without a metric (and that metric being an automated metric) there is no yardstick to measure the complexity and size of the code and therefore no way to improve the complexity and size of the code.

It is true that the complexity of software will grow until it exceeds the ability of the developer to maintain it. Scanning for complexity helps keep code maintainable, which leads to lowering the cost to modify the code.

Inconsistent synchronization

This is an automated scan that may be measured just as any other code metric that can save the bacon of a company all by itself. A scan that produces a report that informs simply that access to an object is synchronized 75% of the time should make everyone gasp. This is a critical concept in modern multithreaded applications, and it is scary to realize that many developers working on multithreaded applications do not understand the importance of this concept.

Most managers, and a majority of developers, will be confused about inconsistent synchronization. They wonder why they should worry about it because either it can't really be a problem or the container is dealing with the threading so they don't have to worry about threading and managing synchronized objects. Some of these ostriches will get extremely lucky and never have this problem rear its ugly Greek mythology hydra head. Others will not be so lucky and find that, like the mythical hydra, once you cut off one head (fix one bug), two more (bugs) pop up in its place.

It only takes one experience with a bug caused by inconsistent synchronization to fall in love with a scan that will point this problem out across your entire code base. Failure to embrace the meaningfulness of this scan leads to problems that only happen in production or that QA can occasionally reproduce but never happen on the developer's machine. Much like build failures that require code from a developer blissfully on vacation, this problem should also be accompanied with the sound of a large vacuum cleaner sucking money out of the company.

Many times synchronization should be avoided and addressed with a different design. However, for cases where it can't (legacy code, which will not have the investment made to refactor, or a fundamental library where the need for synchronization cannot be avoided, etc.), it is a huge benefit to know that you have this scan running and will not have to be kept up at night worrying about the possibility of a nonatomic modification to code that cannot accept multithreaded updates.

Synchronization is like a bathroom with several doors. The beauty of synchronization in the Java language is that once someone (a thread) is in the bathroom and locks a door, all the doors are locked instantly, giving exclusive access to the requested resource (toilet). The processor (toilet) can deal with the currently executing thread (bathroom user) until that thread is done and then another thread is able to access the synchronized resource (toilet). Old-timer Java developers will recognize the sound of flushing as a .notifyAll(). A best-case scenario outcome to a problem with inconsistent synchronization will lead to embarrassment; worst case, it can stop a company in its tracks.

Code test coverage

Measuring how unit tests are exercising the code provides visibility into how much is actually being unit tested. It is surprising to find that the unit tests did not cover much code, but that like cyclomatic complexity, the code that doesn't have unit tests is often the same code that has the most bugs written against it. Code without unit tests is much more difficult to refactor with confidence, and when it does get modified the risk of introducing a new bug is high.

But there is a practical limit to code coverage for most organizations. With a software language that has exception handling, it may be a large amount of work to produce a particular exception dealing with a network failure. A measure of reasonableness must be applied to the coverage metric. It is not necessary for management to produce an edict that all code must be 100% covered at all times, and yet at the same time this is the goal.

When beginning to implement code coverage, a reasonable goal of 80% will pay back huge dividends and produce much happier QA resources. As with so many things, the last 20% takes 80% of the work. This is especially true when retrofitting unit tests and coverage metrics in an existing code base, but the pain eases with code developed with test-driven development (TDD), making the elusive 100% goal attainable.

Developers will resist creating unit tests with the goal of code coverage. In their previous positions, they have always been rewarded for producing new functionality or squashing bugs. In most cases, never before has a measurable metric of quality been introduced into their goals and they have not been financially rewarded for producing quality. In the same way that the discipline to produce source control check-in comments that are readable by humans was introduced to provide value to the ability of the automated build server to produce documentation, the discipline to produce unit tests that exercise the code must be introduced.

Test-driven development is one way to bring in unit tests for the purposes of code coverage. To show the value that this work has to the larger organization, it may be necessary to set aside specific time during the work week to have them gather and be trained how to do TDD. By creating a designated time and place to introduce TDD and letting the developers actually work on doing TDD, it is possible to "put your money where your mouth is" and show that test-driven development is important to the company. Without actually setting aside time to introduce this new concept, the old saying of you get what you pay for is very true and results will be spotty at best. A few developers may pick up on the concepts and begin performing them in their daily work, but more commonly the whole idea will fizzle like a wet firecracker. The importance of unit testing cannot be stressed enough, and the measurement of code coverage gives a real metric to the value of unit testing.

Productive code discussions

Once automated code metrics are firmly entrenched in a development shop, many benefits are realized. The best among these are productive discussions about code, for now it is possible to measure code objectively instead of having a subjective "feeling" about the code. A piece of code may have a bad "smell," but it's hard to say why, whereas metrics point out the why. Instead of spending time arguing over unfounded opinions, there are objective tools to point out good and bad in the code.

Because the build server pointed out the problem, it's not a personal issue between developers. Because everybody has the same measurement, code reviews are free to focus on the big picture, the overall approach, or the algorithm and are not stuck in the quagmire of where a curly brace is placed. A real benefit is realized in the product when a build server points out a problem and the manager is freed from a large number of interpersonal conflicts, for all developers are measured on the same scale.

Instead of developers hogging a meeting room for a day doing a code review while no new work on product functionality is being produced and management frets about a schedule even if code reviews are built into the schedule, the meetings are quick. The above-average developer quickly zeros in on the pattern in use and can evaluate the code rapidly, bringing worthwhile comments to a review. After this style has been in use for a while, it becomes possible to grab a few developers, project the code on the wall, and get good feedback, because the overall style of the entire shop has become consistent and the size of any block of code is reduced to an amount that may be digested quickly.

Because the trivial problems have been removed by metrics and automated scanning of code, pair programming is possible on a level different from a driver and observer approach. Now, instead of catching nits like a forgotten semicolon, concepts such as multithreading and coding patterns are the discussion.

Finally, the window is closed and money has stopped blowing out the window.

Unproductive code discussions

With focus on getting productive code discussions from developers that result in real improvements in a product, it may seem backward to explain unproductive code discussions. We feel it is important to spot some patterns in unproductive code discussions so that these trends may be avoided and a team steered back on course.

As trivial as it seems, the placement of curly braces (begin/end pair or any other block delimiter) can descend into a holy war. It is amazing to hear developers argue the benefits of where a curly brace is located with the availability of tools having the capability to reformat code into any form desired. This was never a topic of discussion even back in vi days for anyone capable of writing a macro to make code look just the way they wanted. The answer is to select one form for a shop and stick with it, and when this discussion comes up it should be ended immediately. Of course good developers already know that the real answer is "on the next line."

Argumentative developers seem to thrive on conflict and will pick any trivial nit to blow up into a skirmish. While arguing may be a fundamental human trait, arguing over academic topics such as encoding a bit of data in an XML stream is best dealt with by publicly noting that this is something that may need to get reevaluated in a future development cycle. Unless it is a clear-cut security violation, note the issue and move on. If a developer can't let the topic go then it may be time to have that developer leave the meeting and quite possibly let them move on to another place of employment. Allowing a code review to degrade into a mean-spirited contest of wills takes the entire team down and wastes time and money.

While not officially a code review, some developers are not comfortable enough to bring up questionable topics in a public setting; these developers prefer to pick around the edges, wandering into a manager's office and then unloading all their concerns. Sometimes, these are legitimate concerns and the best move is to grab everybody involved with the section of code and get them together in one room to hash out the problem. However, if it's a session for the developer to whine, end the session quickly. It is necessary to separate personal issues from technology issues to turn this disaster of private whining sessions into a productive outcome.

AUTOMATION TOOLS

Many tools, whether they are open source or commercial products, exist for performing automation. The platform in use for development, including the operating system or the development environment platform, as well as the delivery platform of the end product, may restrict the selection of tools. Additionally, the software development language in use may dictate a narrow selection of tools. Some development shops (government, government contractors, and others) may have restrictions regarding what software can be brought in due to security concerns.

Plenty has been written on a plethora of Web pages about these tools. Much of it is very focused toward the developer and as such leaves many managers wondering what the benefit is to the bottom line of the company if they let the developers play with these tools. The bottom line benefit is that the speed of development and the quality of the product(s) are increased, leading toward less downtime and better customer satisfaction.

Many of the tools discussed here are focused toward Java development. However, other tools exist for different software development languages, and this section should be viewed as requirements for any tool selection for these particular sections of automation.

In a few years from now these tools may be out of fashion or superseded. Don't take this list as the all time list for past, present, and future. The evolution of software tools may take a different branch in the future, but the concepts will remain. Any doubt that concepts remain for decades can be simply dispelled with revisiting a technology concept, such as regular expressions, which have existed for 40 plus years. The form will undoubtedly change, but the concepts will exist in new forms of the evolution.

The temptation to have one be-all-and-end-all tool to perform automated builds and software development is high in some shops. This is understandable given the historically high cost of software development in that everything should work one way and have a minimal learning curve. It should be clear that the scope of the problem is huge and that one tool will not provide all the necessary functionality as the scope is simply too large. Still, shops frequently select one vendor as the standard and lock themselves into the tools that could lead to a huge amount of rework if the vendor goes out of business or changes the tool drastically in a reaction to market demands. Be wary of selecting a suite of tools from one vendor, for the cost of ownership may be larger than selecting various tools that interoperate using standards.

The IDE—Eclipse

Developers spend most of their time in an editor. An editor used for development is not a word processor that could also be used to create letters, instead it is a specific tool to perform a specific job. A quick digression into the history of editors is necessary to have the background to appreciate where software developer editors are today.

First there was vi, it was (and still is) amazing, and it is possible to write a macro to do just about anything; the problem was that very few developers overall actually invested time into figuring out commands past ":w" or ":q" and most struggled with typing "i" before an insert. But yet vi reigned supreme for years. It was almost as if some developers became ascetics, selecting a life of austerity to become closer to the one true editor. The rest took sips from the big pond of vi, scratching out a macro here and there. As great as it was, though, vi did not have tooling beyond editing.

Other editors appeared; some were touted as easy to use, whereas others added nicer interfaces on vi-like functionality. By the early 1990s, excellent editors such as Brief could be used to edit any language and even had some vestiges of language-specific tooling that could format code in fairly standardized ways. Other editors were tied to specific languages and only allowed editing of a single language; one was Visual Basic. These complete environments provided a ton of functionality for a single language tying layout of GUI forms and editing of code into one environment.

The last branch of editors in the 1990s, and some still exist today, were language-specific and locked developers into a single approach for a problem. Great as they were for solving a handful of problems, the moment a developer started doing something that was not really available out of the box they lost steam. Worse still, extracting a project from the single source was impractical at best and the company was locked into a single vendor unable to jump to a different approach or technology. It's amazing to realize that so-called "standard" languages still have editors that lock development into one vendor and entice that behavior by providing some "hard" functionality with some vendor-specific syntax sugar. Not only is a company locked into a specific vendor for development languages, compilers, and platforms, they are also locked into specific hardware and operating system combinations, which is not a problem if the market for that specific hardware and operation system is large enough, but is if your product is more of a niche that can place the future viability of a company in question.

We currently prefer Eclipse. There are many competitors to Eclipse in the market, and many of these are licensed pieces of software. Eclipse is different, it's free, and the open source nature of the product means that there have been many contributors outside of the core development group producing plug-in projects to extend Eclipse in myriad ways. This rich mind share across the industry may be leveraged to help a development shop improve quality and speed without much investment into a vendor-specific tool.

Eclipse is different from many licensed editors in that it does not promote a single set of objects or approach to development. A software shop is freed from the concern that the code they are producing will not work if they ever choose to move away from a particular IDE.

Eclipse is also different from the editors preferred by the hair-shirt crowd of older seasoned developers. Somehow, 20 or 30 years later, these developers still feel proud that they know how to write a macro in vi and must prove to themselves and others that the investment in macros will pay off on a daily basis. Unfortunately, vi has no out-of-the-box functionality to perform simple actions such as removing unused imports or scanning for unused code. Sure, macros exist to format the code in a consistent style in vi and it is possible to hunt these down or build your own. Eclipse comes with formatting, alerts for unused code, and many more features right out of the box.

Additionally, Eclipse supports grammar-based refactoring tools (for most languages). What that means to you is that for many common tasks in modifying the source code, there are tools that will make those changes and that the kinds of changes made by the tool can be proven mathematically to always be correct, substantially reducing the opportunity for humans to introduce new defects.

Also, within the Eclipse environment, you can add support for your source control, your unit test execution, and your code metric utilities so that the developer always has all the information and tools at his/her fingertips, making them much more productive.

Source control

There are many source control packages: CVS, Subversion, GIT, and others. All do the same thing, which is to track revisions and allow a display of differences between revisions. Regardless of what source control package you do pick, concurrency is the key.

Concurrency, and thinking about concurrency, can be frightening to those unwilling to accept the chaotic nature of software development. Enforcing controls on modifications appears necessary on the surface, for having two developers working in the same file feels like it could lead to a disaster. Instead, the ability to "lock" a file for editing feels so much safer to those with little control over the changes. Like attempting to grip dry sand, the tighter you squeeze the more slips through your fingers.

Instead the free market of concurrent modifications must be allowed, and encouraged, to thrive. Any product of significant size has so many individual files (more have been created because of code metrics regarding the size of a class, size of a method, and cyclomatic complexity) that the real occurrence of developers butting heads over modification of a file is few and far between. If you have a real design and not just a couple of source files that control everything, this is easy to imagine that developers won't be editing the same file. A source control that has concurrency built into it from the start should handle collisions very well. The first developer to check in wins and someone editing the same version must merge.

That merging sounds difficult, for every developer wants their own style, but this fact has been addressed by enforcing a consistent style and using tools that format code automatically as they are being edited, such as Eclipse. Chances are that even though a conflict was detected, it was in two discrete areas of the code and merged easily. Conflicts are rare and are a learning opportunity to increase communication, which the entire process is built around; however, the longer the time between check-ins, the larger the changes, the higher the likelihood of conflicts, and the more painful the merge. The tool itself helps teach developers to make changes in small, manageable chunks or they will suffer painful merges as a result. Leveraging stand-up meetings and the whole process also reduces the need for merging.

Still some developers will not want to check in frequently, feeling that this leads to promiscuous check-ins and increases the builds for no good reason. They would rather work on their desktops and check in when everything is ready. It should be clear by now that this is a disastrous approach and typically is a developer trying to be the "man in a room" even though he is sitting in the open area of the bullpen. This thought process must be broken, and the discipline around frequent check-in is encouraged as the limited communication of a developer desiring to hide in his work space works to destroy the value of the automated build server.

CVS and Subversion have been around long enough that a shop is not held hostage to a single vendor for manipulating the repository. Eclipse handles CVS and Subversion, and other tools, such as WinCVS or Tortoise, can produce visualizations of modification histories. What one tool doesn't do another can do and typically does it well. It might seem like there are many tools to learn, but why pound a screw with a hammer or attempt to drive a nail with a screwdriver? Use the right tool for the job and it gets done well with less effort.

Currently, distributed source control is in vogue, partially because of successful projects using it for open source development and partially because it is the current bright shiny object in the world of source control. The almost magical merging is a huge draw to developers. The basic difference is that in a bullpen all the developers are located together, whereas in many open source projects, contributors are spread over the globe. The other reason to currently stay away from Mercurial or GIT is that it promotes working software on one developer's machine versus the same code running on the entire team's machines. The concept of delaying a check-in until everything is working and not respecting that others are working on the same code base is problematic at best. Developers together in the same bullpen are working as a team toward specific goals set forth in the cycle commitment document instead of on whatever a single developer feels is neat at the moment.

In the past there were other source control products that functioned on locking files. In this approach, a single developer can check out, and lock, a file for editing. On the surface, this seems like a wonderful idea because it completely eliminates any need for merging. These systems advertised that they work like a library; what they didn't say is that there is only one copy of the book so no one else can modify the book once it is checked out. The missing metaphor is that source code is not like a book because it is possible and necessary to modify source code where the library will be upset if you write in a book. Branching was difficult in these systems and generally discouraged. The need for branching and concurrent modification, as well as the desire to avoid vendor lock in, is why we suggest CVS or similar systems over any type of locking source control. By 2010, this approach and the products built on this approach were either dead or dying.

One benefit of source control and the tools that have been developed to support source control is the ability to see and track the rate of change in various areas of a project. This is extremely valuable insight to the health and wellness of your project, as two things are readily apparent. First, new development areas are where the majority of check-ins occur in a healthy project. Second, old files that are touched and retouched are clear indicators of bad design and areas that are costing money to maintain. New development churn is healthy, but rapid changes in existing code that is more than a couple of cycles old are a red flag that something needs serious investment.

Used intelligently, source control manages versions of source code, supports an automated build process, and allows monitoring of the health of a project in ways that no meeting ever could.

A final note about source control, regardless of which product you select, is back up the repository. Do it regularly, but don't worry about constant backups because you have a distributed backup in the form of the code that is on every developer workstation. What you need to be concerned with from your source control backup is history and branches, because that is what you will lose.

The repository—Maven

Somewhere in the shop has to reside the blessed versions of third-party components. A single repository gives everyone one-stop shopping to pick up the proper version. This may sound like a library, as it is a location to get a copy of the proper version, but it is more complex in software development because past versions must be retained to allow for building of previous versions of software. This may seem abstract to someone not involved in writing and maintaining code, but it is a very big problem. Application programming interfaces (APIs) change; some versions may only be valid with the latest compiler version and incompatible with previous versions. All this complexity must be addressed, either by a tool or manually. Clearly, addressing this manually will only be accomplished in development organization, which is not a good expenditure of time and resources that should be creating the next great version of a product.

Simply put, Maven is a brilliant tool. Tying together build, testing, documentation, and the concept of a repository is a huge benefit to a software development shop. Everything Maven does could be done in ANT or Make save one critical piece that neither previous tool provided and that piece is the repository.

The repository concept allows progress from the perfect build machine. This single concept allows builds to be distributed anywhere and single-handedly ensures that all the components are guaranteed to be the same wherever the build was produced. To give an example, it is common for a Java product to use XML and in using XML have a need for a parser that could be provided as a SAX parser from JDom. Previously, it would be unknown what version of JDom was on each developer machine. Maven solves this problem by requiring the use of a definition file (a Project Object Model in Maven parlance), which defines which repository is in use and exactly what version of the component must be used.

Simultaneously, Maven allowed for a free market of experimentation on each developer machine by allowing modification to the definition file and enforced which component version was required to build the artifact. Remember, all changes to the definition file are also tracked in the source control. Freedom and control in the same concept; capitalism in action!

Metrics—PMD, CPD, and FindBugs

At the most basic level, nothing can be improved without measuring. To measure is to introduce a metric, and PMD supplies this metric. Maven, and later Hudson, can execute PMD and its associated CPD to produce reports with each build. This automation of producing reports produced by static code analysis yields the ability to measure the quality of the code base and elevate code reviews to a more productive level.

A tool like PMD is what measures the cyclomatic complexity of code. These reports will point out problem areas in code. Developer resistance of "it's complex software and it will be complex" or "complexity is why our product exists" is a thin veneer on the pride of the developers, for surely they are smart, if not brilliant, and writing complex code is what they get paid to do. The truly brilliant developers will see the new path and embrace it for what it is, a way to get to the "good lazy." Difficult, and expensive to maintain, pieces of code are broken up into smaller chunks. Different patterns of coding begin to appear, valuing the simple and direct over the convoluted and obfuscated.

Other metric side-effect benefits, such as inconsistent synchronization, are found quickly by scans such as FindBugs. Finding these issues is difficult for a human to attempt to scan through thousands of lines of code spread across many modules. Don't accept a developer saying "that can never happen" because it will and it does, usually late at night after everyone has gone home and is sleeping. These problems are nearly impossible to detect with manual QA regardless of how many concurrent QA resources are banging away at the product. Likewise, unless specifically crafted to expose this problem, unit tests will miss this critical issue of product stability.

Copy and paste may be the coolest thing since sliced bread for Grandma to forward emails, but it will kill a piece of software. Not only is it contrary to everything a good developer should have learned, it is dangerous to a business and will cost real dollars to address. Like so many problems, it is better to nip it in the bud early rather than try to retrofit it into an existing code base. There are two reasons why copy and paste is introduced into a product. One, developers are lazy (the bad kind of lazy) and they just don't want to take the time to break out another class. This issue has to be handled and may become a personnel issue. The second is a very good thing on large teams in that it detects two developers who have produced the exact same code. On a good team, they recognize this fact and work together to break the common shared functionality out into a single piece of code. This is one key to a highly productive team.

So what does PMD stand for? Nothing, just cool initials. Both PMD, which also supplies CPD functionality, and FindBugs are open source and have plug-ins available for Eclipse and Maven.

Build server—Hudson

For a build server to be effective, it must be able to be dropped anywhere and execute. Further, it should be able to execute any kind of build to allow experimentation and advancement. The real killer for a custom solution is the ability to execute a standardized plug-in to allow external development of the build server. Pristine-built machines and home-grown automation do not allow advancement outside of the single development shop. The ability to grab new bits to measure your code or perform a build for a new language is crucial to the survivability of your development effort.

If Maven was brilliant, Hudson is dazzling. Here, every concept discussed to date is neatly rounded up, lassoed, and brought to the branding fire before released to the field. Hudson executes a script, which could be any number of things, but also executes Maven natively. Hudson reads from source control, including CVS. Hudson is event-oriented, using changes in the source control to kick off builds. Hudson produces documentation on the whole process without human intervention.

While the scripting portion of Hudson remains a bit of a black art, requiring someone with ANT or Maven knowledge, these skills do exist in the marketplace and are well documented if it is required to start from scratch. ANT scripting is searched for easily on the Internet and there are tons of examples. Maven maintains a great site, which takes a large chunk out of the learning curve to begin producing scripts. Scripting itself isn't the barrier to adoption.

Hudson is capable of executing a build with every check into source control. While this may seem excessive initially, once it is rolling, it is critical to keeping the wheels turning. Build numbers become part of the check-in comments, which document what is in the build itself. Continual builds running on a stack of machines somewhere within the organization are the heartbeat of the development crew. Sometimes Hudson is pumping regularly along at a steady pace and at other times is beating as fast as possible for a quick sprint to the finish line.

The documentation produced tracks what was done, when it was done, and who made the changes along with the improvements, or regressions, in test cases and code quality. Once the organization begins to trust the output from experience with the artifacts produced, the machine is humming along and paving the way for large changes in the software without interruption in the day-to-day production of software.

Another key benefit of Hudson is the ability to run many versions of builds and maintain everything in one location. Because not all customers will be running the same version of software at the same time, it may be necessary to fix a bug in a version that is quite old. Remember, "quite old" is last week to a developer, so having an automated system able to produce builds from a maintenance branch of the source control key provides the ability to maintain a maintenance branch with confidence.

A drawback to any automated system is attempting to employ a technology that is not playing well with a tool such as Hudson. Currently, the OSGI standards from Eclipse do not fit naturally with Maven or Hudson, and while that may be true at this writing, many are working to get everything marching along the same road happily. And we have successfully produced PDE builds, as required in an Eclipse project, within Hudson. If a technology that does not play well with others must be employed to produce a product, the investment in scripting will still pay off even if the initial cost is higher.

There is a build machine, actually a set of build machines in use, and this may not seem terribly different from the holy build machine that no one touches discussed in the beginning of this chapter. The details really make the difference in that Hudson is not based entirely on a magical build script produced by one member of the development staff. The form is standardized so that anyone can modify the build. Hudson is also event-oriented instead of timer-based so that work can flow during the day and give proper feedback. It also publishes the results of all project scans in a consistent location and form so that it is possible to move between individual artifacts without knowing the intricate details of each one.

Bug tracking

A necessary tool missing from the automation discussion so far is a way to enter, track, and close bugs. Bug-tracking software allows larger descriptions, screen shots, and a way to attach log files or other files to a bug report. This software must be able to produce reports of open bugs, bugs sorted by a development cycle target, or developer assignment along with other sorting and searching functionality.

All this documentation in the bug-tracking software helps remove voluminous comments from source code, helping source code remain source code and not degrade into large header comments detailing changes. In this way, a bug-tracking program, along with source control, helps keep the code clean; it does require discipline from developers to enter source control comments to tie the check-in to the bug report, which can be as simple as "Fixes bug #7023." It may seem like merely a footnote to use that check-in comment style, but remember that these comments are being published by the build server and become a reference for support and operations staff.

It is also important to note that a bug-tracking package is not a work order system. This is not the dumping grounds for the whiny pestering desires of some employee, and getting an entry into the bug-tracking system does not mean it will be fixed by close of business today. The bug-tracking system merely tracks defects; management and real thought are required to assign bugs an honest priority to be addressed during a development cycle or assigned to some future development cycle.

The bug-tracking software is also not appropriate to be customer facing. This is a development tool and will contain a lot of dirty laundry in that it shows all your defects. Keep the bug-tracking system internal, even if it means transferring data from a client-facing piece of software that may look surprisingly like a bug-tracking package on the surface. There are excellent programs that are used for communication to customers, and bug-tracking software is not one of them.

We currently suggest Bugzilla as a functional bug-tracking package. It meets all the requirements needed by this type of software without any large overhead of process enforced by the tool that may be counter to the rest of the process. There are no built-in gates or checkpoints and no built-in workflow, which is just fine, as following the six week cycle provides able workflow and process.

Communications

The growth in electronic communication tools has been amazing. Email, instant messaging (IM), and cell phones have given the ability to work from nearly anywhere, with the double-edged sword of the expectation that you will work from everywhere. Where it may be possible to jump on a quick call with a customer while taking your kids to the playground, it isn't possible to create software while driving. The advancements in communications provide real benefit for software development.

Instant messaging

Providing the ability to reach out and ask a question to another developer who may be outside of the office allows work to continue without stopping. A quick, "what's the object I need for the such-and-such API wrapper?" can be sent and a quick reply given. This is awesome, for it doesn't require that both are on the phone at the same time and allows for some level of expectation that the response may be slightly asynchronous.

Beware of using IMs for more than they were meant to be. Like email, instant messaging is not meant to be synchronous. Yes, IM technology may extend to mobile devices such as a BlackBerry, but this does not equate to an instant response. Use the tool for what it was meant to be used for; if you need an instant response, use a synchronous tool such as the telephone and be prepared that someone may not pick up on the other end.

Email

Email is excellent, for it is hoped that it forces the senders to think about what they are writing. It also allows documents to be attached.

· Understand that email is at its heart an asynchronous form of communication modeled after real physical postal systems. This seems silly to point out, but it is forgotten too often that it bears repeating. It is not a joke that emails are sent and then the sender storms into the office of the receiver, stating, with complete justification in their mind, that they sent the email 10 minutes ago and why haven't you responded? Honestly, if it's that important, get off your butt and walk over first.

So what is email good for in a software development shop running the six week cycle? Things such as scheduling time off in the calendar, meeting invitations, and notes for later (such as, "next cycle we need to do . . .") but nothing that needs an instant response.

Joke:

Tech support: Support line, how can I help you?
User: I just sent someone an email, how do I know if they got it?
TS: Did you set "notify on receipt"?
U: No.
TS: Then you can't know.
U: But when will they respond?
TS: (Long pause) Three days.

Wiki technology provides a lightweight method for jotting down quick notes to more complete documentation where anyone can edit, update, and make additions. Simple examples such as how to set up a development machine with links to the installation packages are huge time savers as a team grows. More complex examples may be laying out how a system is linked together. A wiki is online 24/7 and, by its very nature, is another asynchronous tool, but because all can see it, it eliminates the "passing notes in class" flavor of emails entirely.

Documentation tools

There are many tools that purport to document code, some by reverse engineering the code to create diagrams of class hierarchies or other artifacts. While these are sometimes very useful in exploring a new code base that was inherited, there are two problems with these tools: (1) they lie by almost always being out of date and (2) they require manual effort to produce value.

Some of these tools require one or two full-time administrators. Even with administrators, the benefit is small to zero to the organization as a whole. In a competitive marketplace, the cost of two full-time employees is better spent elsewhere if it can be avoided.

None of these tools is fast and automatic, requiring someone to execute the program to produce the models. Some may work within a code editor but are not automatable, whereas others can be at least scripted. Regardless, the pretty pictures from the demos never appear except in the simplest of projects and require someone to work with some other editor to line things up and have them make any kind of sense.

Compare this to unit tests, which not only validate the code they are testing, but also document, in a very real way, the code the unit tests are validating. The code of the unit test itself shows how to use the code it is testing and the interrelationships between the code being tested.

X-unit test frameworks

X-unit test frameworks are testing frameworks designed for testing software without human intervention. These are the tools that support a Test First approach, allowing the inputs and outputs to be defined before the code is written to actually transform the inputs into the outputs.

X-unit frameworks work in conjunction with other tools and by themselves are valuable only to a developer; however, coupled with continuous integration, a build server and code coverage tools provide an ongoing benefit to the teams and the company. Because x-unit tests may be run inside an editor, they are valuable to a developer refactoring or enhancing code because the developers may be sure that they haven't broken or disrupted existing functionality. Used with a continuous integration approach and an automated build server, x-unit tests are executed with every build, facilitating not only testing of existing functionality, but also serving as a communication tool between developers and even bullpens. When code coverage is enabled, x-unit test frameworks provide a method to measure coverage of code by the x-unit test.

One communication benefit of x-unit frameworks is that they document the code they are testing. Because each x-unit test must invoke the code it is testing, it shows the expected form of parameters into the invoked code. The statement of "look at the x-unit, it shows how to call it and what the results are" is extremely powerful as it tests and documents usage at the same time.

Another benefit of x-unit frameworks is that developers must actually invoke their code, which isn't to say that they wouldn't find some other method to fire up the code, but rather that they must actually assemble the parameters and invoke the code just as other developers who would use the code. This promotes smaller parameters lists (lowering complexity) and object orientation (enhancing reusability) and generally simpler interfaces (not GUI interfaces, APIs). It is common for the original form of a parameter set to a method to be discarded in favor of something much more easy to wire together with code, resulting in improved readability and maintainability.

Java development can use the open source JUnit package right off the shelf. The JUnit drops right into many preferred Java development tools, such as Eclipse, Maven, Cobertura, and Hudson, producing unit test checks with each build and metrics for code coverage.

Executable requirement integration test tools

Unit testing frameworks are one thing, but making sure all the parts work together is another. Unless your QA head count is bigger than your development head count, you will be unable to regression test your entire application every cycle for very long into your project. Certainly, you will have to wait until the end of the cycle to find out if adding your new feature broke your old one. A fully mature Six Week Solution team should be able to go to an automated process at the end of the cycle and know if they should or should not pay the bonus at a glance. The team should not have to wonder if they made it; it should be as cut and dried as possible. In order to measure the feature completeness of the cycle and know at all times that you have not gone backward in functionality or stability, you will need an executable requirements tool.

These tools walk a strange line between business and developers, as both are effectively users. An automated acceptance tool allows a requirement to be expressed in the form of a test case that can be read easily by a human. Natural language is generally a component. For example, Cucumber uses the "Behavior Driven Development" template for expressing these requirements in the form of "Given that . . . ," "When the user does . . . ," "_____ should happen."

FitNesse, another such tool, uses a wiki interface to describe the tests in a table-driven format so that they look like this:

WebsiteTrafficCounts		PaymentsSite	
From	To	PageLoads?	Visitors?
1/1/2010	2/1/2010	10	3
12/1/2009	1/1/2010	37	13 (7)

The result cells are colored red (dark gray), yellow (not shown), and green (light gray) to show pass, error, or fail.

Product management, security audits, and due diligence audits are just a few examples of when these types of tests might get widely read by the business.

Of course, so far, all we have described is a test plan repository. The difference with an executable requirements tool, obviously, is that we can run them. We can run a partial or complete set of those requirement statements as tests and get feedback on whether they pass, which ones, and how many, things along those lines. In order to do so, behind each of those tests, a piece of plumbing code is developed that is commonly called a fixture. The job of that code is to drive the application like the end user would and check the behavior to make sure that it is as expected. These fixtures are designed to be highly reusable so that hundreds of tests can be expressed and validated through a single fixture.

There is some debate about who should be writing these tests. It would be ideal for businesspeople to be able to write them to describe their desired behavior themselves, and many people strive to make that happen. However, creating these requirements so that the fixtures are reusable and resilient to product change is a skill that the business is unlikely to want to have to learn. Also, designing the tests to cover all the ins and outs of a feature is usually more detailed than businesspeople want to dive into. So, not surprisingly, we find it most effective to have QA professionals write these executable requirements. Generally, making them readable so that the business can verify the intension or consume the output is quite sufficient.

In terms of automation, these tests generally take much longer to run than unit tests, and therefore cannot be run constantly like unit tests. However, they should be run as often as they reasonably can so that the feedback on changes comes as soon as possible. It is relatively common for developers to keep a copy of the tool on their desktop so they can verify the impact of their changes on the tests before committing new work, but that does not tell them right away when integration of their work with someone else's is going to break something.

It is interesting to note that these requirements will generally start out broken (red or yellow) when they are first written. This is expected because you are presumably describing behavior that does not yet exist. Working to make those tests pass with new functionality is the goal.

Code coverage—Cobertura

Unit testing is great and allows changing software with confidence, reducing the dependency upon manual QA and increasing the effectiveness when manual QA is required. Like everything else, unit tests cannot be improved without measurement. A tool such as Cobertura provides the measurement point by tracking what lines of code in the original source are actually hit by the unit test. Visually seeing what branches of code are executed and tracking the percentage of coverage are both necessary to improve the quality and benefit of unit testing.

Cobertura, especially when embedded in an automated build tool such as Maven or Hudson, can produce reporting to show the percentage of coverage down to the individual file of source code along with pages annotating what line of code was hit by the unit tests. Seeing what code is not tested by unit testing highlights vulnerabilities in the code base and more often than not shows exactly where money is being spent maintaining an existing section of a software product. Tracking the slow erosion of profits through a lack of unit tests due to a manager or executive needing to get one more feature in quickly and a lack of discipline on the development team is the only way to find and plug the holes where money is leaking out of a software product.

It may be tempting to require 100% coverage at all times for every piece of software. A noble goal, but in reality may become like tilting at windmills instead of slaying the real dragons. While striving for 100% coverage, it should be recognized that at around 80% you start to reach a point of diminishing returns for items such as exception case testing and may require several multiples of testing code compared to the code that is being tested.

As is true in many projects, the last 20% of the work requires 80% of the time and resource investment. The goal is complete coverage; however, it may be necessary to compromise the goal with the realities of time to market when it is acceptable to bear the risk.

You can tell a craftsman by his toolbox.

Other Software Development Approaches

9

CHAPTER CONTENTS

Agile Development and Business Goals. DOI: 10.1016/B978-0-12-381520-0.00009-6

INTRODUCTION

A frequent frustration for business and programmers alike comes up very early when discussing any software process.

The question goes like this:

"I have good programmers and a business need. Why do I have to do anything except put them in a room and tell them to get to work?"

It is an important question; nobody wants to drag around a lot of extra administrative costs for no reason. So the real question is:

"What do I need from my development team and how do I get it?"

Delivery

Developing software is an enormous investment. Good programmers are not inexpensive, and systems of any size take a significant amount of time to develop and cost in infrastructure and manpower, whether you are an internal IT department with a big training and rollout budget to manage or a product shop with marketing schedules and sales requests to manage—the problems are the same. In short, software projects are too expensive to let fail, and yet it is estimated that 81% of all IT projects do exactly that. Failures of large software projects cast a long shadow on the few success stories.

Unlike digging a trench or stocking retail store shelves for an expected Christmas rush, it is not possible to simply add more human resources to make software projects finish sooner. All too frequently, the rush to get something out to market hits some blocking factor that causes a large chunk of refactoring. When a project begins to fail is not the point to add resources, for the explosion of jobs in IT and software development over the last few decades has done little to separate those who can from those who can't develop quality software. Endless TLA (Three-Letter Acronyms)-littered resumes were generated and presented, leaving the interviewer in worse shape than the interviewee. A successful delivery starts with the right resources at the beginning, not adding resources in desperation once the schedule is already slipping and the marketing department is whining about when they can actually ship the product.

It is a cliché, but it still holds true:

A successful software project needs to:

- build the right software
- build the software right

Build the right software

This failure point seems so obvious and yet is such a problem. If we don't build software that is what we actually need, we have failed. However, building software that is what we need is difficult. For one, the needs of the system are rarely as clear as expected at the beginning of a project. Software is frequently automating or replacing human effort, and humans excel at making vague decisions based on partial information, patterns of previous experience, and unexpected contextual information. Breaking down the decisions that a human makes to the degree that a computer can make exposes many surprising things:

- Poorly understood requirements
- Adapting business processes
- Changing needs over time of project
- Newly exposed opportunities

Build the software right

Let us be clear. You can do everything else right, everything we have talked about in this book, appear to have successfully completed all features and delivered every cycle, and still have your project fail in under six months due to internal forces. If your company clings to the idea that it is a consulting company ready to whip out anything in a spreadsheet instead of pushing features back into the main product, you have already lost.

Very quickly, a team can find themselves needing to add more and more people to try to get less and less done. An energetic culture can become fearful and resistant. A promising product can become a company-wide expletive. Building a quality project is a multifaceted effort, with some very visible and some very invisible. We give an overview of the measures and warning signs of each.

Building software right is all about getting the most value for your investment. Simply, we can say:

Net Feature Value = Value of a Feature − Feature Development Costs

Visibility and adaptation

From a business standpoint, a crucial component of a good software process is having visibility:

- Visibility into the development plan
- Visibility to see if things are on track or not
- Visibility to know that state of the application
- Visibility into the cost of what is being done

If a project is worth doing at all, it is presumably because it is bringing something of value to your business, and the business needs information to use to make use of that value effectively. Knowing when to send out a marketing release, to change plans due to delays, or to plan budgets with this new software is crucial.

At the same time, things change daily in business. New problems, new integrations, and new opportunities are endless, and the opportunities to change priorities of a project need to be balanced effectively between the opportunity to react to those changes and avoiding changing so much that nothing gets accomplished.

Now that we are pretty clear on what we want out of our team within a cycle, let's look at various software processes and how they can add or detract from those goals.

SIMPLIFIED EVOLUTION OF SOFTWARE PROCESSES

The software development industry has gone through an amazing amount of growth in the few short decades that it has existed. It seems doubtful that our industry has reached maturity, and yet already it is hard to go for five minutes without software somehow touching our lives. Our understanding of our field has evolved from being a branch of mathematics to an engineering discipline to a craft. We have traded theories and proofs for designs and manufacturing and those for skills and tools, and we have done it so quickly that almost every method of work along the way is still in use, and fervently advocated. Here we will walk through the basics of those methods with an eye for what they offer and what they lack in comparison to the Six Week Solution.

Each of these processes has many names and many forms, and each advocate will gladly espouse why their flavor is immune to the challenges of the breed. However, the true drivers from one breed to the next are fundamental dynamics of the industry. Understanding these fundamentals is crucial to anyone running, funding, or investing in software development. These fundamentals are not new. One of our favorite books on the fundamentals of software development is Fred Brook's *Mythical Man Month*, which is more than 35 years old now! However, how to take best advantage of those dynamics has been a perpetual learning process.

First industry driver: automation

Software is simply a way to automate a repetitive task so that it can be repeated with precision. The kinds of tasks we now automate have gotten so built upon each other that we can hardly see that this is all we do, but it is the first step and starts the first method of work.

Process version 0.0: man in a room

Every shop starts here, whether it is the 14-year-old writing Basic on his personal computer, HP starting in a garage, or that skunk works IT project brewing on the sidelines. It is a programmer, a machine, and a solution that need building. This is the root of the myth of the genius programmer. We do not mean "myth" here to mean something that is untrue, but in the sense that it is archetypal imagery of things fundamentally central to the business of software development. It brings images to mind of Dave Packard and Bill Hewlett in their garage or "the two Steves" crafting Apple I.

Philosophically, creating software this way is considered essentially a mathematical exercise. The numerical models and algorithms that form the basis for computer science are deeply mathematical and are still taught primarily by university math departments to this day.

What to take from this

It is fascinating to watch many projects go from this kind of optimistic, encouraging view of developing software to Dilbert-esk drudgery of time clock-punching cubical gofers far more interested in how the break room is stocked than the hopes of the company.

These very dynamic "man in the room" projects are characterized by several factors that should be nurtured on all software projects. First, these projects exert an energy and initiative to overcome any hurdles that present themselves. Blocks to progress are simply not accepted at any point, they are eliminated moment-to-moment as a matter of routine. Second, the team tests the limits of their tools and abilities with "out of the box," creative, inventive problem solving. If necessity is the mother of invention, then she is the "office mom" of these shops. Finally, these shops have a clear vision of what they are trying to accomplish. A small-sized team and limited other resources force these projects to know exactly what problem they are trying to solve and refuse to invest in tempting sidetracks along their pursuit of them.

What to leave behind

On the flip side, there are things that come with this model that are not so beneficial. For example, these teams are commonly very insular. The same vision and focus that keep them moving forward often prevent them from forming deeply collaborative relationships with other stakeholders. This often functions when led by someone with enough vision to create a compelling project, but even then, it frequently misses significant key opportunities by not fully engaging the end user or the marketing folks or not fully understanding the support burden, etc. Projects like this are also commonly plagued by a serious lack of discipline in software development. Crucial quality practices, such as test automation, test-driven development, and continuous refactoring, to name a few, are often dropped. The Portland Patterns Repository (http://c2.com/cgi/wiki?CodeAndFix) is "one year of slamming code, one year of debugging." The motivations are relatively obvious. Getting to a paycheck as fast as possible is seen as more important. Unfortunately, this is trading off a project that makes steady, solid progress for one starting off with a huge pile of technical debt that is likely to be far harder to pay off than, for example, venture capital seed money. This does not seem so risky at first because the scope is small and the gap is easier to cover, but it builds quickly as the project progresses. This scenario is one example of the next big problem that comes with this model that is not so beneficial, which is a gambling mentality. Starting a new software project can feel like a risky endeavor in any environment. As discussed earlier, there are a large number of unknowns to be managed. It is pretty common on projects such as this to find people who are addicted to the risks. Rather than managing the unknowns, they gleefully jump off one cliff after another, enjoying the thrill and the feeling of triumph when they wrestle success from each turn. To quote common public service announcements in Las Vegas: "Please gamble responsibly."

Next driver: complexity

The best "man in a room" projects eventually outgrow this model. The product becomes increasingly complex, core components need increasingly diverse supplemental pieces to support it, and more people need to be brought in to enhance, support, and sell it. As team and product size increase, scaling becomes an issue. Product pieces seem to "not gel" so well, reliability goes down, user trust goes down, maintenance becomes increasingly expensive, and development schedules become increasingly unreliable. Simply put, the complexity of the project outgrows what can be managed in the head of a few "geniuses."

Process version 1: analyze, design, code, test, and maintain

Alright, things are getting too complex, so we need to put some structure around things, right? It's time to plan the work and work the plan. We will break things down into phases, plan out how long each of these phases is going to take, maybe build a few Gantt charts, and we should be all set. First, let us sit down and analyze what we are trying to do. That way, we can get some definition around our goals and make sure that everyone is on the same page. We can get that all documented, everyone can go through it and make sure that we are working on what we think we are working on, and then we will be ready to move forward.

Quite often in almost any process, this step goes on forever. After all, the idea behind the analysis phase is to make sure that we know everything that we need to design the right solution. Because it is impossible to know every detail that you need to know in advance in order to make sure you can create the perfect design, analysis stretches on indefinitely, fueled by a fear of missing something, by the inability to reconcile seemingly conflicting goals, or by a million other details that just cannot seem to get nailed down.

This phenomenon is called *analysis paralysis*, and though it evokes a particular dread from developers who see nothing but endless meetings where they never get to actually build anything, it should fill management with even worse feelings. The reason is that, at the end, we finally finish—well, that probably is not true. We never actually finish, we just decide to quit spending time on it and to move forward with what we have. However, when we do decide to move on, what we have to show for all of the time and effort expended at this stage is a nice fat document. Estimated street value: –$5 for recycling service.

Next, the developers can sit down and design the solution. They can get a good, big picture take on how to structure the application so that things do not get quite so messy, document it all up, and make sure that everyone has the chance to go over that and see if it looks right. We can use some visual dictionary, such as the Unified Modeling Language, to make it something everyone can understand.

Once we have the right design in place, the developers can sit down and just crank out the code. After all, the hard work should be done now, and now it is just filling in the details.

Now we can test to make sure that we hit all the requirements from our initial analysis (I knew that document would come in handy!), patch up anything that does not look right, and then push it into production.

Now, just patch any issues that come up and go. In our experience, the majority of software teams are at about Process ½.

What to take from this

Software is complex. It starts complex, it dallies in the area of being more complex than the most complex physical engineering projects, and then it spikes deep into the realm of ridiculously complex. Getting "genius" developers is far from enough to make a project successful. Organization and development practices at every level are crucial.

What to leave behind

Most of it. Breaking development into these types of phases is the result of manufacturing models where changing from one step to another has high costs. In manufacturing, we have to design before we build because it is expensive to change our mind after we start building. In a simple example, if I am building a wooden box, it stinks to decide it needs to be bigger *after* I have cut the sides down to a smaller size. Now I have to go get new boards. Done correctly, that is *not* true in software, which has no manufacturing costs in that sense, so these phases introduce more problems than they solve.

Next driver: quality

When developing this model, many things still can and do go wrong. It is shocking how often people can read a single document and take away a different understanding of the contents. Natural languages such as English are ambiguous that way. Developers are frequently complaining that their glorious designs are being corrupted by changing requests, and, while the code is less fragile at first, it seems to get shakier every time we touch it. What are we to do? More of the same stuff that got us a little bit of gain so far. Naturally. (See our glossary for the definition of insanity... :-)

Process version 2: waterfall

Welcome to the happy world of processes such as ISO 9001, which are standardized processes for quality control. These have long been the darlings of the manufacturing world, and here we bring all the experience of these processes to bear on the software problem. This is the view that building software should grow from a field of mathematics to be approached as an engineering discipline, with all of the tools that are tried and true for engineering. It is interesting that this is a common view of building software and waterfall processes still have common application. At the time of this writing, searching Google for "waterfall software" brought up pages panning and spoofing this concept at about half of its links. Unfortunately, it is a safe-seeming, easily understandable process that gives a strong illusion of control, and therefore still happens with frightening regularity. Generally, a waterfall revolves around the idea of phases and gates. Figure 9.1 shows a modified waterfall.

Here we show a box for each phase of the project. We are adding a bunch of new phases to make sure that we get all of the parts right. We will do a high-level, architectural design and a detailed design. We will add some prototyping phases so we can try to spot more bad ideas earlier. At the end of each phase is a "gate." A gate is the place where the work for that phase is quality checked

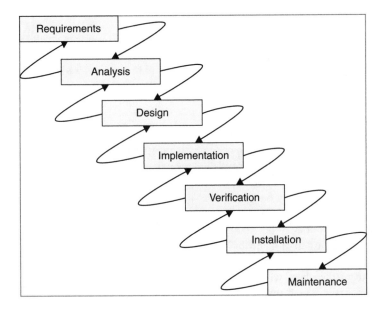

FIGURE 9.1

Modified waterfall process.

ID	Task Name	Start	Finish	Duration	Feb 2010				Mar 2010	
					1/31	2/7	2/14	2/21	2/28	3/7
1	Task 1	1/29/2010	2/4/2010	5d	▩					
2	Task 2	2/5/2010	2/16/2010	8d		▩▩				
3	Task 3	2/5/2010	2/12/2010	6d		▩				
4	Task 4	2/17/2010	2/25/2010	7d				▩		
5	Task 5	2/26/2010	3/4/2010	5d					▩	

FIGURE 9.2

Sample Gantt chart.

and authorized as an input into the next phase. Frequently, these gates are viewed as contractual commitments. By signing off on the decisions made during the phase, stakeholders surrender their ability to make changes later on. Presumably, all factors have been considered and been agreed upon. The modified waterfall attempts to account for finding unexpected problems downstream by providing a mechanisms to return to earlier phases when necessary. For example, if implementation discovers shortcomings in the design, that information can be used to feed back into the design phase for reevaluation. Unfortunately, at this point, there is generally a big Gantt chart with a fixed deadline that is not particularly thrilled with the slip involved with such a step. (For a sample of the famous Gantt chart, see Figure 9.2.)

These projects can span impressively long stretches of time. It is particularly common in large manufacturing organizations such as defense contractors and telecom manufacturers to go to extremes with gates, contracts at gates, and tiny phases for projects that are planned to go for *years*. These projects spend months and sometimes years with nothing delivered except exhaustive documentation. Generally, because the time tables have been fixed very early on, adaptations in requirements or planning are firmly resisted. These projects are the easiest to fall into the death march pattern.

The typical death march cycle starts with a deadline that "cannot be missed" and a scope where everything "has to all be done." When it becomes clear that that task cannot be accomplished, the team is expected to work nights and weekends indefinitely to change that fact. We discuss elsewhere why that fails, but it does. The deadline comes, it goes, and then new deadlines are set (hopefully). Unfortunately, those are generally based on what people want to hear, so the "extra two weeks" the team is given to continue living 24/7 at work comes and goes, and then repeats.

Of course, even when "done," the quality has degraded enough that the cycle continues with adding Band-Aids and patches to try and hold the mess together. Eventually, it is "stable enough." Completely unmaintainable, of course, but the political pressure has now exceeded the defect danger, so it ships. Any team members who are still there take sick days (they cannot take vacation, the project needs them, after all) so that they can send out resumes, which is smart because, sooner or later, the project gets shut down. The users will not actually use the system because what they needed has changed since the project started two years ago, because what they needed was lost along the way, or because the system is too unstable to trust.

What to take from this

It is very important to understand the waterfall model because the concepts involved in it show up in almost every software project. The moment that quality is down, people will suggest phases and gates, even the developers. This extreme (and sadly far too common) model shows in its extremity that the dynamics of software development are fundamentally different than the dynamics of manufacturing. Nearly every process improvement after this is an attempt to learn how to work effectively with the dynamics of software development, evolving now into the Six Week Solution, and undoubtedly will continue to evolve from here.

What to leave behind

Leave behind phases because software can live without them. Some would argue that the phases still exist, but all of them are gotten through in minutes rather than years. We will leave that to the theorists to debate ad nauseum, but the point is, software does not need and cannot afford that kind of overhead. Our time from concept to production should be ridiculously short, which is what people mean by "Internet time" and while it is not instantaneous we already have the means to shorten it enormously.

Next driver: risk

Many other books, articles, and websites have been written on bad waterfall projects. Low estimates for failure rates are around 50%, and high ones exist above 80%. Those kinds of failure rates have given software development a reputation as a highly risky proposition, which it can be. Therefore, it is not surprising that the next steps in software process evolution were all about managing risk.

Spiral development traps

We cannot invest two years and more into software and not know that we are going to get our investment back out of it. No companies can afford that, few can survive it. Spiral life cycles are the next evolution to attempt to tackle that risk. It really only introduces one tool, but it is essential to software development and to the Six Week Solution. That tool is *iteration*. The core concept says that rather than trying to do a waterfall for the entire project, we should break the project into smaller pieces and then go through the waterfall multiple times. For example, rather than attempting to create an entirely new payroll system for your firm in one long project, break it into smaller pieces such as check printing, timecard management, and so on. Then we take the *riskiest* of those pieces and work it through the waterfall for a shorter time, generally something like six months. At the end of those six months, either the risks have been mitigated or the roadblocks are well understood. Then, the business has the opportunity to evaluate the deliverables and either authorize another iteration or cancel the project as appropriate.

Spiral processes get a little more diversified than the previous life cycle models. The methodology wars of the 1980s and 1990s spawned many versions of these processes so generalized statements are a little shaky. Speaking generally, a central attribute of most spiral life cycles is ordering pieces of the project from highest to lowest risk. (See Figure 9.3 for a graphical representation of spiral development.) In reaction to the failure rate of software projects, the goal was to identify projects that will fail as soon as possible to reduce wasted investment.

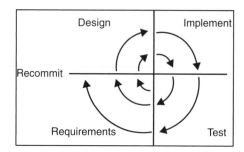

FIGURE 9.3

Spiral development.

The best in breed for this life cycle model is the Rational Unified Process (RUP), originally labeled the Unified Software Development Process. This process was developed in the late 1990s at Rational Software Corporation when three of the most influential thought leaders in the area of software process came together in an attempt to merge each of their processes into a common process and graphical representation of software modeling. The results were mixed but generally idealized for the marketing benefit of Rational Software Corporation. Marketing hype or not, RUP is considered by many to be the pinnacle of the spiral life cycle processes.

The RUP presents a large, complex set of tools for running a software process. Unfortunately, to the unfair criticism of RUP, many shops implementing RUP follow the vein of the waterfall process failures, turn each tool into a requirement, and bloat their project terribly with unnecessary documents, models, and more gates and phases.

What to take from this

Iteration is absolutely essential to software development, and its adoption begins to show where the dynamics of software construction and manufacturing diverge. The commitment barrier between iterations provides business crucial opportunities to manage their investment in a development effort by evaluating whether a project is making tangible progress. These concepts can and will be leveraged to greater degrees. It is also noteworthy, as we move into Agile as the next process model, that Rational has offered RUP with integration to at least one popular Agile process.

What to leave behind

The spiral life cycle, in its best forms, has its roots in a fear-based view of software development. The structures are built around identifying risks to the project and how to combat them. While that is always a worthwhile activity, it takes the focus off of the crucial goals of your project. The goal of the project is not to self-protectively keep itself going, but to meet the business needs that created it in the first place. A project that is canceled after one six month iteration because the risks tackled were insurmountable is better than a two year project that failed, but is still a project that took six months of human and capital investment to not succeed.

Also, the spiral is also still deeply rooted in the phased structure of the waterfall model. It brings far too many manufacturing assumptions and overhead into the software process, very noticeably in the separation of the development phase and the maintenance phase of the software life cycle.

For manufacturing, those are clearly delineated activities. There is a world of difference between designing and building a car and owning and maintaining one. However, there is no functional difference between building software and maintaining it. A new feature request and a bug fix are the same activity. Open up the code, change the structure so that it behaves differently, close it back up, and deploy it. That difference changes everything.

Next driver: steering

Six month miniwaterfalls do not respond fast enough. Opportunities in business come daily, not yearly. Unknowns in the development process get filled moment to moment. Competitive threats pop up unexpectedly and inconveniently. We need to be able to adapt our efforts to the best, most important efforts we can as fast as we can. We need to miss road cones, take necessary detours and shortcuts, and pass slow drivers on the way. In short, we need to be able to steer our projects constantly.

Agile

Agile software processes frequently cite the long history of arms escalation. The most powerful weapons technologies went back and forth between slow, heavy, defensive armor and fast, light, offensive weapons. Shield walls give way to cavalry, which then develop into knights in "shining armor," which are then eradicated by guerrillas with crossbows that can penetrate the knightly armor. The analogy is that the previous processes were slow, heavy, and defensive, but Agile focuses on, well, agility. That is to say, on fast moving, highly responsive, aggressive efforts. We cannot have 80% of our development work be overhead, and we cannot be months and years down the road before we have something of value, regardless of the risks. The difficulty in combating the defensive postures of the preceding processes is enough that one popular Agile process actually lists courage as a core principle.

Prioritizing business value vs risk managements

The flip side, the aggressively pursued goal, is to deliver value as soon as possible, as often as possible. As opposed to risk-based prioritization of the spiral life cycle, Agile prioritizes the business value of the pieces being developed. Instead of eliminating risk after risk to get to a final whole product, Agile grows a product starting on day one by targeting the number one most valuable feature that the business needs and building and delivering it as soon as it can show value. When a spiral may take the first iteration to eliminate three or four threats that may threaten your project down the road, an Agile process has already delivered the most valuable features it could for you to start getting a return on your investment in development as soon as possible.

For an example, let us compare two projects. Project A prioritized their riskiest features first. Those risks were managed adequately, earning the project the green light to continue. The next round of development, then, picked the next most risky things and implemented them, showing that those slightly lower risks were also not going to block the project. Features were delivered, everyone gained confidence that the project could succeed, and development continued. The critical mass of features necessary to earn returns on the investment in development was somewhat delayed because some easy but crucial features had to wait.

In contrast, project B prioritized their most valuable features first. They hit the critical mass of core features early on, and the product was able to go live with a limited set of functionality that was valuable enough to begin gaining customers.

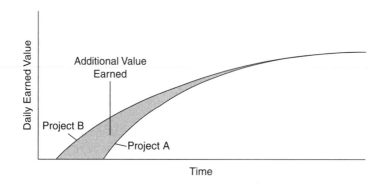

FIGURE 9.4

Earned value—the difference between project A and project B.

The project B development team started paying their own way much earlier than the project A team, reducing the risk of the project by early offsets of development costs, and overall earning the business more money. It is probably obvious at this point that the authors favor a value-based prioritization of development goals. (See the additional value earned between project A and project B represented graphically in Figure 9.4.)

Because the project B team delivered value that could be delivered to a customer, the software was able to begin earning value much sooner than the project A team. If the project was used internally, our value-conscious colleagues on project B quickly have high-value features ready to start providing a return on our investment into development to date, whereas our risk-adverse friends on project A are likely still not ready to start delivery high-value features. While it may not have been the entire solution, the project B approach delivered a savings possibly months or more before project A.

Iteration, though, has an even more dramatic redefinition than that in Agile development. We are not talking about six months, we are talking about weeks, days, and minutes. In the most naïve case, the waterfall is run through in a matter of minutes for changes cut down that small, and then organized finely. In less naïve cases, the whole model is eliminated by a set of co-occurring practices. The shift is profound, and important, from an engineer's process to a craftsman's discipline.

To accomplish this, the process of developing software has to be lightened considerably. Phases and gates are replaced by practices and methods of work that perform consistently. Practitioners create and share catalogues of common structures and solutions to coding problems. They build whole new classes of tooling to increase consistency and to speed and simplify their efforts. They discover what areas can be made more efficient by collaboration, and they draw shamelessly from any and every successful field for any trick, technique, or thought process that can move things along smoothly. These new craftsmen take great pride in their work and have the luxury of knowing that while they may not always be building all the features to make a product a Cadillac, they still need to build it as well as can possibly be done because that quality immediately impacts their ability to continue tomorrow.

The core principles of Agile processes are summed up in the Agile Manifesto. The Agile Manifesto is a statement of values created at a meeting of the creators of a dozen different Agile processes where they tried to express the fundamentals that linked all of their processes together.

Manifesto for Agile Software Development

We are uncovering better ways of developing software by doing it and helping others do it.
Through this work we have come to value:

- Individuals and interactions over processes and tools
- Working software over comprehensive documentation
- Customer collaboration over contract negotiation
- Responding to change over following a plan

That is, while there is value in the items on the right, we value the items on the left more.

www.agilemanifesto.org

The manifesto was later extended on as the role of the developer came more into focus. The addition is called the Software Craftsmanship Manifesto and, as you can see, it extends very directly from the Agile Manifesto.

As aspiring Software Craftsmen we are raising the bar of professional software development by practicing it and helping others learn the craft. Through this work we have come to value:

- Not only working software, but also well-crafted software
- Not only responding to change, but also steadily adding value
- Not only individuals and interactions, but also a community of professionals
- Not only customer collaboration, but also productive partnerships

That is, in pursuit of the items on the left we have found the items on the right to be indispensable.

http://manifesto.softwarecraftsmanship.org/

As a result of these values, these processes look quite differently at things such as team organization and culture, project planning, and best practices. Many of these changes appear at first to be at too low of a level to direct a software project, especially since they are so different from the linear, sequential modes of project planning that we are more comfortable with. However, they form a web of interdependent practices that fit together like the cogs in a Swiss watch to create a system that just keeps on ticking.

Each of the different Agile processes brought a different piece to the puzzle. They also stole shamelessly from each other and blurred the lines between each other. Because these are considered to be the current, cutting-edge processes, we will discuss three popular forms more in depth to discuss their contributions to the Agile process shift.

Scrum

Scrum gets a lot of credit as one of the earliest Agile software processes and the one that helped make Agile mainstream. Taking a lot from innovations in lean manufacturing methodologies, it was named scrum after the rugby term to emphasize that building software is a messy process. The assertion is that most processes hide the mess behind an illusion of control, whereas scrum exposes it so that it can be managed. Scrum emphasizes project management that fixes delivery date and manages scope in a similar manner to what we describe here. It does not speak at all to the development practices necessary to support the planning process, but rather assumes that the team will fumble its way to the necessary pieces. Despite those missing pieces, scrum remains popular and its planning practices have impacted essentially every Agile process.

Like most Agile processes, scrum carries as many cultural norms as explicit practices. Like the sport the name evokes, scrum teams are intended to be run very aggressively. Some of that comes out in the divisive analogy of "chickens and pigs" based on the idea of a joke where a chicken asks a pig to help him start a restaurant that serves ham and eggs. The pig naturally declines, stating "I'd be committed, but you would only be involved." The analogy is that some roles are not invested in the process to the degree that the development team is.

As Extreme Programming (XP) picked up popularity, it also made businesses very nervous. The name evoked images of flannel-wearing snowboarders jumping off cliffs, and it went against so many things people "knew" were right that businesses looking at cutting-edge processes were looking for something that felt safer. Scrum let the development changes be quietly implied and busily sold businesses on the benefits Agility offered them. It also added an impression of respectability and comfort by offering certifications for various roles. Businesses that already felt they were taking risks out on the bleeding edge got to feel like they had some degree of a safety net by leaning on those certifications. Whether or not the certification actually provided anything but resume fodder remains a hotly debated topic.

Extreme programming

Extreme Programming (XP) is an interlocking set of development disciplines (or practices) and values developed initially by Kent Beck with a simple underlying idea. The idea was that if we know that something is good for developing software, what if we took that thing to its logical extreme? For example, if we know that tests help us make better software, what if we test everything, all the time?

Ten years after its public introduction, extreme programming still often causes discomfort in business circles, despite its adoption by companies from start-ups up to Fortune 100 companies such as Qwest. Perhaps the name draws up too many visions of back-flipping snowboarders typing away on laptops on the chairlift. Kent Beck said that he hoped that, in the future, no one would talk about the name XP anymore because it would just be how good software is developed. XP has not fallen too far short of that mark. It introduced many concepts that have become common industry practice. The planning concepts are largely compatible with the six week cycle, and the development practices are highly recommended and complement the six week cycle. XP advocates similar technical disciplines as the Six Week Solution, such as Test Driven Development, Pair Programming, and Continuous Integration, to name a few. A couple noteworthy specifics follow.

The planning game

In XP terms, the cycle would be a release plan and would be looking for iterations inside of that release plan. The two most obvious options are to run two, two week iterations with additional weeks for kickoff and test or six, one week iterations. Having two week iterations nicely divides up the development time in a cycle and gives a natural break at Mea Culpa to evaluate progress and adapt accordingly. However, it is probably a better fit to take one week iterations within the six week plan. In a textbook XP shop, there would not be a need for a planning week or a testing week, as planning would be done in manageable bites as you go and testing would take place all the time, which actually can work extremely well. Where it often breaks down, however, is when scaling up the development organization.

The typical model for scaling XP beyond 12–15 people is to try to form a "team of teams," collaborating the teams together as much as possible in the same ways that individuals inside the teams collaborate. That is actually quite difficult because the number of channels of communication becomes demonstrably more difficult to manage and, in practice, most teams of teams end up with the need for more structured coordination, integration, and hardening phases, just as recommended by the Six Week Solution.

The other advantage of one week iterations is that it makes better use of the XP planning principle called "Yesterday's Weather." The idea is to measure the effort that development requires rather than the time it took and then use that measurement as a planning tool, assuming that a team will do this iteration approximately how they did the last one. Using the one week iteration model, a team has two data points on their progress to use to evaluate their status at Mea Culpa, where as two week iterations would only provide one.

Collocated team

Extreme Programming emphasizes collocation of your team and includes your business in this description. When separated by geography, the speed and richness of communication are hampered greatly and make it far too easy for a project to drift off course without anyone noticing the details of it.

It is currently in vogue that some companies have many remote or work-from-home employees. In many instances, this is a very good economic decision, as it could locate an employee in the same city and even the same office as a customer or reduces the need for office space. With the proper investment in infrastructure, remote employees may be a very good idea indeed. However, when developing software, the need for an on-site customer is huge, for there is no other way for a question to be answered quickly, with all the nuances of face-to-face communication. For this reason, we highly suggest that a product management position exist to fulfill this need in the Six Week Solution's bullpen structure. The project management role has the responsibility to communicate with remote users, understand the needs, and bring that feedback directly back to the developers. In a perfect setup, the customer would be on-site, but the realities of many shops drive the need for the product manager role.

XP drawbacks

Sadly, despite many advantages, XP causes many people in the industry some disquiet. For some, it stems from resistance to the overly exuberant zeal of the initial converts. For some, it was too contradictory to many of the accepted standards that came before it. Most of the concrete complaints revolve around the point that because XP provides such fine-grained control, it takes much more work to steer it and keep it on track. One way this is true is that the customer or product manager has much more fine-grained detail to manage because features are broken down to very fine detail. The benefit of this is the ability to make some very detailed prioritization decisions. Another way XP teams can be hard to steer is that they can change directions on a dime, which sounds great, but it is not an uncommon mistake for the customer to steer the team in circles for lack of long-term vision.

Just as you must hire developers with a critical eye toward the end result, the rest of the company has to play by the same rules. It is not atypical to find marketing engaged so fully in trade shows and sales support that they simply refuse to function on any type of schedule. This "seagull management" (flying in, making a lot of noise, and then flying off again) disrupts the development rhythm and costs far more than it would have cost if the proper entry gates are used. Further, the inability of the birds to properly prioritize strategic goals over moment-to-moment tactical desires has a ripple effect in software that increases the cost to add new features as well as maintain the existing code base. Short-term goals are met at the detriment of long-term success.

Lean software development

This process stays as close as possible to applying the "just in time" manufacturing models popularized by Japanese auto manufacturers to software development. As you would expect from such strong manufacturing roots, it quite rightly emphasizes cutting waste by looking hard at every part of the development process and eliminating anything that does not provide tangible value. It has a strong emphasis on localized autonomy so that each developer can "stop the line," so to speak, when they see that something is going wrong or to fix problems as they see them. Focusing on testing, delaying decision making, and making process improvement a regular part of the process are also key components.

A very useful concept in lean development applies in particular to the Six Week Solution, which is the concept of measuring and minimizing the time between concept and delivery. While many technical aspects of the Six Week Solution are focused on keeping development moving forward, this life cycle also emphasizes the business components such as managing downstream bottlenecks, including documentation, marketing messaging, the end user acceptance process, delivery mechanisms, and training processes. The pace at which the business can absorb a new release or get concepts and feedback to the development team is very important for getting the maximum benefit out of the Six Week Solution.

What to take from Agile

Software development has become a craft where the diligent disciplines of skilled craftsmen are far more efficient and effective than high ceremony quality controls. Establishing a measured regular rhythm of work and focusing on fundamental practices will keep you moving forward smoothly, and most "controls" added on top will impair your project.

What to leave behind

The paradigm shift of Agile development has also come with a culture that often collaborates poorly with the business it is serving. Agile teams often focus on values such as self-organizing teams. The idea is one of decentralized control that gives teams the power to apply their best professional judgment to make the best decisions.

Next driver: the loose customer link

Agile processes pushed off many responsibilities on the customer or business with little direction on how to handle them. The business is responsible for creating a structure and direction for the workload that is given to the development team and put very little structure around that because it is the business's problem. On the one hand, this makes a great deal of sense because the business understands the value of what is being asked for far better than the programmers do, so it is a good alignment of responsibilities. On the other hand, this creates a divide between "sides." This, again, is understood, and there have been various efforts to address it, such as the practice of having an "on-site customer" or a "whole team" view, which attempts to make the business part of the development team. This is necessary, and we encourage these practices. However, that still leaves the development team independent, serving the business, but not part of it. In a bizarre reversal of the scrum's "pigs and chickens" argument, the developers get detached easily from being invested in the impact of their work to the business. If they do not deliver a feature in their time box, well, we just readjust the velocity measurements and try again next iteration. The developers often do not feel the impact of such shifts of schedule on the rest of the business.

This brings us up to the Six Week Solution, which seeks to pull together our best necessary development practices with a tightly wound investment into the needs of the business.

Risks with Using This Approach

10

CHAPTER CONTENTS

Agile Development and Business Goals. DOI: 10.1016/B978-0-12-381520-0.00010-2

INTRODUCTION

No method is foolproof, and no process exists without some risks. The Six Week Solution is no exception. This chapter discusses the following types of risks:

- Small risks
- Large risks
- Things that appear to be risks but actually are not
- Things that do not appear to be risks but are actually potential landmines

We discuss the risks in detail, explain why sometimes what appears to be a risk is not one, and, if it is one, provide methods of mitigating it.

WORKPLACE CHALLENGES

Risk: personality issues

With all the emphasis on committing to very specific deliverable items, the workplace for the Six Week Solution might seem scary enough. But there are more problems: in addition to not having a cube to hide out in and signing a document stating what you will produce for the next six weeks, the staff has to deal with other personalities without any barriers.

Wallflowers

Throughout the process, it should be clear that wallflowers shrink to the sidelines and these are not the resources that excel in an open and driven environment.

Aggressive personalities

Stronger personalities don't mind flying their own personal freak flag. Not illegal or demented freak flags, but don't be surprised if you see evidence of extracurricular activities posted for all to see on the walls.

This may seem extreme and unpleasant for an office. Nonetheless, keep in mind that you are not trying to hire clones of yourself; you want intelligent, thinking, and stimulated individuals. Don't attempt to control the minds of your star performers; let them run and see what happens. The cross-pollination of ideas can challenge some, and others will thrive in the marketplace of ideas. What may seem like a discussion about tweaking a carburetor is really a discussion about an analog computer taking its input from a vacuum produced by an engine.

War Story: Restoring a Plane

Two developers in our office get along wonderfully and disagree on as much as they agree upon. One day the morning coffee discussion had nothing to do with coding (not uncommon) and revolved around the idea of restoring an old woodworking plane that was rusty and neglected but still had lots of quality life left if given a little TLC. The second developer suggested Naval Jelly to remove the rust, pretty nasty stuff but it does the job well on steel and gets the job done quickly. Then the first wanted to put a finish on it that would resist rusting and not be paint, which would flake away with use, and the second suggested cold blue, which is used in touch up and restoration of firearms for exactly the same reason.

What were they discussing? Not coding, but at a different level applying the same skills used in the development of software: using knowledge from outside software development and applying that knowledge. This ability to collate abstract sources of information and apply them to the project at hand is the skill that is needed in the bullpens, not five years of writing code to move a byte from here to there in the language du jour. So what if they spent 10 minutes discussing the difference between FeO_2 (rust) and FeO_3 (blue)?

There is a joke among developers that goes like this:

Manager (upon spotting a developer with his feet up on his desk and arms folded behind his head): "What are you doing?"
Developer: "Thinking."
Manager: "Can't you do that on your own time?"
No, the developer can't. This is what they are being paid to do: think.

WORK ENVIRONMENT

The work environment is a critical component of the Six Week Solution. Developers are no different from any other worker in any other industry or any other time—there are some things that are very important to them (and other things they don't care much about). Also, to optimize the Six Week Solution, consider the workplace ideas discussed in this chapter.

Risk: no offices

The fact that an individual cannot hide in a cube whiling away the hours until it is time to go home may make the work environment stressful to some, which is not a bad thing. The idea that anyone can see what you are doing at any time is a sure-fire formula to either freak people out or force them to realize that they must proceed with care. It's easy to spot the confidence in this environment. Sure they'll check their personal email during the day, and if they weren't getting work done, that might be a problem but the fact is that tons of work is getting done otherwise they'll miss a cycle commitment.

WHY THIS IS NOT A RISK

This openness flows in both directions:

- To conscientious developers, they are working toward goals both near and short term. They are so focused on the goals that there is nothing to hide and no need to sit in an enclosed cube.
- It is only individuals who are concerned about something other than work that need a private cube to hide the fact that they are doing something other than spending time doing what they are getting paid for, which is work.

Risk: noise level

One consideration is the noise level of the open bullpen environment. To some individuals, this is a huge distraction; overhearing conversations disrupts their work. This problem can be solved in a variety of ways: often headphones are enough. But sometimes headphones are *not* enough. To help minimize these risks, the cry room and meeting rooms must be used.

How to mitigate this risk: cry room

There are times when a person talking on a phone is disruptive. For these times, there exists the relief value of the "cry room." Often misunderstood at first ("Do we have to work so hard we need some-place to go and cry?" was actually asked by a prospective employee), the concept is embraced quickly: it is a place to go and have a phone conversation away from your desk.

The origin of the term "cry room" goes back to churches that had an area for families with crying infants to be taken to that was insulated from the main congregation. These rooms typically had a window and speakers to allow members to still participate in the service, but the noise from a crying infant did not escape the room to disturb the congregation. Creating this space in your Six Week Solution bullpen allows personal conversations to be personal.

Reaction to the cry room from outsiders to the Six Week Solution is that it provides a location where things other than work are done (such as a contractor lining up the next gig). Experience from actual practice is that this does not happen. Individuals would much rather be at their desks or take brief visits to the cry room. Additionally, contractors blatantly disrespectful of the current employer to line up future gigs at their desk in the bullpen are brazen enough to do something like that even when sitting directly in front of the boss. Again, those worthy of trust do not abuse it but respect the shared resource for all and use the cry room space only briefly.

How to mitigate this risk: meeting rooms

It's a common practice to have phone meetings with distributed employees or customers. Often, these meetings are also webcast, to share a desktop, walk through a PowerPoint presentation, or project schedule. While it is possible to take these types of calls at a desk, speakerphones are a horrible idea in the bullpen. Additionally, it's typically not only one member of the bullpen involved in a conference call. To help remove the noise from the bullpen, create shared meeting room space complete with a quality duplexed speakerphone and a quality projector. Make these resources easily accessible to use on a moment's notice, with minimal overhead for checking out or reserving projectors. With no administrative overhead to use such a room, there is no barrier to adopting the practice of simply walking in, firing up the projector, and dialing the phone to have a meeting.

Why this is not a risk: the rhythm of the noise level

Beyond personal interactions, though, there is also a rhythm to the noise level throughout the day:

- Early in the morning—between the start of the day and the stand-up meeting—the noise level can get elevated.
- After stand-up, it typically quiets down to a low mumble.
- Preparation for lunch time ("Hey dude, where we going for lunch today?") is another spike in the noise level.

- Midafternoon is typically the time you can hear a mouse crawling in the ceiling.
- Finally, it should be expected that there is another time when the ambient noise rises around 4:30–5 pm, but the bullpens quickly revert to the level of a library.

Once the natural rhythm is understood by everyone, work flows around the natural disturbances.

Risk: if you mismanage any aspect of the Six Week Solution, you are going to have to lie to developers

Most developers have a pretty good B.S. detector, which makes perfect sense since they must work in a logical world, so they are geared to think in this manner. If they hear one story one day and another "spin" on the story a few days later, you can be assured that the B.S. detector went off in their head. This is especially true when dealing with technology, but don't downplay the importance of interpersonal items when talking to developers. If you are condescending, they will pick up on it quickly.

If Mea Culpa is being used to redirect teams instead of making minor course corrections, you are going to have to lie to the developers and lie to cover the fact that you weren't doing your job as a manager and looking far enough into the future, which is not to say that some customer hasn't exploded and you need all hands on deck, but that's a bullet you can only shoot once without losing credibility because the second time you try that trick it will be exposed.

Developers are also good at connecting the dots and making leaps. The concept of "If A Then B" and "If B Then C" allows them to jump to the conclusion that "If A Then C." Developers will see through the smokescreens and detect the conflict in messages. Be true to the goal and don't make knee-jerk reactions to help the developers focus on what you need built instead of spending time weaving conspiracy theories.

Risk: if you mismanage any aspect of the Six Week Solution, you are going to have to lie to customers

Customers are paying you for a product or a service, and because their money is at stake, they also have a low threshold setting on their own B.S. detectors. You may think you have a "spinmaster" in support for any problem, but while the spinmaster can keep the movie rolling, the story gets old after a while. Instead, be up front, explain the schedule and when things will be constructed and released. Involving the customer is another way to show progress without risk because you could give a demo or a URL to a demo site to preview the new feature. This doesn't apply to bugs because you must circle back and address real problems, but tweaks to huge new features can involve your customers. If you find yourself in the situation of delivering a fishy message often, you really need to reevaluate why you are delivering these messages so often.

Poison customers

There are, of course, poison customers. No matter what you do they will not be happy. Short of paying for their therapy so they can work out some personal issues, there seems to be nothing you can do to help them. This problem could have built up over a long period, where lies were spun and nothing ever delivered, and you really need to do some hard thinking about your company and your processes. These people just might never be happy for some other reason; remember that their own involvement with the company they work for may be coloring their use of your product. Unless this is the only customer you have, it might be time to make the hard decision and give them as a lead for a competitor. This is known colloquially as "firing a customer." If they are costing you time and money without any profit, they might as well do that for your competitor.

Instead of lying regarding why there is a problem or why you are not building the requested functionality, it is far better to get ahead of the game and state that you are not building that functionality at this time. Follow that message up with a time frame for when you might be able to begin work or tell them honestly that you are not building it.

Risk: there is no place to hide, physical or virtual

Implementing these concepts provides slackers with no place to hide. However, in the ideal Six Week Solution environment, no developer is hiding from the work. In fact, the very nature of the entire system works against those who would "hide out." The concept of the physical inability to hide has been explained, but this approach also extends to the electronic realm with documentation of cycle commitments, source control check-ins, and so on.

Once a robust source control policy is in place and automated builds are implemented, the level of communication skyrockets. Within minutes, everybody knows who broke the build. Anyone (even including those outside of development) can view the source code. Everybody is communicating and nobody is putting forth much effort to do it! The Six Week Solution and the automation wrapped up in the system capture a lot of the energy typically wasted in software development efforts. Check-ins happen if source control is established in any software process. Many times, the value of source control is simply historical and provides no additional value. Worse yet, a tradition of "documenting" changes in comment blocks within code was fairly acceptable in the past, allowing some future developer to see who did what when. Problem is, these comments in code were useless as they appeared at the header of a file and not local to the changes in the code. This is simply wasted effort that makes the commenter feel good about putting the comments into the code, but it cannot be used in any reporting sense by automated source control tools. So what—there is a huge block of comments detailing the (fictitious) "least squared Boolean approach to database design"? This comment makes the writer feel smart, but no one outside of that developer will ever read it. Better to put a detailed enough comment into the check-in where it can be used by a developer and later product support.

There is no hiding when code is checked in. The automated build reveals to everyone the effort being put into check-in comments and, by association, the code that was checked in. Poor source control commit comments show either an extreme laziness or a total lack of understanding of the code that was created or changed. This may seem harsh, but left on their own, the average developer will not concern himself with comments for check-ins. The comments, even terse comments, show an understanding of what the change was and what impacts and trade-offs were made. More seasoned and mature developers understand the value of a good check-in comment and leave themselves (and the next developer) bread crumbs as a trail to follow for quick resolution to future problems and to speed future development.

Why this is not a risk

Typically, lazy developers are good developers, but this does not that mean comments such as "more changes" or "checked a few things in" are acceptable. That's not lazy, that's disrespectful of yourself and your co-workers. Better comments take the form of "fixed bug 667, which added up to 20% performance improvement when X condition is found," or "refactored Foo.java into two new objects to reduce coupling between packages." The former is blatantly waving a middle finger in the eye of the process for source control check-in comments. The latter is a good way of ensuring that there is no 10 pm phone call from application support asking why the code is breaking.

All these things are a very different way of approaching software development. Not only does software have to function, but it has to function *well*. Communication, both at an intrapersonal level and at a documentation level (check-in comments, etc.), works to elevate the level for all involved.

These bullpen and communication concepts may be a bit uncomfortable at first, but to paraphrase *The Fountainhead*: the first man who first showed his fellow cave dwellers how to make fire was probably taken outside the cave and stoned even though he had changed their lives for the better permanently.

Risk: this is a different culture

The focus to deliver a quality product changes many of the traditional concerns of managing software developers. The difference from the standard view of software development where things get thrown over some virtual wall into a tar pit of delays with very good technical sounding reasons with money disappearing into an endless hole all in the name of software development should be easy to see. The seemingly endless cycle is now put to an end with real deliverables and real product on a predictable schedule.

Why Six Weeks is not a risk

No work environment is right for everyone—certainly most factory-line workers could not trade jobs straight up with their cubicle-dwelling brethren—but some environments are more demanding and rewarding than others. And the Six Week Solution is the same: it is more demanding and more rewarding than most other software environments.

This approach will become a risk to your company only if you fail to acknowledge it is not like most other approaches to developing software and that some people are not going to fit well into this structure. Not only do you see product delivery and improvements on a regular schedule, but the staff working within the structure of the six week cycle feel rewarded and valuable themselves.

Risk: how to sell the Six Week Solution

A business leader once said, "There are two kinds of people in this world: those that are in sales and those who just haven't figured it out yet." It's a simple concept, well understood by salespeople but not universally in the world of software development. Developers are much more likely to think that revenue simply appears out of thin air due to the "awesomeness" of their code.

With a software process based on delivery and compensation only when stated goals are met, selling this concept should be a slam dunk. It should be, but rarely is. The reason is because there are two audiences that must be sold on the change:

- buy-in must happen *at the top* by convincing the executives and
- *on the software shop floor* by convincing the developers.

Risk: convincing the development team

Of the two groups, developers are harder to convince. The groundwork for setting time frames for development has been set by many Agile methods, and the pressure to accept Agile within the software development community is glacial and unrelenting in its force. Plus, all the cool kids are doing it, so most developers will jump at the chance to add something for their resume without much investment. Developers bragging that they are doing the latest Agile method doesn't impact Play-Station time and so they have no resistance to attending a meeting every day even if it means they physically do have to stand up for a few minutes.

If there is developer resistance, it often begins at the mention of compensation. Never before have they been directly responsible for delivering and having compensation tied directly to their delivery of functional product. Other development methodologies, even Agile methods, do nothing to impact compensation if a deliverable is missed. Missed deliverables merely roll into the next sprint with everyone vaguely aware something was missed and management stomping their feet. Now, the delivery of features is not only time boxed into six weeks, but the paycheck varies if it is missed.

Using the word "bonus" throws up some red flags for most developers. In their collective psyche, bonuses always seem to evaporate at the first time of trouble in a company. Developers vaguely understand that a salesperson works on commission and thus is paid for performance, but because they are front-loaded in the process, they focus on creating a software product and not sales and thus don't experience the pay-for-performance approach. Additionally, developers do not universally understand concepts of customer retention, revenue, or other axes of measurements for company performance. This split in viewpoints from quantifiable company performance measurements and front-loaded aspects of software development leads most developers to reject the concept that they will be paid a bonus.

The only way to get around this disbelief is to actually pay the bonus. Only by seeing the check will you earn the trust of developers. Do not delay until the end of the year, pay the bonus as soon as possible after the conclusion of a development cycle, and do not wait until the end of a quarter, biannually, or the end of a year or fiscal year.

Another possible objection from developers is that six weeks is not long enough to produce a significant amount of work. These developers feel that they are not investing in the long-term "real work" that you pay them for. The problem here is one of maturity, for they are not breaking their own work into manageable pieces of work and are attempting to tackle a hill that is just too big.

You have two choices:

- help them understand that any journey of a thousand miles starts with a single step
- help them move on to another position where the employer is willing to continue to repeat the mistakes of the past.

If they want to work on a never-ending death march project, there are places they can go and work in that style of environment; you have to be strong enough to either let them go or get them on board.

The first time I implemented a bullpen, my strongest resistance came from my most senior programmer. He was a guy who had been around the block quite a few times, some of it in jobs where it is federal offense to tell you what he worked on. He preferred to work in dark rooms and set his computer to look like old time green screen machines. He was horrified at the idea of moving into a bullpen, where he would lose his semiprivate office and control of his environment. He stated with confidence that he would never be able to get any work done with the noise and distraction of sharing his space.

Once in the bullpen and feeling the hum of activity and the energy in the room pick us up and help us just fly along, no one wanted to go back.

As for my resisting senior developer, he was the passionate spokesman for the team when they informed me.

Development manager

Risk: convincing executives

Pushing the change to the Six Week Solution up the corporate ladder isn't nearly as hard. Traditionally, software development is a money pit where good money is thrown on top of bad in the hopes that something that can be sold comes out someday. The pitch of getting visibility into the direction of the software on a frequent basis is an easy sell, as you're actually going to show something for the money that was spent in a predictable time frame.

The flip side risk of convincing executives is that they cannot view the bonus structure as optional. It is not optional to be part of the Six Week Solution, and it is not optional to be paid based on business conditions. Further, it is not acceptable to view bonuses as costs that can be cut if there is a bad quarter. It must be viewed as part of the compensation, which is a core principle when adopting the Six Week Solution.

How to mitigate this risk: keep your promises

Empty promises will be met with sarcastic quips at best and worse when the next group lunch happens. When you first implement the Six Week Solution, the initial cycles must be made and bonuses paid promptly. (For further discussion about critical first steps when making the transition to the Six Week Solution, see Chapter 11, "Transition to the Six Week Solution" on page 203.)

The only way to prove that the system works is to prove that it works.

Failure to reward for the behavior desired or deferring bonuses to a quarterly or biannual time span will only serve to undermine the value of the Six Week Solution.

Example Goal Setting and the Boy Scouts

Follow the example set by the Boy Scouts and put fast rewards on achievable goals that build toward a larger goal.

- A few requirements that are met will within a month get the Boy Scout a Skill Award for his belt.
- A larger amount of work is rewarded with a Merit Badge.

Both types of intermediate rewards lead to rank advancement with additional requirements.

Setting a target goal and rewarding it quickly is a proven strategy. When developers see that management is putting their money where their mouth is, they are much more apt to believe the program and get behind it. Expect some grumbling initially, but when the first goal is hit and bonuses are paid stand back and watch the shoulder get to the wheel quickly.

Risk: why are developers getting bonuses?

Outside of the development organization there may be resentment to the perception of bonuses for work developers should be doing anyway. The feeling typically is that they are the group that is supposed to create the product, so why are they getting bonuses?

How to mitigate that risk: two possible responses

- **Response 1:** Salespeople are supposed to sell the product and yet they are given commissions, bonuses, and all kinds of other incentives.
- **Response 2:** The pay structure for developers working within the Six Week Solution is a base salary below market with the chance to make more than the market average when bonuses are factored in to total compensation.

Why this is not a bad thing: the safety to fail

With all the pressure to deliver on every commitment, it may seem like a hostile environment where no type of failure is accepted. In fact, the opposite is true. Failure is baked into the system, and the entire process supports quick recovery from failure. The old adage of "It's not how you fall down but how you pick yourself up" is especially true for this process.

Build failures happen. There is no other way to experiment safely without the safety net of the automated build server. The dependence on the automated build server to catch mistakes is critical to the survival of a group running fast. Someone will forget to check something in, someone will break a unit test, and this must be allowed. There is no need to hang a developer in effigy—everybody already knows a build has failed and they know who did it. A developer yelling "my bad," accepting responsibility, and fixing it quickly is the point.

The unexpected thing is that the build rarely fails unexpectedly. With communication open and daily stand-up meetings, you'll know ahead of time that a developer or set of developers is doing something risky, such as upgrading a third-party library, and that this action is going to have the risks of compilation errors or unit test failures. The only bad failures are unexpected, and the process works to rectify these problems quickly by not letting them fester for days or weeks.

Why this is not a bad thing: nobody bats .1000

Large mistakes happen. They happen less frequently if there is a good anthology of unit tests and integration tests, but they still happen. And some of those mistakes will make it into production.

Roberto Clemente, a baseball player for the Pittsburgh Pirates from 1955 to 1972, said that he was more valuable hitting .330 than swinging for a home run every time. He struck out over 2,500 times and got on base only one-third of the time, yet he was still a Hall-of-Fame player! When you really take a step back and think about it, if one-third of developers' original lines of code make it into production after testing and other changes, they are doing very well.

We had a bright and talented developer who usually hit it out of the park. He made a large mistake, but it was not caught because changes can pass unit testing and even manual QA—only to show up in production.

As painful as it was, because a problem leaked through to production and only reared its head under heavy load, this was not something to have the developer drawn and quartered or shot at dawn. Because of other controls built into the system of code analysis and good source control procedures, the problem was contained and resolved in a timely manner.

Development manager

Why the short-term fix won't work for the long term

The moral is that many managers will opt for the simple solution without truly understanding the problem. This is true when the problem is difficult; maybe it's a problem that only happens under heavy load when many users are pounding on the system. The difference is that the software works, but fails in specific situations. A manager not versed in things such as multithreading will approach this problem the same way as some simple failure and come to a completely wrong solution.

Often the solution picked by the technologically ignorant manager is only squeezing a balloon, causing a problem to pop up elsewhere. They may select a solution that may work for a while, but it only serves to mask the real problem and does not solve the problem. Management must trust that:

- they have hired well
- developers understand the magnitude of the problem
- their own continued welfare depends on solving problems quickly for their own benefit as well as that of the company. (For further discussion about this topic, see the "Band-Aid Fixes" section on page 194)

This approach is contrary to a management approach based on fear of the unknown—whether it is that the manager is not well versed in the technology or that they don't know the skills of the employees they have hired.

Likewise, pulling everybody together to solve a single problem is detrimental as well. This approach shows how blind a manager is to the technology and displays an enormous distrust in the staff. Strongman approaches seldom work with developers and work even less well with an educated staff that is well aware of their own free agency; in most instances, developers can walk out the door, taking their right to work someplace else with them and leaving management holding the bag.

A well-organized team will elect a member to chase the bug without a formal meeting. Each bullpen has a leader, and all can contribute. Too many cooks spoil the pot. Let your team correct the problem and move on.

Finally, yelling at someone for a bug that a manager cannot fix directly is a surefire way to upset every developer in your bullpens. If you've hired well, then the employees are not going to shrink in fear of forehead veins pumping and red ears. If all the support mechanisms are in place (automated builds, unit testing, etc.), the problem can be solved quickly.

RISK: ABANDONING QUALITY FOR BONUSES

Planning iterations with four dials

Traditionally, planning a manufacturing project has four dimensions or dials that can be controlled, each at the expense of the other. Those dimensions are:

- Scope
- Time
- Resources
- Quality

Note that these are explicitly fixed. Using this process, you cannot modify the time factor.

Managing these dimensions is like playing Whack-A-Mole at your local Chuck E. Cheese. If you want to reduce the time a project will take, you can increase resources, reduce scope, or reduce quality. If you want to get more done, you have to add more time, more resources, or reduce the quality of your product. If you want more and faster, you'll probably need more resources and less quality.

This, really, is the temptation to create a design deficit on your team. (For a detailed discussion of Design Debt, including strategies on how to deal with it, see the sections "The Value of Quality" on page 118 and "Design Debt" on page 196.) You have a deadline and list of things you want to get done. Adding resources is never as simple as it seems, as new people are actually a detriment to progress before they grow to be a benefit. Therefore, we have to "make do" with lower quality. After all, "We don't have to build the Cadillac of software." It is hoped that our discussion of design debt and design deficits has made it clear by now that there is only one setting for the long-term success of your project, which is with the *quality dial* turned all the way up.

Risk: if you are a screwup, everyone will see it

With all the emphasis on communication, direct or indirect, a resource who is struggling will be readily apparent. Two large clues are a huge number of check-ins for the same thing over and over again or no check-ins and getting "Tuesday/Friday" answers. (See the story in the section entitled "Tuesday/Friday Problem" on page 28.)

One risk to watch for is a large number of check-ins within the same set of files. Don't be deceived, developers are crafty folks, and it may seem like it's just a file in this module and that module. Look for the pattern, as couplings between those modules contain the answers. Lots of bug reports and check-ins all orbiting the same code produced by the same person(s) throw up a huge red flag. Thankfully, the build server makes this quick "dashboard" inspection possible. "Stupid coder tricks" become visible with the static analysis. The source control reports the check-ins. All the clues are there, you just have to look for them.

Tuesday/Friday is another challenge that is visible at the daily stand-up meetings. A feature is slipping for some reason and it's Tuesday. When questioned, the developer states confidently that it'll be done on Friday. Then Friday comes around, "Well, no, there were some issues," but the developer states confidently that it'll be done on Tuesday. Rinse, lather, and repeat. Something isn't clicking. It's time to question the individual, rescope the feature, or get more team members on the problem (which will lead to rescoping).

Example: the really nice guy

This guy was perfect. Good in the interview and a great personality too, including all the business feel-good points of a firm handshake and great smile. He was excited at the prospect of the six week cycle and getting incented to produce. We all felt like we couldn't have found a better candidate, and was it mentioned that he was a really nice guy with a great smile?

Then the work began. Initially, he did pretty well. A few rough spots needed some coaching, but we all wanted him to be successful. First couple of cycles showed he was okay but not great, yet good enough to keep on, we all thought. Nobody wanted to go back to the well and find another candidate. There was so much work to do, surely we had work for him to take on that was at his level and provided good mentoring examples.

Things never improved. To make the situation worse, the work wasn't getting any easier. There were big challenges to tackle and it was going to take a lot of effort by several developers to make it happen. This is when things started to crumble.

First, there was weekend work. Not so bad if a couple of quiet hours on a Saturday would be productive, but this started to become the norm. Added to the trouble was that he was a try/buy consultant and not an employee, which meant additional pay and not much forward momentum.

Next, the number of check-ins was out of control. Not only was there a large volume of check-ins (not a bad thing in itself!), but the check-ins were all in the same files. Worse yet, the source control history showed bug fixes and then reversal of the fixes to attempt to fix another problem.

Finally, the quality of the work began to show in automated builds and static code analysis. The sheer number of "Cut & Paste" violations jumped up dramatically in a period of two weeks. Not only were problems not getting fixed only to be undone again in another attempt, now there were multiple locations in the code base to fix the same problem!

Clearly he was floundering, flopping around in the code like a trout snatched up onto a beach while fishing. Thankfully, the six week cycle gave all the documentation necessary to approach the developer and point out the problems that needed to be corrected in the code and his approach to coding.

When shown all the documentation, he stayed on for a week, pledging to work on improving the coding approach, but then he didn't show up the following Monday. Sometimes, problems solve themselves.

MANAGEMENT CHALLENGES
When to cut losses

Cut losses as quickly as you can, it really is that simple. Leaving a festering wound alone leads to more problems than addressing it quickly. The longer you wait, the more damage that gets done, and the damage is to your product and the teams working on the product.

Mistakes happen to everybody. Maybe the scope was just plain wrong and it's an opportunity to coach developers how they can use the first week of the cycle and Mea Culpa to communicate the trouble. Possibly there was a one-off mistake however it was driven into the product. The real sign is the ongoing problem, they are just not "getting it."

Don't let a problem child hide out in the bullpens for several cycles. This is a disaster waiting to happen. If you have to, move to a Performance Improvement Plan (PIP) quickly and either get the problem resolved or part ways. This isn't something to threaten developers with; your survival as a company depends on having the correct people with the correct skills and mindset on the floor all working together to be successful.

Example of a bad hire: "The Rocket Scientist"

Long before the Six Week Solution, we once hired a brilliant developer. This guy had worked for NASA, aced all the interview questions, and was extremely outgoing and seemed like a great guy all around. The interview was perfect, but something didn't feel right. All the developers and manager who interviewed got together right after and all thought he was a technical fit and would fit into the office group well. We were all proven wrong, and later every interviewee admitted that something just didn't feel right.

We extended an offer and he was able to start the following week. Monday comes and he shows up, happily handing in his own personal card referencing game characters. Red flags went up, that little voice started talking, and the B.S. bell was ringing. We all ignored it.

He went to work, gladly taking his first assignment. And that's when the trouble really began. No one in the position previously had done anything correctly in his view, and it all needed to be rewritten for very good reasons, which he explained. The manager let him start in on some of the perceived trouble spots. A year later, the same trouble spots were still being rewritten. Eighteen months into the project, things were still being rewritten and this product had been in daily use for almost seven years when he joined the company! He had never moved on to another project during his whole tenure, still banging away at these mysterious trouble spots. Nothing had been produced, and in the intervening months his attitude had gone from gregarious to surly and insulting.

Finally, a decision was made to put him on a PIP to help him understand that he needed to produce something. With an insane level of documentation, the company was finally able to shed a resource that had never produced anything and upset every staff member he had worked with.

The Six Week Solution provides tools to have good checkpoints at reasonable intervals where a significant amount of work can be done. These checkpoints are the tools to track progress and cut losses earlier than letting projects stretch out for months upon months.

Example of a bad hire: the professor

Sometimes, a hiring decision is made for you. This is the way things happen through either nepotism or the willpower of some higher up. Compounding upon a bad situation is a bad attitude coupled with a willingness to tell an entire staff that they are merely at a kindergarten level.

First day, almost minutes after introductions, he began telling everyone on the team why they were clueless and that there was another way—his way. Nearly powerless to stop the assault on the code base and design for fear of losing the job entirely, everyone on the development team began changing their behavior. The central tenants of the design of the entire product were summarily destroyed.

All the warning signs presented themselves. Not using source control became rampant. Code was placed directly into production without any unit testing and minimal brute force QA efforts.

Access to the production systems was taken and changes were made without any communication to the rest of the teams. At one point, several customers were running the same version of the software produced through the automated build server on who-knows-what revision of the database.

The code was a mess of spaghetti. Approaches that would have set off every alarm with static code analysis sailed into production gleefully without the automated harness wrapped around stored procedures in the database. And no effort was made to put such procedures in place because it simply wasn't necessary when the developer was clearly as good as he thought himself to be.

If the code was a mess, relationships within the bullpen got even messier. Whispered conversations became the norm for fear of retribution from The Professor's higher-up sponsor. Open and clear communication was destroyed. When communication did occur between anyone and The Professor, it was only for The Professor to degrade the listener.

Finally, with the damage so widespread that even The Professor's sponsor could see the problem was the green light given to release him from employment. The damage to the teams was long lasting, and even almost a year after his departure, problems caused by The Professor's changes are still being discovered and corrected; some are now so widespread that the cost in both dollars and downtime to process the corrections is so great that choices are still being deferred to future cycles.

The moral of the story

Letting employees go, whether you think of it as firing them or euphemistically "freeing up their future," is difficult. It requires documentation and, more personally, the admission that you screwed up jeopardizing the fortunes of the company, yourself, and every team member who works in your software shop. Making the wrong selection is expensive. Retaining that wrong selection is even more expensive. Cut quickly and don't let the wound fester into something worse. You—and everyone you hire—exist in the company to produce value, not run a psychiatric ward. Even the clinically insane can appear charming for short periods of time, but the long-term risks outweigh the brief honeymoon.

Once you have the information, act. It may feel comfortable to give another chance with coaching, but if the recipient does not respond to the coaching, it is time to cut them loose. Hesitation will be sensed in every bullpen and will cause questions to a leader's ability to actually lead. Move quickly and with confidence.

Cultural shift within the company

All this change goes hand in hand with a cultural shift in the company. No longer will seagull management approaches be tolerated. It's time to grow up the development side of the house and the whole company with it. The discipline of getting things into the framework of the six week cycle will take time, but with growth it is possible.

We've got a minor bug: why does it have to wait for the next cycle?

Often defects are addressed as they are uncovered. This is even truer with Internet-based businesses that don't have to wait to stamp a CD and send it to customers, as a SaaS (Software as a Service) company can easily post a new build to correct a defect and continue. So why then does a bug fix have to wait until the next cycle?

There are several reasons driving the decision to delay correcting a bug:

- The severity plays a huge role in selecting where (that is, in which cycle) to correct a bug. If you have a product that produces reports and a number in a report is incorrect, then that's a severe problem, but if you have been doing test-driven development (TDD), hiring smart, implemented automated builds, and performing code quality checks, how did this problem get into production?
- More typically, the bug that someone thinks must be fixed right now is merely political posturing for someone who doesn't agree with the process. Nine times out of 10, the huge bug is actually usage so rare that you have to 'spin around twice on Tuesday when there is a full moon' type of situation to replicate. Simply put, if there is a work-around and it's not heinously manual or keeps people up 24 hours a day, it can wait until another cycle.

Another problem individual is a partner or new customer who is flexing muscles to drive a better deal at renewal time. In this case, weak leadership promises something to be changed right away and wants it out the door. A much better option is to value the input candidly and present a plan for when the suggestion will be implemented. Remember, you never have to wait more than 11 weeks for a reasonable-sized feature to appear in the product; if it's a huge new concept, pieces can be brought into the product in each cycle.

The "Next Client-Facing Release" is not an option

Every cycle is expected to be client facing and may be deployed. For this reason, there is a great deal of pressure to keep the entire body of work functional at all times. This is why TDD, along with automated builds and measurement, is so crucial to the Six Week Solution.

Balancing the desire to not fix a bug quickly is the knowledge that every cycle produces a build that may go in front of a customer. For this reason, a discipline of back-patching is sometimes necessary to allow a release in the field to be patched for a quick fix, thus keeping the wheels on the bus for a couple of weeks. The best way to approach this is to explicitly call out the requirement in a cycle commitment document and go through all the formal processes that would occur for the build produced at the end of the cycle.

Temptation of giving up the rules under pressure

When faced with the screaming executive threatening to fire everybody, there is a huge temptation to give up the rules and just go with the flow. Typically, all processes cave in and yield to the onslaught with a promise that things will return to normal after this one death march or crisis passes. We all know these words are lies before they even leave the lips.

Another situation is that some group has decided that many features simply must appear in the next cycle, even though they are conflicting or there is a real resource problem, be it human or machine. Strong personalities are pushing for everything right now, and there seems to be no way around having to deliver it even though these requirements were just delivered and the true scope is not known. The only way to combat this is to add requirements into the cycle commitment documents to call out the need for scoping, investigating, or refining the requirements. Sometimes this can go all the way to prototyping a feature to get better requirements definition, for much of the time someone is merely playing buzzword bingo with requirements, and the company as a whole needs to know what it means to the company and its profits.

Web 2.0

An actual request from a partner was that they could do more with our product if we only provided data in a "Web 2.0 format." Instantly, developers began making jokes not only about the requirement but about the members of management who were blindly repeating this phrase over and over in every meeting, feeling very happy about their mastery of a new phrase and being able to use it in context.

What did the partner really want? Could it mean that they really wanted up-to-the-minute blasts in less than 140 characters through a Twitter feed? Did they want a Really Simple Syndication feed to update their Google home pages or could they really need some sort of service a different product could send a request against and get data back for presentation in another product? In this real-world example, the senior manager never spent any time defining the desires and kept repeating "Web 2.0 format."

The partner in this case was a reseller and could provide a ton of business to the company. Instead of pulling developers to work on whatever this "Web 2.0 format" was, it would be better to call out a line item on the cycle commitment to investigate what the partner's real need was for scoping in a future development cycle. It's only six weeks away and requires guts to understand instead of a round-heeled approach to servicing a partner.

Issues regarding the bonus

Bonus payments are a sticky subject when they are first introduced. On the business side, other departments are not getting a bonus for "just doing their job." On the software development side, there is a great deal of suspicion. How and when to pay this bonus are also issues that need to get worked out from the beginning and not left up to daily variations in the business. Being wishy-washy on either side will cause more difficulties.

Outside of the software development group, news of a bonus every six weeks will spread like wildfire. In the current process, it is instantly a problem because everyone, including the folks who deliver breakfast burritos to the office in the morning, will think they should also get a bonus and resent those who do receive compensation in this manner. It must be made public that the development group has put at risk base compensation and that these bonuses are only paid when everything, and we mean everything, on the cycle commitment list is complete and functional. These are performance-based Management By Objectives and have an actual artifact that can be interacted with to prove that an item was or was not created in an objective manner equal to any revenue goal; either it was hit or not.

Developers are initially suspicious of a bonus every six weeks. Seasoned ones have heard promises of bonuses based on company performance many times in their careers and, most times, they feel it was not paid or not paid to the promised level due to something outside of their sphere of influence. These same developers may also exhibit a natural distrust of authority due to their age grouping, for Generation X'ers are naturally independent and unimpressed by authority (Holtsnider & Jaffe, *IT Manager's Handbook*, p. 69). The only way to get over this resistance is to begin paying the bonus. Pay it in a timely manner as close to the end of cycle as possible with the next run of payroll. As respect is earned and not given, proving the honesty of the bonus payout must likewise be earned.

Paying the bonus on time is not pandering to a bunch of whiny developers who don't believe they will actually get paid. The rules for paying the bonus are hard and fast to the original cycle commitment document within the accepted confines of rescoping during Mea Culpa. Either everything is complete and can be demonstrated or the bonus doesn't get paid. However, if the company has not yet accepted the discipline to use the entry gates of the cycle kickoff week and Mea Culpa, it may be difficult to gauge what actually took the time because there still was a manager/senior leadership position somewhere in the company who went around all the checkpoints to directly pressure/threaten developers. In the maelstrom of conflicting desires, a balance must be struck, and there are times when this is a soft balance, although the correct path of every cycle is to stick to the cycle commitment documents.

If you find yourself constantly re-working the cycle commitments one the following events is occurring: the development staff is trying to pull the wool over your eyes, the scope of the cycle targets was not gauged properly to begin with, or the company is not all singing from the same songbook. All three are risks and are difficult to manage for if you are getting snowed by developers or individuals outside of the development organization that are not working within the system. The scoping issue rests clearly on the shoulders of management within development and product management. If it is a personnel issue, then have the guts to make a change. If it's a scoping issue, then more effort needs to be placed in functionally decomposing the individual features to ensure a quality delivery.

A final note regarding cycle bonuses: make sure that everyone in the company understands—and we mean *everyone*—that these bonuses are *not* tied to company performance. It is not acceptable to say that cycle bonuses will not be paid this quarter because of a slow sales quarter. It may be true or it may be political double talk, but this kind of statement is exactly why developers had some resistance to having their compensation adjusted for the six week cycle in the first place.

Band-Aid fixes

With the constricted time frame of six weeks, it is sometimes extremely tempting to do something quick and dirty. There are times when this quick-and-dirty approach is a good thing, such as when you are not sure about how a feature will be accepted and you are doing it to test the waters before spending more development dollars. However, when fixing defects or refactoring for large chunks of a code base to handle more volume or perform better, a Band-Aid is the wrong choice. When being tempted to produce a Band-Aid, always remember that you will have to live with this code in the product for at least 11 weeks and unwinding it can cost even more.

Squeezing development into six week chunks may seem like it does nothing but drive Band-Aid on top of Band-Aid. Sometimes, it may seem like you are caught in some sort of socialist experiment of producing collective poetry with factory workers. (As ridiculous as idea that sounds, it was actually tried in the old Soviet Union.) With each successive Band-Aid, the cost to unwind the bad decision continues to escalate. You must always be on guard for the innocent-looking fix or change that can spiral out of control in the future.

There are two different approaches for many data-intensive pieces of software:

- Either things are calculated on the fly quickly enough to be presented to the user or some level of precalculation or
- roll up is performed to manage the response time for a user.

If you really have a need to produce a Band-Aid, it is much safer in the case of the dynamic calculation for roll ups as a Band-Aid to produce some sort of persistent artifact either in a file or in a database that will also bring additional costs to unwinding in the form of migration of that data to another form. More often than not, the cost to unwind a bad decision once it had been persisted to disk in some form is several times more expensive than waiting to fix a bug or add a feature the right way.

Even though the compressed time frame seems to drive to Band-Aid fixes and favor that mode of thinking, you must remain vigilant at all times to resist the temptation and follow the process.

A huge temptation to be alert for is to throw on a Band-Aid when the company feels behind. This may be because there has not been a major new feature to sell in a while or something more technical, such as a product that is chewing up disk space at a rapid rate. The temptation to Band-Aid a couple of quick wins with the thought that the company just doesn't have time to do it "right" at the moment with the justification that if this Band-Aid isn't thrown on right away the company won't be around to have anything matter is flat wrong. There is never time to come back and do it right, for there is always another bright and shiny object for the next customer. Be honest with yourself, have a design in mind, and work the plan to get to the desired position and don't jump into a death march while calling it a six week cycle; if you are thinking that folks are going to have to work nights and weekends then you are sacrificing the future for a very short-term objective.

QUALITY CONCERNS

When the time frame is locked into six weeks and the number of resources assigned to the project is constant, there should be a large concern that quality may suffer as a result of attempting to put too many items or units of work that are too large into a single six week cycle. Every single person in the company must understand that it is far better to have a single function that works well than 10 that are sloppy. But there are still factors at work to push to get just a little bit more into a cycle or just a small tweak done in a cycle that conspires to destroy quality.

The fixed time and scope provide predictability in the process. Quality must be approached differently. Manual QA covers only one dimension of quality and typically focuses on the front end, vainly searching for answers in the presentation that might uncover huge issues in data without ever really drilling down into underlying data. Human QA efforts are still necessary in anything that a person will actually use, but without a large suite of automated tests and automated integration tests, the quality of the overall product will suffer.

Business would like to move as fast as possible, and the phrase is not "as fast as humanly possible." Automation, from the assembly of automobiles to robo calls during an election year that annoy you at dinnertime, is employed everywhere to move faster and solve real problems. However, in software development, automated testing suites are localized to small islands of development, whether those islands are a single development shop or sometimes a single developer in a large group. Without automation of the testing for unit tests and integration tests, you are doomed to follow your QA department into random clicking in the hopes you'll uncover the problems before a customer finds them.

With a fixed time frame and a fixed number of resources, quality is typically left to suffer. This is why we stress automation so strongly throughout the process, for without automation you are left to forever regression test the exact same things and the only answer is to hire more QA resources.

Like Sisyphus from Greek mythology who was cursed to push a huge boulder up a hill only to watch it roll down the hill again, your QA team will barely get through the current round of regression testing to find out that 25 new features and hundreds of new builds have passed since the last fully regression tested build. Clearly, to survive in an environment without automated testing, QA resources must be masochists who have completely forgotten their safe words.

Developer temptation to cut quality to meet the cycle

Another area to be wary of is developers falling for the temptation to cut corners in the process to ensure that they meet a cycle commitment. It is very tempting to skip a unit test, especially near the end of a cycle, to show some feature functioning. This always backfires, for it leads right into QA finding a bug at the last moment that causes a developer to hack a fix quickly, and there is a good chance that the fix they just hacked will make it into production, where something else will be found and another hack produced. This trap ends up costing more than calling out the problem at Mea Culpa and rescoping the feature or assigning new resources to help get the item delivered with quality.

DESIGN DEBT

Another risk of developing software in six week iterations is creating a huge backlog of design debt. Design debt is not something that typically appears in a day due to a single bad decision, but something that builds up over time, much like sludge in a car's engine, which seems to sit innocently, not causing any harm. Then one day a critical part of the oil delivery system is clogged and you are left with no option except to rebuild or replace the entire engine. At that point, it really seems sad that someone would choose not to spend $30 on an oil change every six months to save a few bucks and is now faced with a $3000 or higher repair bill to replace an entire engine. Yet this happens every day in software development with crazy requests cranked out at high speed. It may seem like a good idea to charge, taking the hill and counting the costs later, but the cost in real dollars and time lost is always higher. Put another way, is it more important to give a single customer some tidbit or give every customer a high-quality piece of functionality?

While it does feel good to deliver something quickly that a customer has requested, if that functionality is shoehorned into a bad design, it will cost more to correct later than to do it right the first time.

Another large contributor to the design debt problem is the rush to get a product to market. Again, cutting corners for something that is good enough today is a very tactical decision and sometimes necessary for the short-term survival of a company. With no product (being realistic, not discussing shell games of vaporware or attempts to "FUD-up" a competitor), there are no sales and without sales there is no company. The saying that nothing really happens until someone sells something is very true. So now you have a product with some real design debt that is in the marketplace, functional and hopefully delivering real value to one or more paying customers. This tactical decision to ship something that may not be 100% what you wanted to ship is exactly why the six week cycle approach can pay some real dividends. Go ahead, ship it because it works well enough for today and will keep the ship afloat. Now you have six weeks to correct the problem and get the "real" version out or at least can take a step to replace the bad design in each six week cycle driving toward the ultimate goal.

Design debt is bad, but having no plan to work design debt out of your product is even worse. It is impossible to find some uber developer to spend a couple of days with your code and exorcise the design debt demons with a couple of words of Latin. Instead of living with design debt and auguring in even deeper, have a plan to work on each and every design debt over a course of several cycles, taking small steps along the way, to achieve the final goal.

Design debt may be necessary, but what you are working to avoid is code rot. Code rot happens from a bad idea that is functional and so convoluted or brittle that no one wants to touch it but maybe an original author who many times has scampered on to another job once they realized the corner they had painted themselves into! Code rot is even more expensive to tackle and often ends up affecting code far removed from the actual rot just to make sure you cut everything out.

This book is a cookbook on how to handle these risks.

HARD TO TRANSITION

Waterfall cultists—there is no other word for them—will push back hard when asked to give up their beloved methodology. Before you begin extolling the virtues of the Six Week Solution, however, ask them a direct question:

"How *successful* has your method been?"

Ask the hard questions. Don't accept namby-pamby "Well, we didn't have enough java programmers" or "We did fine but we missed the deadline by just a couple of years" kind of answers. Push back. What has waterfall done for them—or for you—lately?

Possible solution: hire an outside development team

The changes outlined in this book are drastic. Some individuals will resist change merely out of some personal need to be contrary. We once took over a development organization where the majority of the developers had quit and had stopped producing long before we took over. Several QA resources were hanging on, and when presented with a goal and bright future, said with sarcasm, "We'll see." A few months later they, too, were all gone.

If a transition just isn't going to happen, it may be time to go fish. There is no reason to overlap the development resources, as a new set of developers will make mistakes in any existing code base but they will have the freedom to change things that the original team was married to and wouldn't change. You can build a new team, separately, from the original team or hire a team of outsiders. Either way, you have a blank slate to build the team in the manner you wish without the baggage and history of the existing team.

Risk: business wants a death grip on the assembly line

With all the talk of process, it may suggest that you have a death grip on creating software and nothing will happen without you knowing about it and only the things you want to happen do get done. While it would be comfortable to think that an assembly line that runs at some feet per second produces X widgets per hour, it's not really possible when creating software.

Frequently, good software needs some spark of inspiration, and this is the antithesis of locking down the process. Remember that at its core, creating software is a creative process and is not quantified easily. Stop pretending that management controls every aspect of the process and let your racehorses run.

It is not suggested that small items be selected from the approach presented in this book and implemented independently. The whole process must be embraced throughout the organization. Once you agree to everything, bullpens, bonuses, cycle documents, source control, automation, and everything else outlined in this book, you don't get to go back and change your mind. You agreed to this approach, now burn the boats and advance.

SMALLER BUT STILL POTENTIALLY PROBLEMATIC RISKS

"One piece at a time"—that's how Johnny Cash outlined stealing a Cadillac from the assembly line. Take on a little bit every day and continue working toward the end goal. As long as you are advancing, you are making progress. The challenge is not to end with an engine from a '54 and a transmission from a '74 when you are ready to integrate. Taking manageable chunks of work and completing them within the time frame of six weeks, you continue advancement of the product and show measurable gains while allowing opportunities to revisit past successes and have them all integrate smoothly.

Half-ass requirement requests

Remember—you are going to send off a team of developers to work on these requests for 240 paid man hours—six weeks. You need to be very, very precise about what you want *them* to do and very precise about what you agree to do *for the requestor*. The requestor can be The Business, it can be a member of your own team, or it can be a third party—regardless of the source, though, make sure you are very specific about what is required.

There need to be consequences for not following the rules

One of the core items of the Six Week Solution is that there are direct consequences—positive and negative—to actions taken by developers. This holds true not only for code development but for professional behavior too.

In addition to the carrot-and-stick/whip of bonuses, other companies use a wide array of incentives and penalties. Some states, for example, have "snow days." Others have "wave days" based on the conditions of the surf. Depending on your location and the makeup of your team, you can use either one of these to your advantage.

Too flat/too hierarchical

It is a fine line, but a Six Week Solution can be too structured or too free-form. You need some management in place—to interact with other management, among other things. But you can have too many middle managers, too much process. No Six Week Solution teams can contain one or more Large Bureaucracy Dropouts who fill their first couple of days with "It took me five days to get a form signed" stories; even management of development must be focused on delivery.

We suggest two layers of management: the front-line technical manager who is the bullpen lead and a manager above the front-line technical manager. The bullpen leads deal exclusively with technical issues and not with personnel and salary; this includes not managing developer time-off, etc. The bullpen leads do have input to personnel issues, but in a more casual manner as it should be expected that they report that "Frank is takin' names and kickin' ass" and "Fred shows up late almost every day for stand-up," etc. The multibullpen manager has more responsibility for personnel decisions such as hiring and recommendations for raises.

Even with this flat structure, it is too hierarchical for some developers. Unfortunately, as team oriented as bullpens are, it is not a democracy where all input is equal. While there is shared responsibility, there is not shared risk, for the bullpen leads should have more compensation riding on the outcome of development cycles. This exists for a reason, for while a single developer may be enticed to explore some resume-padding technology during a cycle while ignoring cycle commitments, the entire team will suffer and no one knows this more directly than the bullpen leads. It may be fashionable in the 2000s to go to work in jeans and call everybody by their first names, but without leadership, software development dissolves rapidly into a free for all instead of everyone pulling in the same direction to accomplish a shared goal.

For further discussion about this topic, see the section on "The Bullpen" on page 62.

No clear career path

As we have said, the Six Week Solution is relatively unique. Some companies and some developers thrive in it. However, some developers are looking for a more structured, "ASP programmers with X years of experience" kind of place. The Six Week Solution is not necessarily going to provide that. It might, but it might not. It is a team coding environment—individual rewards come about because the person did what the team needed, not what he/she thought was best for him/her.

In addition, there are not hundreds of management openings available for a developer in a Six Week Solution environment. There might be one bullpen lead over five to 12 developers, maybe a lead QA person, and possibly a manager over the department. Not a whole lot of opportunity for those who want to make the jump into the Pointy Haired Boss ranks, but for someone who wants to be an incredible developer, the structure simply rocks. This is not to say that you only want code pigs in the bullpen for those who only live to code; these types typically don't have the personality to survive in the bullpen and tend to drive both the team and themselves into a man-in-a-room style of development.

Developers with backgrounds in government or government contracting work should also generally be avoided. It is the rare individual who can make the shift from a "time and grade" approach to advancement and the lack of advancement possibilities in the bullpen structure to really excel in the environment. There are a few who can make the leap, so the fact that such a background is on a resume does not immediately disqualify them from consideration as a team member, but be careful.

Set up and executed correctly, a developer is free to become a better craftsman without worrying about political consideration. Developers are not in endless meetings worrying about what some outside manager's agenda or concerns over budget are. The priorities are clear and set every six weeks so the developers are free to focus on the best solution for the given priorities instead of being jerked around for the latest topic du jour just when they are in the groove of development.

People will go over your head

It should be expected that patterns of behavior from before any attempt to implement the Six Week Solution will persist simply because those patterns have been successful in the past. One of these patterns is to call your boss and demand that some feature be created or bug fixed right now. Once you have sold the methodology up the chain, and achieved buy in, this is less of a risk, but there are situation where this behavior will be attempted even after implementing the Six Week Solution successfully.

There is no way to stop someone from attempting this approach, but you do have the tools to diffuse the problem. Gauge the real opportunity presented by the feature or bug. Is it really critical or only being positioned as a critical issue? Nine times out of 10, the real motivation is political; someone is trying to make a splash to justify their existence, embarrass one group to prove a need for an additional head count, or one of the many myriad other games that get played in a modern office that have nothing to do with being a successful company.

In the other cases, it's a real issue and you do need to do something, but the question is "When do you need to do something?" If it's a bug, get a grip on how gnarly it really is. If there is a work-around, how long will the work-around last? If it will last only two days then your answer is different than if it was annoying but a work-around is easy and doesn't take too much time. If it isn't a dire emergency, you can use the Six Week Solution to position a change for the next development cycle or renegotiate the scope for another feature using the Mea Culpa meeting.

In the case that there really is an emergency failure and things will not wait until the next cycle or Mea Culpa, then you have to make a decision and reduce the scope on one or more features or drop something entirely. It won't make everybody happy, but in these situations you can't try to make everybody happy and compromise for that only leads to a half-hearted fix/patch that will break at some point in the future. A better choice is to understand the scope of the problem and address it with the quality that is expected.

Remember, it is no longer that status quo of "We have to fix this right now!" Use the structure to fit work into time frames that allow for quality. If you fall into the trap of jumping for every little nit that someone objects to or small bugs, people will learn to expect that behavior. Stay true to the methodology and the end result will be of higher quality.

Another source of someone going over your head will be sales, and toward the end of a quarter or fiscal year these requests get more interesting. This area really isn't even a problem for development, as the statement of "We could sell this if only we had some feature that . . ." is the same as a salesperson telling their boss that "We could sell this if we drop the price. . . ." Both are issues for sales management to handle and not something that development should handle.

However, these requests do provide good insight to any barrier to sales that may be occurring in the marketplace. Be sure to record these for consideration when selecting what work goes into a future development release. Sometimes, you can be bold enough to look at a feature request and know it will fit into one cycle and can give a date. While nothing beats already having the functionality build into your product, being able to announce a date confidently (even if you do have to wait until cycle kickoff) is the next best thing. Chances are that some other prospect or customer will need the same functionality, so do not disregard requests communicated by going over your head but do work them into the process.

Transitioning to the Six Week Solution

CHAPTER CONTENTS

Agile Development and Business Goals. DOI: 10.1016/B978-0-12-381520-0.00011-4

INTRODUCTION

"Okay," you say, "this all sounds great, but there is no way I can move my company in this direction. The business will never participate, the developers all have offices, and marketing will not understand."

We promise that the initial pain of the transition will be well worth it. At first, the uniqueness of the approach and the participation of all aspects of the business will have people very excited. Before you know it the entire company and your customers will fall into the rhythm. There is a predictable comfort to the process that everyone will appreciate.

BEFORE YOU DO ANYTHING, THOUGH

Even before the work of putting people into the proper roles and moving forward with the Six Week Solution, there are some basic infrastructures that must exist. While the full benefit of the system will not be realized for a while, these early wins put you in position to succeed.

Use source control

A source control system must be in place to enable rapid changes. The source control system must support the concurrent nature of development, not lock files to one user, and allow branching and support labeling of individual files and groups of files. If you already have a source control system, congratulations and move on, but be sure you begin stressing the point of good check in commenting.

AUTOMATE THE BUILD

You must also now automate your builds. The changes you are about to make require that you have a viable build server to continue down the path. Not having an automated build server will hamper the development efforts immensely, so this is a very important piece of the puzzle to move forward.

Unless you put the build server at the top of your priorities now, it will linger at the bottom of some list of infrastructure investments and there will always be something more important. It is the rare business that sees value in the build server once they are receiving builds directly from a desktop for the soft costs of reworking old builds and maintaining old scripts always get swept under the rug.

If you have the time, delve into code metrics right up front. As stated earlier in the book, it is impossible to improve what you cannot measure, and code metrics put an objective measurement on code instead of basing your measurement of quality on how someone feels about the code. Start with easy wins such as scanning for dead code to help dust the cobwebs off of sections of code that have been cheaply maintained for a while. Look at cyclomatic complexity next, as this will have a high correlation with code that is causing you trouble.

If you are starting from scratch, invest some time in coming up with your metrics and what scans you will enable initially. This is a fine line because some scans can be so tight or restrictive with certain settings that you will never achieve a level of zero violations. Be strict, but also reasonable. With cyclomatic complexity, it would be extreme to set this at four levels, but ridiculous to loosen the setting to 50. For cyclomatic complexity, we chose 10 as a reasonable point based on experience and seeing where the size of the code exceeds the ability of developers to maintain.

SELLING THIS IDEA UP THE CHAIN
Senior management backing

This transition really works best if you get the buy in from the top first and then enlist top leadership to help sell the idea back to the staff. They need to make hard decisions about the change of work area and compensation. Get senior management engaged, get them excited, and let them explain it to the company. Part of the beauty of this process is that anyone can understand and explain it.

There are many reactions to the Six Week Solution from senior management because they haven't seen developers work and succeed in an environment like this.

A technology manager may have the reaction of "It will never work, they can't write code with all those restrictions." This is easy to handle because this process does work and has been successful. The question is more that they feel themselves that they couldn't work in an open environment with high communication.

Product managers and marketing may come back with "How do I decide when I will do a release?" Here again the answer is simple because you know your company and how frequently they can absorb an update; initially, it might be biannually, but you will be paving the way for quarterly updates in the future once all involved are comfortable.

Other resistance from various leadership positions includes the idea that they think it will not scale beyond a small group of developers. But it can and does scale because we have run this process successfully with multiple bullpens.

Finally, because of expectations rooted in the past, leadership may feel that nothing of value can be produced in six weeks—it will surely take longer. They are missing the point because there typically are work items that can fit into the six week time frame nicely and other larger projects can be spread over several cycles with well-defined checkpoints and achievements.

It is human nature to resist change, and software development is no different. Additionally, to senior management, software development has been such a black hole and budget unknown with constant slips and budget overruns that they may want to stick with the devil they know over the devil they don't know. Drive home that this is a proven process, vetted at several companies, and the initial pain of the change will pay off.

Creating the work environment

It will take senior management to create the environment of the bullpens. Like automation and compensation, the bullpen is core to the entire methodology and is crucial to the Six Week Solution. Attempting to open up communication in a standard cubicle office space is lying, for as soon as a meeting is over, the denizens scurry back to their own private cubes and continue to work as they always have. You need to be different to achieve change, and nothing is as different in the modern office from the cubicle as the bullpen structure.

It is unlikely that you have the perfect area for a bullpen as there are many physical problems with creating a bullpen environment. Office building architecture is often not conducive to large open spaces, with support pillars at regular intervals that would break up any attempt to have a large open space. For the most recent implementation of the Six Week Solution, we looked at 10 different office buildings and only two of them had the uninterrupted footprint to make the bullpen possible. If you are lucky to be in a building that would allow a large work area for the bullpens, it will take some planning to get the space created before you can move everybody and equipment into the bull-pens. This planning may require other groups to move or otherwise be restructured physically, and senior management must be involved to pull this off.

If it is absolutely impossible to create a bullpen, you would be much better served to move developers into an open area with folding tables than to keep them in individual offices. In one implementation of the Six Week Solution, we actually took over the CEO's large office, as it was the only space we had in the building that was large enough to colocate all the developers and testers.

SELLING IT TO SALES AND MARKETING

Core concepts in the Six Week Solution such as compensation tied directly and measurably to performance should resonate very well with the sales department. The idea of fitting releases inside of quarters should make marketing perk up, as they will have visibility into everything that is being developed and a schedule. If the approach is communicated to these groups, it should be an easy sell.

Sales department

When a salesperson can state—without making a call to anyone—that "our next development cycle kickoff is on mm/dd/yyyy. I will be at that meeting and will explain how important the feature is to you. I should be able to tell you the following Monday when we can expect that feature to be available," everyone is better served inside the company and the customers.

Sales will learn quickly that answers for the request of new features will not come outside of cycle boundaries, which works in everyone's favor by keeping development focused and delivering better quality when the time comes to really work on a feature instead of attempting to squeeze it in. We have been through this situation several times, and without fail when approached reasonably regarding the scope of a feature request, it is far better to state truthfully when the feature can be addressed and when it will appear in a production release than to promise some imaginary date and death march to that date.

This cannot be taught in a day, and if you are digging out of a hole of slipped scheduled and half-baked features, you can only address it by producing a history of reliable deliveries with minimal defects. Solid software goes a lot further than endless patches and fire drills.

Marketing department

Marketing should be receptive to increased communications and the focus on a plan for scheduled releases. With new, production-ready builds coming twice a quarter, they will have more control over the big-bang releases and be able to schedule appropriately for announcements.

Release numbers: a small but important point

For the sanity of all involved, including both staff and customers, we strongly recommend that you address the issues of release numbers right at the start. It may be tempting to operate with two names for a release, one used for external communications and another for internal developer use, but this ultimately leads to confusion for employees and customers. Our suggestion is to call the software what it is and don't try to get cute with "a," "b," etc. Settle on a major version and then add the cycle, year, and build number to the entire version. For example, Version 6.210.202 can be translated easily to version 6, second development cycle of 2010, build #202. Take a step back and ask what value "5.1" or "5.2" really had in the marketplace. The answer is resoundingly "None!"

Customers outside of IT and development really don't care if it's version 5.1 or 5.2 because they have version 5 and that is enough to remember. The other numbers exist for you to quickly identify what build is running, map that back to the actual code that went into that build, and be able to correct a defect quickly if necessary. That's the value of version numbers: once we get past the first number of code name, it's clear that those numbers exist only for your internal use.

This version number discussion is a big deal as it relates to your automated build. Without an automatic mechanism to stamp each build with a unique identifier (really just an incrementing number, reset for each cycle), someone will forget this crucial step and you'll have two builds in production with the same "version" and be scratching you head trying to figure out why something is broken even though you fixed it already. Don't worry about the number being high, as in our experience no one except the support organization really cares about what build it is and there is no perception difference between build 172 and build 2170. In fact, high build numbers really point out that your automation was working at each time the build ran; it executed every unit test. Don't attempt to hide the build number, publish it and publish it automatically.

The new process warrants an announcement, including the potential for changing how versions of the product are named. This should be big news as the development group is getting more in tune with the needs of the customers and how they do business. This announcement is the first project that marketing can get involved with.

DETERMINE YOUR AGGRESSIVENESS ON CYCLES AND COMPENSATION

Transitioning developers will be the most difficult part of the change. As detailed in Chapter 10, "Risks with Using This Approach" on page 177, developers won't believe they will ever get paid.

How to pay developers really comes down to two options:

- One choice would be to keep the base compensation at the status quo with a small bump for each person realized in the form of a cycle bonus.
- The other choice is to be very aggressive and make the cycle bonus a significant part of the total compensation with a very aggressive bonus on each cycle.

The first method will not be met with much resistance from developers, as it impacts total pay in a very insignificant way. They will like the "extra" money every six weeks, but their livelihood will still be independent of the process and just as secure as it always was.

Note on Base Pay vs Bonus

Since working with this method of compensation in several organizations now, we have noticed several trends, some good, some bad.

Risk-adverse individuals will not want to put much at risk for each cycle; consequently, they really have nothing to lose if a cycle is missed. These people will negotiate for a higher up-front pay rate and a minimal bonus. This leads to problems, as if they only have $100–$200 riding on the success of each cycle, they really haven't bought into the process and while they will take the extra cash when a cycle is hit, they really don't care if the target is missed completely.

Another type of developer has the confidence to "go big" and will put a much larger amount at risk if it means that the total compensation is above market. These developers will be agitated if a cycle is missed and may take some corralling to keep on track if they see that others are slacking, for they understand that it's an all-or-nothing proposition. There must be a reasonable cap initially on each cycle bonus or these gunslingers will double down and go for $10K or more each cycle! Restraining this excitement is a challenge, but it's better to have this motivated person than the person who is merely keeping a seat warm in the bullpen.

Your challenge is to pick one or the other, for mixing both types side by side will lead to some interesting management challenges as you referee the two opposites.

To help entice the interest in the bonus, it should be made clear that unless there are outside circumstances allowing you to increase base pay, raises will only come via an increase in the bonus paid each cycle. Smart developers quickly do the math and realize that if they risk more, then 20% of a bigger amount at risk is much larger than a smaller amount! Plus, it's a pretty dramatic statement to tell employees they are getting a 30% increase in their bonus as a raise when the time does come for adjustments.

The more money that is at risk for each developer, the more aggressive you can be with the cycle commitment list for each cycle. Introducing this financial motivation into software development assures you of not having to live through another death march or dealing with slipping schedules.

Either end of the spectrum may be appropriate for your organization. You have to make an honest assessment of the team you have or wish to build and the comfort level of all involved.

One other quick note: accounting is generally not used to paying out items eight times a year. Someone will need to explain the new system to them.

SET EXPECTATIONS FROM THE START

It must be clear from the very beginning, and reiterated, that a cycle bonus is not a *guarantee* unless everything on the cycle commitment list is met. Some developers you have simply will never be comfortable with this approach, and once you have locked in on your own comfort level with bonuses, if the developers don't want to play then they need to move to another place of employment.

Restructuring event

This transition in the approach to compensation is a chance to restructure as you are changing everything about the job, compensation, work environment, and even the job description; take advantage of all this to set expectations properly.

This is either a human resource (HR) nightmare or an HR dream, depending on your point of view. On the one hand, you are signing a new employment agreement with every member of your development staff. On the other hand, it is a restructuring that gives you the window to make some hard changes that may otherwise be painful. Use this opportunity to make these hard changes and trust your gut instinct. If an individual or group of individuals will not adapt, then you need to let them go now as it will be much more painful to make this move later.

This is another time to saddle up and make some hard decisions. You need to think about the people you inherited and make hard choices regarding who to keep.

Legacy fortresses

We are sure there is one person in your group who has their legacy fortresses solidly constructed to resist any change. It may feel like you cannot upset this team for fear of losing them. We have done this process four times, and once cut the entire development team. Yes, there is some short-term pain but the company and customers adapt quickly and are very happy to trade up for the increased quality and transparency.

PICK THE DATE FOR THE CUTOVER

You need to pick a good date for the cutover. We would strongly suggest you do it at the beginning of a quarter and make a big deal about the cutover. Perhaps send all of the developers home for a week prior to the cutover to prepare the space. Make sure everyone is involved and fly in stakeholders who are not on-site. Strongly discourage business meetings the week of the cutover.

Treat it as what it is: a huge change for the entire company.

The fact that compensation is changing is also important to keep in mind. Because bonus compensation is typically based on quarters, this is another reason to cut at the beginning of one.

Other considerations may be the fiscal calendar that the company operates on, for making a huge change in January may cause too much disruption in various sections of the company. Instead, wait until April to be in the business Q1 (if the fiscal year closes at the end of March).

Another approach is to align with the yearly review to help bring up the change in compensation. Yearly reviews are when compensation would change, so it's going to change in a different manner this year to help align with the overall change in physical layout and process.

All things considered, introducing the change in the fourth quarter has many advantages. This window of time will not affect pending sales much for you're not going to introduce any amazing new features that will close deals and it will give everyone a good break once two cycles are under their belt to come back recharged if the Q4 of your business coincides with November through December.

USE THE LANGUAGE OF THE PROCESS

In all of your opening moves, introduce the language of the Six Week Solution and get everybody to use it consistently. Because it will take a while for everyone to start thinking in terms of cycles, the sooner you introduce the terminology the better, and keep reinforcing it throughout the initial change and with every cycle meeting once things get rolling.

We encourage you to read a prepared statement at the beginning of each meeting to define the purpose of the meeting (perhaps straight from Chapter 4 on page 37; the meetings are Cycle Kickoff, Cycle Sign-Off, Mea Culpa, and Cycle End).

TRANSITIONING THE DEVELOPMENT TEAM
Starting a new team

If everything is totally new, then you have built the team with bullpens in mind and there simply is nothing to transition inside of development and you will spend the majority of time working to transition the remainder of the company. But you may not be that lucky.

Taking over an existing team

If you are taking over an existing team, and one that has been missing deadlines, there is value to doing a shock-and-awe transition. Walk in and clearly state: "This is how we are going to do things." This will cause people to jump, and the cockroach developers will scurry away when this light is shined on them. Go big and make it an event, as you have nothing to lose in this situation since the existing team is already missing deadlines.

We once entered a company where we came in from outside and intentionally kicked over the server. The server had been acquired using questionable means; regardless, it was being used to run Quake. We were a software company, not a video game company.

It may not be necessary to break something, but you have to do something to jump start the process and get interest. Once we did an alternate approach and presented the change very gently. Instead of getting people excited one way or another, it was greeted with a "we'll see," and the existing development staff worked intentionally to attempt to sink the process until it was clear to all that they would need to move on for their health as well as the health of the company.

Transitioning from Agile

Transitioning from a shop that is already doing Agile development should not be a large departure from what they are already doing. Agile shops will already know the value of time boxing and setting goals. They may also be doing scrum meetings, so the stand-up is not really a change for the existing procedure.

Transitions may be necessary where a shop has picked up a few concepts from various Agile approaches but not embraced everything. The shop is on the right course, so you will only have to adjust by a few degrees. If they are already setting goals, having stand-up meetings under the name of scrum and time boxing, the biggest resistance you may have is that six weeks is too long! They have planning under their belt, but the horizon of planning may be too short term.

The other concept to introduce is automation and quality checks. Prying build scripts away from a team that is successful may be a challenge, but once they see the value of automation through the feedback it provides, good developers will jump on board. Metrics on code are another challenge, as they may have been seen as something that will only slow them down in delivering value quickly, which is one of the reasons that there are six weeks in each cycle. Once they realize the ease that future changes are made, the resistance to code metrics fades.

Transitioning from "wingin' it"

Moving to the Six Week Solution is a challenge if there is no structure and releases are coming at erratic intervals with questionable quality. It will take a "big bang" event to clear the way to make the change. Developers are going to require training to rethink their own roles in the organization. And like codependent drug abusers, the rest of the company must admit that they have been enablers for development with their own actions.

Start with senior management and then sales and marketing. This will be quite a shake-up in development, but it may surprise you to find that some of the developers will welcome the change as they have only been repeating the only process they have ever known within the company.

Transitioning from a "death march"

If you are in a death march, transitioning to the Six Week Solution should be easy, but because you are already behind your deadline, this move can be very difficult. The product or feature has already slipped and your staff is tired and grumpy. Maybe some rats have already left what they think is a sinking ship, and maybe some of those rats were highly valued developers. You're drowning, and the whole company is thrashing about kicking and splashing and going nowhere fast. Someone has to have the guts to stand up and say: "Stop. Breathe. Think about what you are doing." That is the perfect time to implement a change, for what will a couple of weeks cost you that you haven't already spent in the last couple of years going through a death march? The answer is "nothing" in the long term.

Once you have chosen to stop the madness, the difficulty is not the process but rather choosing what to do first. Sight unseen, we can guess that your feature backlog is huge and that the original ship date has slipped several months. If you are running without automation and code metrics, implement those steps first. While implementation of automation is under way, begin selecting the targets for each cycle and planning your way out of the mess you are in. Approach the processing holistically, planning office moves in parallel with feature/defect targeting.

Take a hard look at the existing staff, for these are the same developers who are currently performing the death march. Are they too poisoned on the product or the company to truly implement and embrace the change? Also look at the company and find the holdouts who will not accept change, as these too have to go, for the entire organization must be ready to move forward and change how things were done in the past.

CREATING THE BASELINE—YOUR FIRST SIX WEEK CYCLE

Make the first cycle like spring cleaning or, to go with a baseball analogy, like spring training. If you have your code metrics in place, then set goals to reduce violations or attack some explicitly called out violations that are exceptionally heinous. If you like spring training, then go with identifying some technology that can be replaced or updated in your code and implement the practice of writing the unit tests before changing the technology. Developers should relish working on these focused tasks and being rewarded for their work.

Use this cycle to teach the entire business how to interpret the results of the build server. Teach the QA resources how to deploy the builds. The support organization also needs to get involved and begin learning the value of the reports produced from the build server, especially the change log.

Spend time explaining the process and each component of the process. Use the stand-up meeting to reiterate what is changing. Keep driving the points home or you will find that the newness will wear off very quickly and everyone will revert to their daily routines. You need to ensure that you have transferred as much information as possible to truly empower the employees to make the right decisions independently.

Selection of the cycle commitment items must be done with care. You do not want to set a precedent that sandbagging the scope is acceptable, but at the same time you don't want to burn out with the very first attempt. As attractive as it may be, given that everyone has compensation riding on a successful outcome, to shoot the moon right away, that approach will fail. Picking cycle commitment items is where the real art of management comes into play, so it can be a little stretch but not so much of a stretch that it breaks.

Another point to plan for during the first iteration if you have an existing product is the inevitable emergency bug fix for that product. It will come, and at the worst possible time. If you are maintaining a legacy product, keep the old build alive and be ready to jump back but also temper that attraction (and it will be attractive because that is what everybody is comfortable doing) with the concept that most things can wait and it might be a great commitment item for the second cycle.

Conclusions

CHAPTER CONTENTS

Agile Development and Business Goals. DOI: 10.1016/B978-0-12-381520-0.00012-6

INTRODUCTION

The Six Week Solution is a unique and powerful process of creating software. This process has several features that distinguish it not only from the classic methods of software development (now commonly called the "waterfall" approach), but also from the newer, more dynamic methods of software development (of which the "Agile" process is perhaps the most famous).

Those distinct features are as follows.

ALIGNS SOFTWARE DEVELOPMENT WITH BUSINESS NEEDS

The Six Week Solution formally ties the needs of your business with the goals of your software development team.

For further details on this topic, see the following sections: "Why the Six Week Solution Is Different" on page 28, "Software Development Sometimes (Accidentally) Succeeds" on page 32, and "True Negotiation" on page 83.

DEVELOPERS ARE COMPENSATED BASED ON THEIR PERFORMANCE

One of the unique features of the Six Week Solution is its implementation of a risk/reward compensation system for the development team. While it is a radical approach—some companies reward technical people for performance, but not very many—the compensation piece of the Six Week Solution is not a random little idea dropped in the middle of an otherwise rigorous process. It is a core component of the solution.

This book discussed not only the mechanics of how to structure the compensation piece (see the section called "Compensation" on page 79 and "Developer Compensation: COD" on page 45.) but also dealt with the challenges of the issue in our chapter "Transitioning to the Six Week Solution" (see the section called "Determine Your Aggressiveness on Cycles and Compensation" on page 207).

ADDRESSES BOTH CORE BUSINESS AND CORE TECHNICAL COMPONENTS

This duality is a critical component of the Six Week Solution and is one of its key differentiators from other Agile processes. Agile Scrum, for example, addresses some of the *business* components the Six Week Solution does, but does not fully address the critical aspect of bringing tight discipline.

SIMPLE TO DESCRIBE TO EVERYONE IN THE COMPANY

A one-sentence description of the Six Week Solution is:

The Six Week Solution is a unique methodology that aligns the goals of the software development division with the goals of the company.

Throughout the book we discuss how important it is for everyone in your company to understand the uniqueness of the software development method that you are using. We give specific examples of why this understanding is important.

DESIGNED FROM THE GROUND UP TO PRODUCE REVENUE-GENERATING SOFTWARE

There is a lot of software being written these days. Some of it even addresses real-world needs and, as a consequence, generates revenue. But a lot of software is not like that. The Six Week Solution:

- Raises revenue
- Reduces expenses
- Increases profit

If you run a development shop, you may know firsthand how unusual this feature of this process actually is.

For further details on this topic, see the section on "Successful Software Development: Manages the Cost of Change" on page 33.

TIES DIRECTLY INTO YOUR INVESTMENT IN YOUR SOFTWARE DEVELOPMENT

You get the software you need written instead of some resume-padding projects created by your developers. As discussed throughout this book, writing software is not cheap. The Six Week Solution provides you with a direct method of addressing that issue.

Another important point discussed is that software development is too expensive not to align it with the goals of your business. By "expensive" we mean not only dollars, but resources, potential market share, and value to the company as a whole.

For further details on this topic, see the section called "Avoid Speculative Investments" on page 100.

ACCOUNTS DIRECTLY FOR QUALITY

You get functional software fast that has been tested carefully. While most companies test the software before they release it, companies using the Six Week Solution incorporate testing to the core of their process. Testing is not an afterthought but in fact a key component of your software development if you use the Six Week Solution.

For further details on this topic, see Chapter 7, "Assuring Software Quality" on page 117.

ALLOWS YOU TO HIT YOUR SHORT-TERM GOALS WHILE ADDRESSING YOUR LONG-TERM GOALS AT THE SAME TIME

You get real, releasable software code for this quarter while also testing code for release *3, 6, and 9 months out*. Software development is no different from the rest of the company: the focus in today's hypercompetitive corporate climate is results for this quarter first and then, much later, longer term thinking. The Six Week Solution allows you to do both.

For further details on this topic, see "Why Six Weeks?" on page 41 as well as Chapter 6, "Managing the Cost of Change" on page 89.

REWARDS SUCCESS AND PENALIZES FAILURE

Your star resources will shine brightly and the wallflowers just hanging on will be exposed when you implement the Six Week Solution. Many parts of today's corporate culture are competitive environments that constantly weed out nonperformers. Software development teams have traditionally *not* been like this; they were often seen as places to hide, to coast. The Six Week Solution exposes a very bright light on everyone's work. If you ain't keeping up, it will be obvious not only to your teammates, but also to your boss.

For further details on this topic, see the section called "Compensation" on page 79.

WHAT TO DO NEXT

Check out www.6-weeksolution.com.

Glossary

Term	Definition
Agile Manifesto	Statement of common values and goals crafted at a meeting of the creators of most major Agile methods that has been signed by thousands of software developers. This topic is discussed in detail in the section called "Quality and Software Craftsmanship" on page 129.
Automated Testing	Software used to be tested very manually: each new feature was tested painstakingly (and slowly). Now many software development teams automate their testing process as much possible. Not only does automation bring speed to the process, it increases the quality radically.
Build Process	Mechanism for turning a pile of code into a deployable product by compiling, measuring, testing, and packaging software.
Build Server	Machine that performs the build process. In the Six Week Solution, we suggest that this machine is not on a developer's desktop.
Bullpen	Most Agile teams work in a single open office (we call it a "bullpen"), which facilitates intrateam communication. Team size is typically small (9–12 people) to help make team communication and team collaboration easier. Larger development efforts may be delivered by multiple teams working toward a common goal or different parts of an effort. This may also require a coordination of priorities across teams. http://en.wikipedia.org/wiki/Agile_software_development
CLM	Career-Limiting Move
Code Coverage	Measuring how unit tests are exercising the code provides visibility into how much is actually being unit tested.
Continuous Integration (CI)	Technique used in software development where developers check in their work frequently, often right after they have completed making a change (regardless of how small that change might be).

Continued

Term	Definition
Continuous Integration (CI)—*continued*	Proponents of CI praise the quality of the resulting code: every member of the team is almost always working on the latest version.
	Detractors point to, among other things, the (somewhat) radical changes required in work styles; coders used to working for days or weeks on their own suddenly have to adapt to working much more collaboratively.
	Some developers—and some people in general—do not want to work in such a dynamic environment. The Six Week Solution is such a workplace and has no place for "rugged individualists."
COTS	Commercial Off The Shelf software
Cowboy Coder	An often derogatory term for a programmer writing code all by himself—even if he/she is technically part of a team. One guy writing code at 3 am is often called a "cowboy coder."
CPD	Cut & Paste Detection
	Either the manual or the relatively automated method of formally searching for duplicate code. No one is questioning the validity of reusable code: objects, to mention one small concept, are prime examples. But cutting-and-pasting code—almost regardless of its applicability—has become a big problem. The problem is so common that there are now many plagiarism search tools; one site selling these tools calls cutting-and-pasting source code: "... the single most widely distributed method of producing less-than-perfect programs."
	http://www.anticutandpaste.com/
Crontab	"Crontab (CRON TABle) is a file containing the schedule of cron entries to be run at specified times. cron is a unix ... utility that allows tasks to be automatically run in the background at regular intervals by the cron daemon."
	http://adminschoice.com/crontab-quick-reference
Cry Room	Room near a bullpen in the workplace layout for the Six Week Solution that people can use to make personal phone calls. (Some churches have relatively sound-proof rooms for parents to take their infants during the service; these are called "cry rooms.")
CVS	Concurrent Versioning System; one of the most popular open source control packages.
Cycle Kickoff	First week of the Six Week Solution (also known as "Week 1"). This is an important time for the six week cycle process; all stakeholders should be heard from at this point in the process to have their views represented adequately. "I need feature X" is a 100% valid statement for the week of Cycle Kickoff, but at no other time should it be uttered. It will be said many times after Cycle Kickoff, but only during that first week do you actually have to hear it.
	This topic is discussed in detail in the section "Week 1: Cycle Kickoff" on page 48.
Cycle Sign-Off	Last day of the six week cycle, when the cycle is complete or incomplete, is the day to have a Cycle Sign-Off meeting.
	This topic is discussed in detail in the section "Cycle Sign-Off" on page 50.
Cyclomatic Complexity	Cyclomatic complexity measures the number of paths through a section of code. It is especially useful for planning unit tests and reducing the difficulty of maintenance of code. This topic is discussed in detail in the section "Cyclomatic Complexity" on page 145.

Term	Definition
Death March	As it applies to software development, a "death march" is a destined-to-fail software project.
	This topic is discussed in detail in the section "Death March" on page 24.
Design Debt	Unworkable or otherwise bad code that remains in the current software and thereby prohibits rapid progress on the software.
	Note that design debt requires a considerable investment of time and people to correct.
	Design debt is discussed throughout the book, but is detailed in the section "The Value of Quality" on page 118 and "Design Debt" on page 196.
Design Deficit	Rate at which poorly structured code (design debt) is being added to your product. A continuous design deficit points to a fundamental flaw in your development process.
Design Rot	Elements of code that, for a variety of reasons, are left unmaintained but still exist in the software. Business rules can change or new teams of developers with different priorities can be brought in—there are many reasons why designs can rot—but when they do, it is a problem that can mask other problems.
Extreme Programming	Also known as "XP."
	A type of Agile methodology, XP emphasizes both speed and quality of software releases.
Feedback Loop	Feedback loops are one of the means in a process of getting information about the process that are then used to alter the direction of that process.
	In software development, feedback loops are mechanisms used to identify internal drivers for a change in a project and are inputs for correcting the course of the project appropriately. Each one provides measurable status on the progress of the project, which brings change drivers out as soon as possible. At the same time, it provides a checkpoint where responding to changing factors can be accomplished almost immediately.
FUD	Fear, Uncertainty, and Doubt
	A tactic used in some (note that we did not say "all") sales departments to cast confusion about a competitor's product. Examples of FUD are discussed throughout the book.
Gantt Chart	Type of chart used most commonly in scheduling; project managers often use Gantt charts to manage complex project scheduling issues. Because they often (although certainly not always) are used by businesspeople, Gantt charts are sometimes referred to disparagingly by technical personnel.
	The real strength of a Gantt chart is that it illustrates dependencies well; for a software release schedule, for example, software cannot be tested until it is built. Knowing that exact dependency in advance, you can schedule your testers elsewhere.
	But businesspeople have come to rely too much on Gantt charts at the expense of getting the task done; "paralysis by analysis" is what is often meant when Gantt charts are referred to negatively.
Go/No Go Decisions	Moments in a process where the decision to proceed with the project is made. "Go/No Go" decisions are common and difficult in software development.

Continued

Term	Definition
Greenfielding	Starting from scratch. If you are "greenfielding" a software development team, for example, you are not using legacy code or legacy processes. You are starting something brand new.
IDE	Integrated Development Environment
	An IDE allows a developer to modify, compile, and test code. They are code-specific tools *not* found in word processors. Eclipse is an example of an open source IDE.
Inconsistent Synchronization	A critical concept in multithreaded programming that, left unattended, could lead to disastrous outcomes.
	Example: an integer that is nonatomic that is being modified by many threads concurrently, leading to inconsistent and unexpected results.
K.I.S.S. Principle	Keep It Simple Stupid. An axiom with value in and out of the software development industry.
Lord Baden-Powell of Gilwell	Founder of the Boy Scouts.
	http://www.usscouts.org/aboutbsa/bsahistory.asp
Man in a Room	Term for an individual coding by him/herself. He/she may or may not have had the original idea for the software, may or may not be part of a team now, and so on. But they are acting, they are coding, and they are creating software, *all by themselves*. While this method certainly has its advantages, it has many negatives too.
Mea Culpa	For purposes of the Six Week Solution, this is the formal section of the process where expectations about what can be accomplished for this cycle are reset. It occurs at Week 3.
	Detailed discussion of Mea Culpa can be found in the section "Week 3: Mea Culpa" on page 51.
	It means "my fault" in Latin, in case you were wondering.
Metrics	One definition of metrics—specifically software metrics, one of the major concerns of this book—is that they are elements of your software that you can measure. Software can be a lot more vague than it looks: what is "good" software, what is "releasable" software, what is your product, and what is someone else's product? Metrics go a long way toward answering those and other questions. A common software metric is cyclomatic complexity. One important note about metrics: they do not *fix* the problem, they only help you *measure* the problem. This may be obvious in theory, but in actual practice, it is easy to forget. Metrics have their place, but they are not the be-all and end-all.
NIH (Not Invented Here) Mentality	Way of thinking in software development (and elsewhere) that rejects an idea/tool/method not originated inhouse, regardless of the value of the idea in question.
Pair Programming	Method of programming where two programmers work side by side: one writes codes and the other watches, criticizes, corrects, edits, validates, etc. In theory, software generated by paired programmers has already been looked at by another set of eyes before it even gets put into the build.

Term	Definition
Performance Improvement Plan (PIP)	Formal plan between an employee and his/her manager that details areas where the employee needs to improve their performance in order to meet the expectations of management.
PMD	A source code analyzer that identifies potential problems. (http://en.wikipedia.org/wiki/PMD_(software)) At the most basic level, nothing can be improved without measuring. To measure is to introduce a metric, and PMD supplies this metric. Maven, and later Hudson, can execute PMD and its associated CPD to produce reports with each build. This automation of producing reports produced by static code analysis yields the ability to measure the quality of the code base and elevate code reviews to a more productive level.
Product Manager	Individual responsible for defining the present and future direction of an organization's product. Precisely what this means varies radically from company to company and from industry to industry.
	Within the Six Week Solution, the job description of the Product Manager is well defined.
	Product management must have a very strong understanding of both the business needs and the development dependencies of their company. They must be able to articulate guidance in both directions. The perfect individual can understand everything about your technologies; perhaps they have developed sometime in the past. They also can stand in front of a customer and explain the features of the product in great detail. However, it is very hard to find both of these skill sets in the same person. You may need to split the role into two people: one developer focused and one marketing focused. (For further details, see the section "Product Management" on page 71.)
Project Manager (PM)	Individual responsible for supervising, organizing, directing, and coordinating the completion of a particular undertaking. PMs typically work under strict time and money constraints. The concept of project management has evolved into an enormous discipline: estimates show that there are now over 300,000 certified Project Managers. http://www.preparepm.com/faq.html
Proof of Concept (POC)	Formal presentation by one organization to demonstrate the viability of a second organization's product. While cars, weapons, and all kinds of other technological products are shown routinely as viable, for purposes of the Six Week Solution, we care about POCs for software.
	POCs often radically modify the direction that your software development is taking. POCs are useful not only for demonstrating the viability to a potential external customer, but also to force your *internal* teams to show that their stuff works
Refactoring	Changing the internal source code that does not change the external face of the product.
Repository	Library of precompiled "known good" artifacts used to produce a build.
ROI	Return On Investment
	ROI is a common business metric for evaluating the monetary yield on a particular speculation. "If I invest in two more developers between now and the end of the quarter," for example, "will I get a software release sooner?"

Continued

Term	Definition
RUP	Rational Unified Process; a software development process created and sold by Rational Software Corporation.
Scrum	Specific type of Agile programming technique that involves, among other things, a daily meeting (called a "scrum") where every member of the team provides an update. Another key feature of the scrum method is well-defined time periods for software release.
Seagull Manager	Manager that flies in, makes a lot of noise, and then flies off again. In corporations, a manager that only shows up occasionally, yells and stomps a lot, and then disappears again. Obviously not a complimentary term.
Software Sign-Off	Formal step of releasing software.
	This topic is discussed in detail in the section "Cycle Sign-Off" on page 50.
Software Testing	Performed by members of the Quality Assurance (QA) team, software testing is the process of verifying that the software works as the development team claims it does. Note that QA people do not verify that the software works "correctly," as "working correctly" can mean all kinds of different things to different people. The Six Week Solution has a strong component that defines what "working correctly" is supposed to mean for an organization.
	The job of QA and testing is to verify that goals have been met (not to question the validity of the goal itself).
Software As A Service (SAAS)	Software delivery mechanism where software is deployed remotely, on the seller's servers; the purchasing customer is saved the costs of maintaining the hardware and software and enjoys the benefits of only using the software.
Source Control	All source control packages do the same thing, which is track revisions and allow a display of differences between revisions.
Stand-Up Meeting	Many Agile practices—and the Six Week Solution—use a daily stand-up meeting as a technique to accomplish a variety of goals. (Trading statuses and sharing discoveries make every member of the team feel both *accounted for* and *accountable*.)
Stupid Coder Tricks	Dumb things developers do to save time and effort.
	"Copy and Paste and Tweak" is an example of this. These are tricks developers use to get their code into the build. Cutting and pasting is a core technique for writing code (and writing lots of other things, too... :-). But the intellectual sloppiness that comes with unchecked cutting and pasting can cause enormous short-term (testing) and long-term (usability) problems.
Subversion (SVN)	Recent addition to source control options; includes enhanced features over CVS.
TDD	Moment-to-moment development of features is generally called Test Driven Development.
Test-Driven Development (TDD)	Moment-to-moment development of features.
The Flavors of Scrum	Different methods of implementing the particular Agile methodology called "Scrum." There are many types of Agile methodologies and several different subsections of scrum.
Time Boxing	Scheduling technique that defines portions of your overall tasks into distinct time periods. Often used more globally, as in: "I'm going to timebox the kitchen

Term	Definition
	remodeling to keep my time and money costs down. If they can't do it in three months, I'm not going to do it."
TLA	Three-Letter Abbreviation (examples include ROI, CLM, and, of course, TLA)
UML	Unified Modeling Language is a graphical representation of object relationships.
Unit Testing	Method of software testing that verifies that individual portions of the software work correctly. A unit is the smallest piece of testable code and varies from software to software.
	Unit testing is performed by code (which tests code)—this is *not* performed by a QA resource.
vi	One of the first text editors written; it was originally written for UNIX systems in the mid-1970s.
Waterfall software development	Methodology that requires each piece of the development process be completed before the next one is started. The software flows down (like a waterfall) through the team until the completed product is delivered.
XP Programming	Extreme Programming
YAGNI	"YouArentGonnaNeedIt" is an Extreme Programming practice that states:
	"Always implement things when you actually need them, never when you just foresee that you need them." http://c2.com/xp/YouArentGonnaNeedIt.html

Sources

- The first (http://www.cedmagic.com/history/project-gemini-computer.html) computer could only hold so many lines of code in its less than 160,000 bits of core memory.
- "The perfect is the enemy of the deadline." - Bill Wallace, engineering group manager for GM's Volt battery, Source: http://blogs.techrepublic.com.com/tech-manager/?p=2321&tag=nl.e053http://crankypm.com/2009/11/translation-cranky-product-manager/
- http://collaboration.csc.ncsu.edu/laurie/Papers/XPSardinia.PDF [Fear of Pair Programming]
- Wikipedia: http://en.wikipedia.org/wiki/Pair_programming [Fear of Pair Programming]
- YAGNI http://c2.com/xp/YouArentGonnaNeedIt.html
- (Agile programming) http://en.wikipedia.org/wiki/Agile_software_development
- Cost of change graph (Barry Boehm) [http://www.amazon.com/Software-Engineering-Economics-Barry-Boehm/dp/0138221227]
- Customer's Bill of Rights: http://epf.eclipse.org/wikis/xp/xp/guidances/concepts/xp_rights_A1C4DF21.html
- Project Management: estimates are that there are now over 300,000 certified Project Managers. (http://www.preparepm.com/faq.html)

Index

Note: Page numbers followed by *f* indicate figures.